When You're Entertaining INTERNATIONALLY

When You're Entertaining INTERNATIONALLY

by the editors of SPHERE Magazine
wine editor/Paul Kovi

Platt & Munk, Publishers/New York

Design: Barbara Griffler; Associate Designer: Sandra Gelak
Editorial: Margot Goldsmith

Library of Congress Catalog Card Number: 77-85244

ISBN: 0-8228-7721-X

Contents

Acknowledgments

Thousands of recipes and hundreds of menus have appeared in the pages of SPHERE since the magazine's inception in early 1972. From these, and from others planned for future issues, the best of the international recipes and menus were selected, and then reviewed and edited for inclusion in *When You're Entertaining Internationally.* Each of the recipes, menus and Party Plans has been rigorously kitchen-tested. Sue Spitler, SPHERE's food editor for over five years, supervised much of this formidable task; for her patience, dedication and expertise, we are grateful.

For the wine suggestions accompanying the menus, we thank SPHERE's invaluable wine editor, Paul Kovi. Mr. Kovi, a partner in New York's famed Four Seasons Restaurant, has for many years been recognized as one of America's most knowledgeable men in the areas of both wine and food. We are proud of his association with SPHERE.

Many photographers, both in the United States and abroad, have their work displayed on the pages of *When You're Entertaining Internationally.* Their names and the pages on which their work appears are listed on page 222.

Elizabeth Rhein supplied additional material for this book.

Joan Leonard
Editor, SPHERE Magazine

Chicago, Illinois
August 1977

Introduction

When You're Entertaining Internationally is more than just a menu cookbook: it's a selection of thirty-two unique and individual events, each with its own special foreign flair. Within each menu the editors of SPHERE Magazine have included nearly everything you need to know to make party preparation as easy as possible.

The thirty-two, full-course menus in *When You're Entertaining Internationally* range from the foods of far-off places like Turkey, the South Sea Islands and the pampas of Argentina, to closer-to-home locales such as the Spanish-style cooking of old St. Augustine, Florida, and a traditional Christmas in Nova Scotia. Each menu is also designed for a specific type of party, often one that typifies the area or culture from which the foods come: there are a Russian Easter dinner, a Finnish coffee-table menu, a British sweet trolley and many more. Of course, you can easily adapt any menu to your individual needs.

To simplify the work of party preparation as much as possible, each menu includes a complete party plan. This tells you exactly when to prepare each item on the menu so that everything will be ready exactly when you need it.

Recipes for each menu are printed in an easy-to-follow, step-by-step format. Every recipe in this book is from SPHERE Magazine, and has been subjected to SPHERE's rigorous testing. None requires unusual cooking equipment to prepare.

Full-color, captioned photography accompanies each menu and illustrates nearly every recipe. You'll see just how the food will look when it is ready to be served, and you'll pick up interesting ideas for serving it most attractively, too. To add to the international feeling, we've also included photographs of the countries and regions where the foods originated.

Especially for this book, SPHERE's wine editor, Paul Kovi, has made selections of wines and other beverages that will best complement each of the menus. He has chosen both foreign and domestic wines; though most of them are widely available, if you cannot find a particular label in your area just ask your wine seller to recommend a similar variety.

So whether you are holding a formal dinner party, a casual outdoor buffet or anything in between, look to *When You're Entertaining Internationally* for a menu that fits the occasion perfectly — and offers all the information you'll need to have as much fun at your party as your guests do.

A French Picnic Luncheon

BEACH PICNIC MENU

- **VERGE CHEESE SPREAD**
- **BEEF SALAD OLIVIER**
- **PAN BAGNA**
- **GRILLED FISH WITH ORANGE SECTIONS**
  MELONS FILLED WITH STRAWBERRIES

- Recipes included

A gourmet picnic as pretty as a summer scene would have to be the product of a Gallic imagination. Renowned French chef and restaurateur Roger Vergé has devised such a beachside luncheon for a leisurely afternoon near ocean or lake.

A snowy cheese spread dotted with chives makes a zesty dip for crisp fresh vegetables. Beef Salad Olivier is a potpourri of beef, prunes and potatoes topped with Mustard Dressing.

For a continental sandwich offering, sample Pan Bagna — crusty rolls layered with tuna, vegetables, anchovies and eggs. And if the fish are biting that day, grill your catch and garnish it with orange sections and rosemary for an aromatic delight. Succulent melons stuffed with fresh strawberries create a simple, yet elegant, ending for the meal. Serves 4.

Wine Suggestion: My good friend Roger Vergé has chosen a rosé, Château de Selle, for his picnic. I also recommend Concannon's Zinfandel Rosé.

PARTY PLAN FOR BEACH PICNIC MENU

1 Day Before:

Make Vergé Cheese Spread; refrigerate spread and romaine leaves, separately, covered.
Prepare Beef Salad Olivier through step 2 in recipe; refrigerate dressing and prunes separately.

1 Hour 30 Minutes Before Serving:

Complete Beef Salad Olivier.

45 Minutes Before Serving:

Make Grilled Fish with Orange Sections.
Make Pan Bagna.
Prepare fruit for dessert.

VERGE CHEESE SPREAD

Makes about 1½ cups

1	cup large curd creamed cottage cheese
½	cup dairy sour cream
¼	cup snipped fresh chives
2	tablespoons olive or vegetable oil
1	tablespoon white wine vinegar
1	tablespoon Dijon-style mustard
½	teaspoon salt
	Freshly ground pepper
	Romaine leaves

Combine all ingredients except romaine leaves. Serve spread on romaine leaves.

For creative outdoor eating, choose Beef Salad Olivier, Pan Bagna and strawberry-stuffed melons.

Kaiser rolls hold tuna, eggs, anchovies and vegetables in Pan Bagna.

BEEF SALAD OLIVIER
Makes 4 servings

	Mustard Dressing
	(recipe follows)
1	**cup water**
20	**pitted prunes**
5	**medium potatoes**
1	**pound cooked beef brisket, cut into ¼-inch slices**
8	**cornichons or small sour pickles, sliced lengthwise**
8	**onion rings**
	Snipped fresh parsley
⅔	**cup olive or vegetable oil**
½	**cup white wine vinegar**
2	**tablespoons Dijon-style mustard**
2	**teaspoons salt**
	Freshly ground pepper

1. Make Mustard Dressing.

2. Heat 1 cup water and the prunes in medium-size saucepan over low heat to boiling; remove from heat. Let stand covered 30 minutes; drain.

3. Heat potatoes in salted water to cover over medium heat to boiling; reduce heat. Simmer covered until tender, 15 to 20 minutes; drain. Pare and slice warm potatoes. Arrange potatoes, beef, cornichons, prunes and onion rings in baking dish, 10 x 6 x 1¾ inches. Pour Mustard Dressing over salad. Let stand at room temperature 1 hour. Garnish with parsley.

MUSTARD DRESSING
Place all ingredients in jar with tight-fitting lid; cover and shake.

PAN BAGNA
Makes 4 sandwiches

2	**tablespoons olive or vegetable oil**
1	**tablespoon lemon juice**
	Freshly ground pepper
4	**Kaiser rolls, 4 to 5 inches in diameter each**
	Tomato slices
	Green pepper rings
1	**can (7 ounces) solid white tuna in water, drained, flaked**
	Onion slices
	Anchovy fillets
2	**hard-cooked eggs, cut into quarters**

Place oil, lemon juice and pepper in jar with tight-fitting lid; cover and shake. Slice each roll horizontally in half; brush cut surfaces of each roll with oil mixture. Layer tomato slices, green pepper rings, tuna, onion slices, anchovy fillets and 2 egg quarters on bottom half of each roll; cover with tops of rolls.

GRILLED FISH WITH ORANGE SECTIONS
Makes 4 servings

1	**dressed whole firm-fleshed fish (3 to 3½ pounds)**
	Salt
	Pepper
4	**orange slices**
3	**oranges, peeled, cut into sections**
	Rosemary or parsley sprigs, if desired

Sprinkle inside of fish with salt and pepper; arrange orange slices inside fish. Place fish in lightly greased hinged grill.* Grill 4 inches from hot coals until fish barely flakes with fork, about 20 minutes on each side. Serve with orange sections. Garnish with rosemary sprigs.

*TIP: *To prepare Grilled Fish with Orange Sections without hinged grill, place fish on heavy-duty aluminum foil, with several holes punched in foil, 4 inches from hot coals.*

Serve creamy Vergé Cheese Spread and orange-accented grilled fish at your gourmet picnic.

A Sukiyaki Table

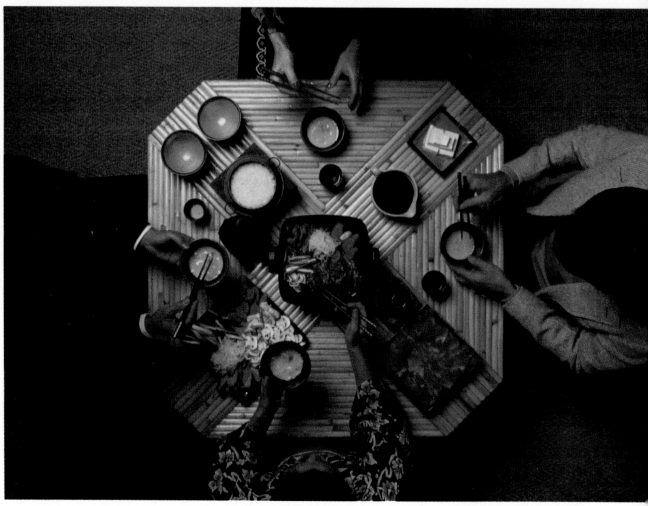

"Artistic and appetizing" are key words at the Japanese sukiyaki table.

SUKIYAKI MENU

- YAKITORI
- ASPARAGUS WITH
  PEANUT DRESSING

- SUKIYAKI
  STEAMED RICE

- ORANGE BASKETS
  TEA OR SAKE

• Recipes included

The freshest of foods, arranged with a keen eye to color, texture and shape, are the essence of sukiyaki. Though this Japanese term refers to the main dish itself — cooked atop the dinner table — sukiyaki also signifies a culinary ritual of grace and artistry.

To simulate Japanese custom, try serving the meal at a low coffee table or card table resting on bricks. An electric skillet or a heavy pan over an electric hot plate will be necessary for the tabletop cookery.

The first course is Yakitori, skewers strung with pieces of marinated chicken breasts and green onions, or chicken livers and green pepper. For a cooling intermission, follow with chilled asparagus lightly tossed in a peanut dressing.

Platters of paper-thin beef, shimmering bean thread noodles and vibrantly colored vegetables herald the central event of dinner. The cooking process harks back to feudal Japan when peasant farmers used plowshares as skillets to braise small game over open fires (*suki* means plow; *yaki*, braised). But you can gently simmer the foods in a sake-soy sauce right at the table, then have guests help themselves to the Sukiyaki, dipping it in beaten egg. For dessert, Orange Baskets draw dinner to a close on a note of refreshment. Serves 8.

Wine Suggestion: Besides the appropriate sake, you might present your guests with a light, young red wine, such as the Petite Sirah by Fetzer Vineyards, or a deliciously fruity young Beaujolais from France.

Skewer, then broil bits of chicken, livers and vegetables for the Yakitori appetizer.

Chilled Asparagus with Peanut Dressing is a refreshing vegetable course.

PARTY PLAN FOR SUKIYAKI MENU

1 Day Before:	Make Orange Baskets.
That Afternoon:	Prepare Sukiyaki through step 3 in recipe; cover and refrigerate sauce, noodles and carrots separately. Prepare Asparagus with Peanut Dressing through step 1 in recipe.
3 Hours Before Serving:	Prepare Yakitori through step 2 in recipe. Complete step 4 of Sukiyaki recipe; refrigerate ingredients. Complete step 3 of Yakitori recipe; refrigerate covered. Make peanut dressing for Asparagus with Peanut Dressing; cover and let stand at room temperature.

1 Hour Before Serving:	Cook rice; rinse with warm water in strainer. Reserve.
15 Minutes Before Serving:	Complete Yakitori. Heat rice in strainer over boiling water. Complete Asparagus with Peanut Dressing; refrigerate.
5 Minutes Before Serving Sukiyaki:	Complete Sukiyaki.

YAKITORI

Makes 8 servings

3 tablespoons sake (Japanese rice wine) or dry sherry
2 tablespoons soy sauce
2 teaspoons sugar
1 pound chicken livers, trimmed, washed, drained

½ cup mirin (Japanese sweet wine) or sweet white wine
½ cup soy sauce
2 tablespoons sugar

1 green pepper, cut into 1-inch pieces
2 whole chicken breasts (about 8 ounces each), split, skinned, boned
1 bunch green onions, trimmed to 3 inches, cut into 1½-inch pieces

Cayenne or sansho (Japanese seasoned pepper)

1.   Place sake, 2 tablespoons soy sauce and 2 teaspoons sugar in container with tight-fitting lid. Cover and shake. Cut each chicken liver into bite-size pieces; place in small bowl. Pour sake mixture over chicken livers. Let stand at room temperature several hours.

2.   Mix mirin, ½ cup soy sauce and 2 tablespoons sugar in small saucepan; heat over medium heat to boiling. Remove from heat and reserve.

3.   Drain chicken livers; discard sake mixture. Thread chicken livers alternately with green pepper onto 8 bamboo skewers. Cut each half of chicken breast into 4 pieces; thread chicken pieces alternately with green onions onto 8 bamboo skewers.

4.   Heat broiler or hibachi. Place skewered chicken and livers with vegetables 3 inches from heat. Cook, basting frequently with reserved mirin mixture, until brown, about 3 minutes on each side for livers and 5 minutes on each side for chicken. Serve immediately with cayenne.

ASPARAGUS WITH PEANUT DRESSING

Makes 8 servings

2 pounds fresh asparagus, pared, trimmed, cut into 2-inch pieces*

3 tablespoons smooth peanut butter
2 tablespoons soybean paste**
⅓ cup sugar
¼ cup soy sauce
2 tablespoons sake (Japanese rice wine) or dry sherry
1 teaspoon grated fresh or canned gingerroot

1.   Place asparagus pieces in 1 inch boiling salted water in medium-size saucepan. Heat to boiling; reduce heat. Simmer uncovered over medium heat 2 minutes. Drain; rinse with cold water. Pat dry on paper toweling. Refrigerate covered until cold.

2.   Mix peanut butter, soybean paste and sugar in small bowl. Stir in remaining ingredients gradually. Just before serving, pour peanut butter mixture over chilled asparagus; stir gently to coat asparagus. Serve immediately.

*TIPS: *3 packages (10 ounces each) frozen asparagus, cooked according to package directions, can be substituted for the fresh.*

***Soybean paste can be purchased in Oriental and specialty food shops. Two tablespoons peanut butter can be substituted for the soybean paste.*

On next pages: Sukiyaki ingredients simmer in a soy sauce blend, then are dipped into beaten egg.

2   **packages (7 ounces each) fresh shirataki (bean thread noodles) or 2 cans (8 ounces each), drained**

1   **pound fresh carrots, pared, sliced diagonally into ½-inch pieces**

4   **bunches green onions with tops, sliced diagonally into 3-inch pieces**
1   **pound fresh mushrooms, thinly sliced**
1   **bunch (8 ounces) Japanese chrysanthemum leaves or watercress**
¾   **pound tofu (soybean curd), fresh or canned, cut into 1-inch cubes, if desired**
2   **pounds lean beef (boneless rib eye or top loin steak), very thinly sliced***

1   **piece (about 1 inch square) beef suet**

8   **eggs, beaten, if desired**

1   **tablespoon water, if desired**

1   **cup soy sauce**
½   **cup sake (Japanese rice wine) or dry sherry**
½   **cup sugar**
⅛   **teaspoon monosodium glutamate**

   Warishita Sauce (recipe follows)

1.   Make Warishita Sauce.

2.   Place noodles in boiling salted water to cover. Heat to boiling; reduce heat. Simmer uncovered over medium heat 3 minutes. Drain; rinse with cold water. Pat dry on paper toweling. Cut noodles into 3-inch pieces.

3.   Place carrots in 1 inch boiling salted water. Heat to boiling; reduce heat. Simmer uncovered over medium heat 3 minutes. Drain; rinse with cold water. Pat dry on paper toweling.

4.   Arrange noodles, carrots, green onions, mushrooms, chrysanthemum leaves, soybean curd and beef on large platters or trays.

5.   Heat electric skillet or portable cooker at serving table until very hot (425°). Rub hot cooking surface on all sides with suet until well greased. When very hot but not smoking, add ¼ of the beef slices, being careful not to overlap slices. Brown on both sides; push meat to 1 side.

6.   Add ¼ of the green onions; cook and stir 2 minutes. Pour in ½ cup of the Warishita Sauce. Add about ¼ of each of the other ingredients except eggs and water. Cook just until hot, about 2 minutes. Let guests serve themselves from the cooker. Dip cooked food into individual dishes of beaten egg.

7.   Repeat procedure with remaining ingredients as cooker becomes empty. Add 1 tablespoon water and lower temperature if food sticks.

*TIP: *Have butcher slice meat, or freeze 30 to 40 minutes until meat is firm enough to slice into ⅛-inch-thick slices.*

WARISHITA SAUCE   *Makes about 2 cups*
Place all ingredients in container with tight-fitting lid; cover and shake.

ORANGE BASKETS   *Makes 8 servings*

8   **large oranges or tangerines**
2   **cups orange juice***

1   **envelope unflavored gelatin**
¼   **cup water**
2   **tablespoons sugar**
2   **teaspoons orange-flavored liqueur**

1.   To form orange basket shells, cut 2 wedge-shaped sections of peel on top half of each orange, leaving ½-inch strip between sections for "handle." Loosen peel with spoon; remove wedge-shaped peels. Loosen entire fruit from inside shell with spoon; remove fruit. Squeeze juice from orange sections; measure 2 cups juice and reserve.

2.   Sprinkle gelatin on water in small saucepan; let stand 5 minutes. Add sugar to gelatin mixture; cook and stir over low heat until gelatin is dissolved, about 5 minutes. Remove saucepan from heat; stir in reserved orange juice and the liqueur. Pour about ¼ cup of the mixture into each of the orange shells; refrigerate until gelatin mixture is firm, about 3 hours.

*TIP: *Add reconstituted frozen or fresh orange juice to juice squeezed from orange or tangerine fruit to measure 2 cups.*

North African Dinner Party

Serve Marrakesh Soup (left), then set out the exotic main courses.

NORTH AFRICAN DINNER MENU

- **HORS D'OEUVRES EGYPTIAN STYLE WITH YOGURT-GARLIC SAUCE**
- **SANGRIA COCKTAIL**

- **MARRAKESH SOUP**

- **MOROCCAN LAMB STEW**
- **ORIENTAL RICE**
- **KASBAH SALAD WITH TANGIER SALAD DRESSING**
- **HONEYED BREAD**
- **LIME WATER**

- **ORANGES PERFUMED WITH CINNAMON AND ROSE WATER**
- **ARABIC COFFEE**

• Recipes included

From Cairo to Casablanca, North Africa curves around the Mediterranean, touching the Middle East at Suez and Europe at Gibraltar. In between lies a region of vast contrasts: from forests to deserts, mountains to lowlands, crowded cities to sparsely inhabited countrysides. North Africa is mystery, color, sensuality — a million different faces and thousands of years of history. A dinner that captures the sights, sounds and moods of North Africa in the flavors of its foods can only be an exciting and memorable occasion.

Start your culinary sojourn in the east — with Egyptian-style hors d'oeuvres. These tiny "fried" cakes subtly combine ground fava beans, cumin, onion, parsley and coriander, and are matched with Yogurt-Garlic Sauce. To accompany the appetizers, set out glasses of Sangría Cocktail, a tart wine mix that speaks of the Moorish-Spanish influence in Africa. Soup from the heart of Marrakesh is a golden chicken broth laced with spices and adorned with slices of lemon. Your guests can enjoy the soup in bowls, or in the Arabic fashion — sipping it from cups.

The entrée is an exotic alliance of lamb, almonds, raisins, onions and eggs, known in North Africa as *tajine*. This refers to any combination of ingredients prepared in a shallow ceramic African *tajine* or casserole. Serve the stew with pungent Oriental Rice, and a salad tingling with red pepper-cumin-lime dressing. As dinner progresses, pass baskets of bread to be eaten North African style, dipped into honey and soft butter.

Flavored waters, such as our Lime Water, are popular in many Mediterranean countries for cleansing the palate between courses. Oranges Perfumed with Cinnamon and Rose Water and cups of cardamom-sparked Arabic Coffee are a fitting conclusion to an unforgettable dining experience. Serves 8.

On previous page: Egyptian hors d'oeuvres and Sangría Cocktail are novel party openers.

Tajine combines lamb, eggs, raisins and almonds in a savory stew.

PARTY PLAN FOR NORTH AFRICAN DINNER MENU

1 Day Before:
Prepare Marrakesh Soup through step 2 in recipe.
Prepare Moroccan Lamb Stew through step 2 in recipe; refrigerate.
Prepare Lime Water through step 1 in recipe.
Prepare Hors d'Oeuvres Egyptian Style through step 2 in recipe.

That Afternoon:
Prepare Oranges Perfumed with Cinnamon and Rose Water through step 1 in recipe.
Prepare Sangría Cocktail except do not stir in wine.
Prepare Kasbah Salad through step 1 in recipe.

30 Minutes Before Guests Arrive:
Complete hors d'oeuvres; cover and keep warm in 200° oven.

As Guests Arrive:
Complete Sangría Cocktail and serve with hors d'oeuvres.

35 Minutes Before Serving:

Complete Moroccan Lamb Stew.
Make Honeyed Bread.
Make Oriental Rice.
Complete Lime Water.
Complete Kasbah Salad.
Complete Marrakesh Soup.

15 Minutes Before Dessert:

Make Arabic Coffee.
Complete Oranges Perfumed with Cinnamon and Rose Water.

HORS D'OEUVRES EGYPTIAN STYLE   *Makes 24*

Yogurt-Garlic Sauce (recipe follows)
1   can (19 ounces) fava beans, drained

1   small potato, cooked, mashed
½   cup minced onion
⅓   cup snipped fresh parsley
¾   teaspoon ground coriander
½   teaspoon ground cumin
½   teaspoon salt
¼   teaspoon red pepper sauce

1   egg, beaten
⅓   cup bread crumbs

1   tablespoon olive or vegetable oil
    Fresh dill, if desired

1½ cups unflavored yogurt
1   tablespoon snipped fresh dill
2   teaspoons olive or vegetable oil
2   cloves garlic, crushed
    Snipped fresh dill, if desired

1. Make Yogurt-Garlic Sauce. Place beans, ¼ at a time, in blender container; cover. Blend until smooth.

2. Combine beans, potato, onion, parsley, coriander, cumin, salt and red pepper sauce in medium-size bowl; cover. Refrigerate no longer than 24 hours.

3. Stir egg and bread crumbs into bean mixture. Shape mixture by 1½ teaspoonfuls into small flat cakes.

4. Brown cakes in oil in skillet until crisp on both sides; drain. Arrange on serving dish; garnish with fresh dill. Serve warm with Yogurt-Garlic Sauce.

YOGURT-GARLIC SAUCE   *Makes 1½ cups*
Mix yogurt, 1 tablespoon dill, the oil and garlic; cover and refrigerate. To serve, garnish with snipped dill.

SANGRIA COCKTAIL   *Makes about 2½ quarts*

1   cup brandy
¾   cup Curaçao
⅔   cup fresh lime juice
½   cup fresh orange juice
2   quarts chilled Spanish dry red wine

Mix all ingredients except wine in large pitcher; cover. Refrigerate 3 to 4 hours. Stir in wine. Serve in glasses over ice, if desired.

MARRAKESH SOUP

Makes 8 servings (about 1¼ cups each)

2½ quarts chicken broth
3 stalks celery with leaves,
     sliced
2 cloves garlic, halved
2 medium onions, sliced
8 parsley sprigs
2 lemons, cut into quarters

¼ teaspoon ground ginger
¼ teaspoon ground turmeric
¼ teaspoon ground cinnamon
   Dash crushed saffron

8 lemon slices
   Snipped fresh parsley,
     if desired
   Whole grain bread

1.   Heat chicken broth, celery, garlic, onions, parsley sprigs and 2 lemons in large kettle or Dutch oven to boiling; reduce heat and cover. Simmer 30 minutes.

2.   Strain soup. Return broth to kettle. Stir in remaining ingredients except lemon slices, snipped parsley and bread. Cook over low heat 15 minutes; cool. Cover and refrigerate until cold.

3.   Heat soup to boiling; ladle into bowls. Float lemon slice in each bowl. Garnish with snipped parsley. Serve with bread.

MOROCCAN LAMB STEW

Makes 8 servings

5 pounds boneless lamb,
     cut into 1-inch cubes
2 tablespoons olive or vegetable oil
2¾ cups chopped onions
2 cloves garlic, chopped

⅓ cup snipped fresh parsley
2 whole cloves
1 teaspoon ground ginger
¼ teaspoon crushed saffron
4½ teaspoons salt
1 teaspoon pepper
2 cans (16 ounces each)
     tomatoes, undrained
2 bay leaves

2 large Bermuda onions,
     cut into quarters
3 tablespoons butter or margarine
⅔ cup blanched almonds
1 tablespoon butter or margarine
¾ cup golden raisins

5 hard-cooked eggs, halved

1.   Brown lamb, ½ at a time, in oil in 5-quart Dutch oven; remove lamb. Sauté chopped onions and garlic in pan drippings until brown.

2.   Stir in parsley, cloves, ginger and saffron. Cook and stir 2 minutes. Stir in salt, pepper, tomatoes and lamb. Add bay leaves. Heat to boiling; reduce heat and cover. Simmer, stirring occasionally, until meat is tender, about 1½ hours.*

3.   Heat stew to boiling; reduce heat. Simmer uncovered until slightly thickened, 20 to 30 minutes. Remove bay leaves.

4.   Sauté onion quarters in 3 tablespoons butter in large skillet until golden. Cover; keep warm. Sauté almonds in 1 tablespoon butter in small skillet until golden. Stir in raisins. Cover; keep warm.

5.   Turn stew onto large heat-proof serving platter. Arrange onions and eggs around edge of platter. Sprinkle almonds and raisins on center of stew.

*TIP: *Stew can be prepared to this point in advance. Cool slightly and cover. Refrigerate no longer than 24 hours.*

ORIENTAL RICE

Makes 8 servings

¼ cup butter or margarine
2 cups chicken broth
2 cups water
1½ teaspoons salt
½ teaspoon ground turmeric
2 cups uncooked regular rice
   Pepper strips, if desired

Melt butter in 3-quart saucepan. Stir in chicken broth, water, salt and turmeric. Heat to boiling. Stir in rice. Heat to boiling; reduce heat and cover. Simmer until rice is tender, about 15 minutes. Garnish with pepper strips.

KASBAH SALAD

Makes 8 servings

   Tangier Salad Dressing
     (recipe follows)
8 to 10 cups bite-size pieces
    romaine
4 medium tomatoes, sliced
2 cucumbers, thinly sliced
8 to 10 green onions,
    cut into 1-inch pieces
1 cup drained pitted
    ripe olives
¼ cup snipped fresh parsley

1. Make Tangier Salad Dressing. Arrange romaine in large salad bowl. Arrange tomatoes, cucumbers, green onions and olives on romaine. Sprinkle with parsley; cover and refrigerate.

2. Toss salad with dressing.

¾ cup olive oil
⅓ cup fresh lime juice
2 teaspoons red pepper sauce
½ to 1 teaspoon ground cumin
¼ teaspoon pepper

TANGIER SALAD DRESSING

Makes about 1 cup

Shake all ingredients in jar with tight-fitting lid; refrigerate.

HONEYED BREAD

Makes 8 servings

1½ cups honey
2 sticks butter or margarine
    (1 cup)
   Assorted breads, sliced

   Heat oven to 200°

Divide honey between 2 shallow serving dishes. Place 1 stick butter in center of each dish. Place dishes in oven until butter is slightly melted. Dip bread slices in mixture.

LIME WATER

Makes 2 quarts

5 limes
2 quarts bottled natural
    spring water
8 large mint leaves

8 lime slices
8 mint sprigs

1. Peel limes. Place peels and spring water in large pitcher. Add mint leaves; cover. Refrigerate at least 24 hours.

2. Remove lime peels and mint leaves from pitcher. Garnish water with lime slices and mint sprigs; serve water with dinner.

Oranges Perfumed with Cinnamon and Rose Water is offered with Arabic Coffee.

ORANGES PERFUMED WITH CINNAMON AND ROSE WATER
Makes 8 servings

8	to 10 oranges, peeled, sliced
⅓	cup honey
½	cup fresh orange juice
¼	cup brandy
¼	teaspoon ground cinnamon
1½	cups whipping cream
1	teaspoon rose water*
	Mint sprig, if desired

1.   Arrange orange slices in large shallow dish. Heat honey in small saucepan until hot. Stir in orange juice and brandy; pour over oranges. Sprinkle with cinnamon; cover. Refrigerate at least 3 hours.

2.   Beat whipping cream and rose water in chilled small bowl until stiff peaks form. Place oranges in serving dish; garnish with mint sprig. Serve with whipped cream.

TIP: *Rose water can be purchased in drugstores.*

ARABIC COFFEE
Makes 8 servings

3	cups water
1	cup ground coffee
16	to 18 cardamom seeds
	Sugar, if desired

Measure water, coffee and cardamom seeds into regular, drip or percolator coffeepot. Prepare according to manufacturer's directions. Serve with sugar.

Colonial Holiday Feast

Christmas in New England is a more-than-three-centuries-old custom, beginning long before the American Revolution. The austere holiday practices of the Puritans gave way in the 1700s to a celebration complete with sumptuous dinner. It was a repast eagerly anticipated all year. And the traditional Christmas feast that evolved features native foods combined with English favorites.

Cream of Chestnut Soup — an old-world treat transplanted to the new land — is garnished with parsley and dollops of whipped cream. The American turkey became popular at the holiday table. But many New Englanders did, and still do, prefer their English Christmas goose — served here with an apricot dressing and potatoes.

The Indians of New England taught colonists to plant crops and adapt to the new foods of the region. Squash with syrup from local maple trees, and succotash are two Christmas dishes derived from these tribes. The abundant cranberries of the area blend well with oranges for a sweet-tart meat and fowl accompaniment. And golden Blueberry Corn Muffins are another by-product of the help given settlers by the Indians. Rounding out the festive spread are Creamed Onions and a zesty watercress salad.

For dessert, colonials took comfort in both a traditional steamed pudding with hard sauce and the fruits of the New World. Serves 8.

Wine Suggestion: As a balance to the richness of this Christmas spread, offer the full-bodied, dry red Hungarian wine, Egri Bikavér, or a well-developed Zinfandel — three or four years of age.

Set a bountiful table with New England Christmas favorites, including Cream of Chestnut Soup (left).

PARTY PLAN FOR CHRISTMAS DINNER MENU

3 Days Before:

Make Tart Cranberry-Orange Relish.

2 Days Before:

Make Maple Butternut Squash.
Prepare Cress Salad with Old-Fashioned Mustard Dressing through step 1 in recipe.

1 Day Before:

Prepare Cream of Chestnut Soup through step 3 in recipe; cool slightly. Cover and refrigerate.
Make Fruit Dressing; cover and refrigerate.
Make Creamed Onions; cool slightly. Cover and refrigerate.
Make New England Succotash; cool slightly. Cover and refrigerate.
Make Blueberry Corn Muffins; cool thoroughly. Wrap tightly in aluminum foil.
Make Hard Sauce.
Thaw goose if frozen.

5 Hours Before Serving:

Remove New England Succotash from refrigerator.

4 Hours Before Serving:

Complete Christmas Goose with Fruit Dressing and Roast Potatoes.
Prepare watercress and greens for salad; cover and refrigerate.

1 Hour 30 Minutes Before Serving:

Complete step 2 of Grandma's Steamed Applesauce Pudding with Hard Sauce recipe; refrigerate mold.

45 Minutes Before Serving:

Heat New England Succotash covered in oven until hot.

20 Minutes Before Serving:

Heat Cream of Chestnut Soup until hot; complete step 4 of recipe.
Heat Maple Butternut Squash until hot.
Heat Creamed Onions until hot.

10 Minutes Before Serving:

Heat Blueberry Corn Muffins in aluminum foil in oven until hot.
Complete Cress Salad with Old-Fashioned Mustard Dressing.
Complete Cream of Chestnut Soup.

At Serving Time:

Complete step 3 of Grandma's Steamed Applesauce Pudding with Hard Sauce recipe.

15 Minutes Before Dessert:

Complete Grandma's Steamed Applesauce Pudding with Hard Sauce.

CREAM OF CHESTNUT SOUP

Makes 8 servings (about ½ cup each)

1¼ pounds chestnuts*

8 parsley sprigs
2 celery leaf sprigs
3 whole cloves
1 bay leaf
¼ teaspoon dried thyme leaves
1 quart water

2 cups chicken broth
½ cup whipping cream
⅓ cup port
1 teaspoon salt
¼ teaspoon pepper

1. Slit chestnut shells crosswise on rounded side making an X; place in jelly-roll pan, 15½ x 10½ x 1 inch. Roast 8 minutes. Remove shells and skins while nuts are warm.

2. Tie parsley sprigs, celery sprigs, cloves, bay leaf and thyme in cheese-cloth bag to make a bouquet garni. Heat chestnuts, bouquet garni and water in 3-quart saucepan to boiling; reduce heat. Simmer uncovered 25 minutes. Remove bouquet garni.

3. Place chestnuts and cooking liquid in blender container; cover. Blend on high speed until pureed, about 1 minute.

4. Return chestnut mixture to saucepan; stir in chicken broth. Heat to boiling; reduce heat. Stir in whipping cream, port, salt and pepper gradually. Heat until hot but not boiling.

Whipped cream
Snipped fresh parsley

Heat oven to 450°

5.   Pour soup into tureen. Top with dollops of whipped cream. Sprinkle with snipped parsley.

TIP: *3 cans (6 ounces each) chestnuts can be substituted for the fresh. Drain chestnuts and proceed with step 2 in recipe.

CHRISTMAS GOOSE WITH FRUIT DRESSING AND ROAST POTATOES   *Makes 8 servings*

Fruit Dressing
  (recipe follows)
1   goose (8 to 10 pounds)

6   large baking potatoes, pared,
      cut lengthwise in half
    Salt
    Pepper
    Paprika

2   tablespoons flour
1   cup water
1   teaspoon salt
½   teaspoon pepper

    Orange segments
    Parsley

1.   Make Fruit Dressing. Heat oven to 350°. Fill goose cavity loosely with dressing. Tie drumsticks together with heavy string. Place goose breast side up on rack in open shallow roasting pan. Insert meat thermometer so tip is in thickest part of inside thigh muscle away from bone.

2.   Roast goose uncovered until thermometer registers 185°, 3 to 4 hours. After 2 hours, drain all fat from roasting pan. When ⅔ done, cut string holding legs. Season potatoes with salt, pepper and paprika. During last hour of roasting, place potatoes in roasting pan.

3.   Remove goose and cover loosely with aluminum foil; let stand 30 minutes before carving. (Remove all dressing from goose before carving.)

4.   Remove potatoes; keep warm. Drain all but 2 tablespoons fat from roasting pan. Stir in flour. Cook over low heat, stirring constantly, until mixture is smooth and bubbly. Remove from heat. Stir in water, 1 teaspoon salt and ½ teaspoon pepper. Heat, stirring constantly, to boiling. Boil and stir 1 minute.

5.   Serve goose surrounded with potatoes. Garnish with orange segments and parsley. Pass gravy.

Succulent goose with Fruit Dressing and potatoes is accented by a cranberry-orange relish.

½ cup water
⅓ cup chopped dried apricots
½ teaspoon salt
½ teaspoon dried rosemary leaves
½ teaspoon ground sage
½ teaspoon pepper

½ pound pork sausage
2 cups soda cracker crumbs
2 large apples, unpared,
    chopped (about 1½ cups)
½ cup minced celery
¼ cup snipped fresh chives
2 tablespoons light cream
    or milk

FRUIT DRESSING   *Makes about 5 cups*

1. Heat water, apricots, salt, rosemary, sage and pepper in 3-quart saucepan to boiling; reduce heat. Simmer 5 minutes. Remove from heat.

2. Sauté sausage until brown; drain fat. Stir sausage and remaining ingredients into apricot mixture.

MAPLE BUTTERNUT SQUASH   *Makes 8 servings*

1 butternut squash (about
    3 pounds)

¼ cup butter or margarine
¼ cup maple syrup
½ teaspoon salt
¼ to ½ teaspoon ground
    nutmeg
⅛ teaspoon pepper

1. Cut squash into 8 pieces. Remove seeds and pulp; do not pare. Heat 1 inch salted water (½ teaspoon salt to 1 cup water) to boiling. Add squash and cover. Heat to boiling. Cook until tender, 15 to 20 minutes; drain.

2. Pare and mash squash. Heat squash and remaining ingredients over medium heat until hot.

TIP: Maple Butternut Squash can be made 2 days in advance. Store covered in refrigerator. To serve, heat over medium heat until hot.

CREAMED ONIONS   *Makes 8 servings*

½ cup dark raisins
¼ cup sherry

2 jars (16 ounces each)
    whole onions
3 tablespoons butter or
    margarine
3 tablespoons flour
¼ teaspoon salt
⅛ teaspoon white pepper

1 cup light cream

1. Combine raisins and sherry; reserve.

2. Drain onions; reserve onions and ½ cup liquid. Heat butter in 3-quart saucepan over low heat. Stir in flour, salt and pepper. Cook over low heat, stirring constantly, until mixture is smooth and bubbly. Remove from heat.

3. Stir in cream and reserved onion liquid. Heat, stirring constantly, to boiling. Boil and stir 1 minute. Stir in reserved raisin-sherry mixture and onions. Heat until hot.

NEW ENGLAND SUCCOTASH   *Makes 8 servings*

1 jar (22 ounces) molasses
    baked beans
2 cans (12 ounces each) whole-
    kernel corn, undrained
5 slices bacon, cut into ½-inch pieces
1 large onion, sliced
1 tablespoon packed brown sugar

Heat oven to 325°

Layer half each of the beans, corn, bacon pieces and onion slices in 2-quart casserole; repeat. Sprinkle with brown sugar; cover. Bake 1¼ hours; remove cover. Bake until onion is light brown, about 45 minutes.

TIP: New England Succotash can be made 1 day in advance. Store covered in refrigerator. Let stand at room temperature 4 hours before heating. To serve, heat oven to 350°. Heat succotash in covered casserole until hot, about 45 minutes.

TART CRANBERRY-ORANGE RELISH

Makes 3½ cups

1 orange, unpeeled
1 pound fresh cranberries*
1 cup sugar

Cut orange and remove seeds. Pass cranberries and orange through food grinder using fine blade. Stir in sugar and cover. Refrigerate at least 1 day, no longer than 1 week.

*TIP: *Frozen cranberries can be substituted for the fresh. Do not thaw; pass through food grinder in frozen state.*

CRESS SALAD WITH OLD-FASHIONED MUSTARD DRESSING

Makes 8 servings

¼ cup mayonnaise or
salad dressing
2 tablespoons red wine
vinegar
1 tablespoon Dijon-style
mustard
1 teaspoon salt
½ teaspoon sugar
1 cup vegetable oil
2 tablespoons snipped fresh
parsley

2 bunches watercress
1 head romaine lettuce, torn
into bite-size pieces
(about 4 cups)
1 head iceberg lettuce, torn
into bite-size pieces
(about 4 cups)

1. Mix mayonnaise, vinegar, mustard, salt and sugar in small bowl. Beat in oil gradually; beat until thick and creamy, about 2 minutes. Stir in parsley; cover. Refrigerate at least 3 hours, no longer than 2 days.

2. Remove stems from leaves of watercress; discard stems. Combine watercress leaves, romaine and iceberg lettuce in large bowl; toss with dressing. Serve on individual salad plates.

BLUEBERRY CORN MUFFINS

Makes 1 dozen

¼ cup butter or margarine,
softened
¼ cup granulated sugar
¼ cup packed brown sugar
1 egg
½ cup milk
¼ teaspoon salt
¼ teaspoon ground nutmeg
1 cup all-purpose flour
½ cup cornmeal
2 teaspoons baking powder

½ cup canned blueberries,
rinsed, drained
1½ teaspoons flour

Butter or margarine,
if desired

Heat oven to 400°

1. Mix ¼ cup butter, the sugars, egg, milk, salt and nutmeg in large bowl. Stir in 1 cup flour, the cornmeal and baking powder just until ingredients are moistened. (Batter will be lumpy.)

2. Toss blueberries and 1½ teaspoons flour; fold into batter. Fill 12 greased, medium-size muffin cups (2¾ inches in diameter) ⅔ full.

3. Bake muffins until golden, 20 to 25 minutes. Remove immediately from pan. Serve with butter.

GRANDMA'S STEAMED APPLESAUCE PUDDING WITH HARD SAUCE *Makes 8 servings*

Hard Sauce
(recipe follows)

¼ pound ground suet (about
   1 cup)
½ cup packed light brown
   sugar
1 egg
½ teaspoon ground cloves
½ teaspoon ground allspice
½ teaspoon ground cinnamon
½ teaspoon salt
¾ cup applesauce
1 cup all-purpose flour
½ cup dark raisins
½ cup chopped dried apricots
¼ cup slivered almonds
½ teaspoon baking powder

1 cup powdered sugar
½ cup butter or margarine,
   softened
2 teaspoons rum extract
1 egg white

1. Make Hard Sauce.

2. Measure suet, brown sugar, egg and seasonings into large mixer bowl. Beat on low speed, scraping bowl constantly, 30 seconds. Beat on high speed, scraping bowl occasionally, 2 minutes. Stir in remaining ingredients. Spoon batter into well-greased, 1-quart mold. Cover tightly with aluminum foil.

3. Place mold on rack in deep kettle; add 1 inch water. Heat water to boiling; reduce heat and cover kettle. Steam until wooden pick inserted in center comes out clean, about 1½ hours. (Add boiling water to kettle, if necessary.)

4. Remove mold from kettle; cool slightly and unmold. Top with small amount of Hard Sauce. Pass remaining sauce.

HARD SAUCE *Makes about 1½ cups*
Mix sugar, butter and rum extract in small bowl until smooth. Beat egg white in small mixer bowl until stiff peaks form. Add sugar mixture. Beat 2 minutes on high speed; cover. Refrigerate at least 1 hour, no longer than 1 day.

Raisins and apricots dot the traditional steamed applesauce pudding.

A Yucatecan Brunch

Lime Soup begins the brunch menu.

EGGS MOTUL MENU

• **LIME SOUP**

• **EGGS MOTUL**

**ASSORTED FRESH FRUIT
COFFEE**

• Recipes included

Eggs Motul for brunch is an easy way to make the acquaintance of Yucatán cooking. The foods of Mexico's Mayan region are not as familiar as enchiladas or *molé*. But their unusual blend of flavors and fresh attractive appearance recommend them to even the most experienced culinary traveler.

Start with soup. Chicken-based Lime Soup is highlighted by coriander and garnished with tortilla wedges.

Our colorful egg dish introduces most of the standard ingredients of Yucatecan cuisine: peppers, beans and a variety of vegetables. Layers of fried eggs and crisp corn tortillas — one spread with Black Bean Puree — are topped with a zesty tomato sauce. Then peas, chopped ham and cheese are sprinkled over, to create this lively luncheon offering. An assortment of luscious fruits, like grapes and papayas, and coffee are all that are needed to complement the authentic meal. Serves 8.

Wine Suggestion: Open a bottle of fine Moët & Chandon Champagne or illustrious Korbel Natural from California to serve with this unusual cuisine.

The foods of Mérida's market (above left and below) are the basic ingredients in Yucatecan cookery.

PARTY PLAN FOR EGGS MOTUL MENU

2 Weeks Before:	Prepare Eggs Motul through step 1 in recipe.
2 Days Before:	Complete step 2 of Eggs Motul recipe; let cool to room temperature. Refrigerate covered.
1 Day Before:	Prepare Lime Soup through step 1 in recipe; refrigerate chicken and broth, separately, covered.
1 Hour Before Serving:	Heat Yucatán Tomato Sauce over medium heat, stirring occasionally. Heat Black Bean Puree over low heat, stirring occasionally. Complete Lime Soup. Complete Eggs Motul.

Zesty Eggs Motul is complemented by cooling fruits.

LIME SOUP (Sopa de Lima)   *Makes 8 servings (about 1½ cups each)*

1	broiler-fryer chicken (3 to 3½ pounds), cut up
10	cups water
6	peppercorns
3	coriander or parsley sprigs
1	stalk celery
1	medium onion, cut into quarters
2	teaspoons salt
½	teaspoon dried thyme leaves
2	tablespoons vegetable oil
1	medium onion, chopped
1	medium green pepper, chopped
2	large tomatoes, peeled, seeded, chopped (about 2 cups)
2	limes, halved
3	tablespoons snipped fresh coriander or parsley
	Salt
	Pepper
	Lard
8	corn tortillas, cut into 8 wedges
	Lime slices, if desired
	Coriander leaves, if desired

1. Place chicken pieces in Dutch oven. Add water, peppercorns, coriander sprigs, celery, quartered onion, 2 teaspoons salt and the thyme. Heat to boiling; reduce heat. Simmer uncovered, removing film occasionally, until chicken is tender, about 1½ hours. Remove chicken; strain broth and reserve. Cool chicken; remove meat from bones.

2. While chicken is cooling, heat oil in Dutch oven over medium heat. Sauté chopped onion and green pepper in oil until tender, 3 to 4 minutes. Add tomatoes; cook 5 minutes. Add reserved broth, the juice from 2 limes, and ½ squeezed lime. Stir in snipped coriander; simmer 20 minutes. Add chicken; heat until hot and bubbly, about 10 minutes. Taste and adjust seasonings.

3. Heat lard (1 to 2 inches) in skillet to 350°. Fry tortilla wedges until crisp and golden, 2 to 3 minutes. Drain tortillas on paper toweling. To serve, place 8 tortilla wedges in each soup bowl; add soup. Garnish with lime slices and coriander leaves.

EGGS MOTUL (Huevos Motuleños)   *Makes 8 servings*

2	cups Yucatán Tomato Sauce (see recipe, page 42), heated
2	cups Black Bean Puree (see recipe, page 43), heated
	Lard
16	corn tortillas
	Butter or margarine
16	eggs
2	packages (10 ounces each) frozen peas, cooked, drained
2	cups chopped ham
¼	cup grated Parmesan cheese

1. Make Yucatán Tomato Sauce.

2. Make Black Bean Puree.

3. Heat lard (1 to 2 inches) in skillet to 350°. Fry tortillas in lard until crisp and golden on both sides, 2 to 3 minutes. Drain tortillas on paper toweling. Spread each of 8 tortillas with ¼ cup of the Black Bean Puree; place on individual serving dishes. Melt butter in skillet over low heat; fry eggs until set. Place 1 fried egg on each tortilla spread with Black Bean Puree; top with another tortilla and fried egg. Spoon ¼ cup of the Yucatán Tomato Sauce over top egg; garnish each with ⅓ cup peas, ¼ cup ham and 1½ teaspoons Parmesan cheese. Serve with grapes and papayas.

A Mayan Meal

A sprawling hacienda produces Yucatecan henequen, or sisal.

BAKED PORK DINNER MENU

• **SEAFOOD COCKTAIL**

• **YUCATAN-STYLE PORK**
   BAKED IN CLAY
• **CLASSIC VEGETABLE TRIAD:**
   BLACK BEAN PUREE
   SQUASH WITH PEPITAS
   CORN PUDDING
TORTILLAS

• **CARAMEL CUSTARD**
   ROSE WINE

• Recipes included

Mexico's Yucatán peninsula is strewn with ruins — magnificent reminders of its Mayan past. The region's ancient heritage, with an overlay of Spanish influence, also lives on in many of its foods. And Yucatecan dishes make a menu tantalizingly different from other Mexican offerings.

Begin dinner with a first course of delicacies from the sea. Shrimp, crab and conch are stirred together with a piquant peppery tomato sauce. A classic specialty, the pork entrée, *cochinito pibil*, demonstrates famous Yucatecan pib cookery. This style of cooking starts with a deep pit lined with stones kept heated by a fire. Raw meats wrapped in banana leaves, then placed in a container are deposited in the pit. More hot stones are laid on top and the entire hole filled with earth. The result is meat of incredible tenderness.

In our version, a paste of spices — including earthy achiote, a favorite Yucatecan flavoring — covers the pork. Plantain leaves, then Baker's Clay envelope the roast while it cooks in the oven to a delectable juiciness.

The vegetable triad presents traditional Mayan complements, beans, squash and corn. The bean dish is a puree of black beans, peppers, onion and garlic, accented with *epazote*, another typically Yucatecan herb. Our squash is *chayote* — a mild-flavored variety — sparked with *pepitas*, tiny shelled seeds toasted in oil. And Corn Pudding combines whole-kernel corn with pimientos and cornmeal.

Set out sweet rich Caramel Custard, a legacy from Spain, for dessert. Serves 8.

Wine Suggestion: If you wish, serve a rosé throughout this dinner — Simi Winery's Rosé of Cabernet or Amourosé from Sichel, for example. For a fuller-bodied red wine, sample a Barbera from Heitz Cellars, or the Italian Gattinara from Troglia.

Pib-cooked pork teams with squash, bean and corn side dishes.

PARTY PLAN FOR BAKED PORK DINNER MENU

2 Weeks Before:
Make Yucatán Tomato Sauce.

2 Days Before:
Prepare Classic Vegetable Triad through step 1 in recipe.

1 Day Before:
Complete step 2 of Yucatán-Style Pork Baked in Clay recipe.

That Afternoon:
Prepare Caramel Custard through step 3 in recipe; refrigerate custard and raisins separately.
Complete steps 2 and 3 of Classic Vegetable Triad recipe; refrigerate squash and corn, separately, covered.
Measure and label ingredients for remaining recipes; refrigerate perishables.

3 Hours Before Serving:
Complete Yucatán-Style Pork Baked in Clay.

30 Minutes Before Serving:	Complete Classic Vegetable Triad.
	Complete Seafood Cocktail.
10 Minutes Before Dessert:	Complete Caramel Custard.

SEAFOOD COCKTAIL (Ensalada de Mariscos)

Makes 8 servings

---

1   cup Yucatán Tomato Sauce,
      chilled (recipe follows)*

8   ounces cooked shrimp
8   ounces frozen crabmeat, thawed,
      cut into 1-inch pieces
1   can (8 ounces) conch, diced**
      Lettuce cups
      Snipped fresh coriander or
        parsley, if desired
      Lime wedges

1.   Make Yucatán Tomato Sauce.

2.   Combine shrimp, crabmeat and conch in large bowl. Stir in Yucatán Tomato Sauce. Line 8 cocktail dishes with lettuce cups; fill each cup with about ⅓ cup of the seafood mixture. Sprinkle with coriander. Serve with lime wedges.

TIPS: *Remaining Yucatán Tomato Sauce will be used for Yucatán-Style Pork Baked in Clay.

**Cooked shrimp, crabmeat or other shellfish can be substituted for the conch.

41

YUCATAN TOMATO SAUCE
(Salsa de Jitomate Yucateca)

Makes about 3 cups

4	dried ancho chili peppers*
⅔	cup boiling water
6	large tomatoes, peeled, seeded, chopped
4	to 6 fresh or canned hot green chili peppers, seeds and stems removed
2	medium onions, cut into quarters
1	large clove garlic
2	tablespoons olive or vegetable oil
2	tablespoons orange juice
1	tablespoon cider vinegar
1	tablespoon lemon juice
1	teaspoon salt
¾	teaspoon cayenne pepper
½	teaspoon sugar

1. Remove stems, seeds and veins of ancho chili peppers while rinsing under cold water. Cut ancho chilies into 1-inch pieces; place in ⅔ cup boiling water. Let stand 45 minutes. (Do not touch eyes while working with chilies; wash hands immediately after preparing chilies.)

2. Place ancho chilies and water in blender container with tomatoes, green chili peppers, onions and garlic; cover. Puree until smooth. Heat oil in 10-inch skillet over medium heat; add tomato mixture. Heat to boiling; reduce heat. Simmer uncovered, stirring occasionally, 15 minutes. Stir in remaining ingredients. Simmer until raw taste disappears, about 30 minutes. Add water if sauce becomes too thick.

TIPS: *Yucatán Tomato Sauce tastes best when made 2 to 3 weeks before serving to blend flavors. Sauce can be stored covered in refrigerator.*

*Anchos are reddish brown, heart-shaped chili peppers with a strong, but not overpowering, flavor. They can be purchased in Latin American grocery stores. One tablespoon ancho powder can be substituted for each ancho pepper. Omit step 1.

YUCATAN-STYLE PORK BAKED IN CLAY (Cochinito Pibil)

Makes 8 servings

2	cups Yucatán Tomato Sauce (see recipe above)
1½	tablespoons achiote*
2	tablespoons salt
1½	tablespoons minced garlic
1½	teaspoons ground cumin
1	teaspoon dried oregano leaves
1	teaspoon pepper
2	tablespoons orange juice
2	tablespoons lemon juice
1	tablespoon cider vinegar
	Baker's Clay (recipe follows)
¾	pound plantain or banana leaves**
1	pork loin roast, boneless (3 to 5 pounds)
	Lime wedges
	Heat oven to 500°

1. Make Yucatán Tomato Sauce.

2. Heat achiote in water to cover in 1-quart saucepan to boiling; reduce heat. Simmer uncovered 5 minutes. Let stand overnight.

3. Place achiote and liquid in blender container; cover. Blend until seeds resemble coarsely ground pepper. Combine mixture with salt, garlic, cumin, oregano and pepper in small bowl. Mix orange and lemon juices and vinegar in small bowl. Gradually add 1 to 2 tablespoons of the liquids to the seasonings mixture, stirring until paste consistency. Reserve remaining liquid.

4. Make Baker's Clay.

5. Dip plantain leaves in boiling water until soft, about 3 minutes; dry on paper toweling. Arrange 3 layers of leaves vein side down in 18-inch square. Place pork fat side up on leaves. Score fat; make 1-inch cuts into meat between strings. Rub meat with seasoning paste, placing paste in cuts. Brush with reserved liquid. Wrap roast in leaves; tie with string. Roll Baker's Clay on floured waxed-paper rectangle, 20 x 18 inches. Place roast in center of dough. Wrap roast securely with dough; seal seams. Place seam side down in aluminum foil-lined shallow roasting pan. Insert meat thermometer so tip is in center of thickest part of meat and does not rest in fat. Roast until thermometer registers 170°, about 2½ hours.

6. Crack clay with hammer; peel clay from leaves. Open leaves with 2 forks; carve roast. Serve with lime wedges and heated Yucatán Tomato Sauce.

TIPS: **Achiote is a dried red tropical seed that adds orange color and light earthy sweet flavor to foods. It can be purchased in Latin American grocery stores and supermarket specialty sections.*

**Aluminum foil or parchment paper can be substituted for the plantain leaves.

BAKER'S CLAY

3½ cups all-purpose flour
1½ cups salt
1   tablespoon ground cumin
1¼ to 1½ cups water

Mix flour, salt and cumin in large bowl. Sprinkle mixture with water, ½ cup at a time, mixing until flour is moistened and dough almost cleans side of bowl. Gather dough into ball. Wrap in waxed paper.

CLASSIC VEGETABLE TRIAD
Makes 8 servings

Black Bean Puree (recipe follows)

Squash with Pepitas (recipe follows)

Corn Pudding (recipe follows)

1. Make Black Bean Puree.

2. Make Squash with Pepitas.

3. Make Corn Pudding.

4. Serve vegetables warm in 3 serving dishes.

BLACK BEAN PUREE (Frijoles Negros Puré) *Makes 3 cups*

½   pound black beans*

1   dried ancho chili pepper**
¼   cup boiling water

1   small onion, minced
1   hot green chili pepper, halved, seeds and stem removed
1   to 4 cloves garlic, crushed
1   to 2 teaspoons salt
1   teaspoon dried epazote leaves***
¼   cup lard

1. Rinse beans in cold water. Heat beans in water to cover in 2-quart saucepan over medium heat to boiling. Remove from heat; cover. Let stand overnight.

2. Heat beans to boiling; reduce heat. Simmer uncovered until beans are soft, 2½ to 3 hours. (Add water to saucepan if beans become dry.) Cool. Pour beans into blender container; cover. Puree until smooth. Return pureed beans to saucepan.

3. Meanwhile, remove stems, seeds and veins of ancho chili pepper while rinsing under cold water. Cut ancho chili into 1-inch pieces; place in ¼ cup boiling water. Let stand 45 minutes. (Do not touch eyes while

Young rope makers separate the rough strands at the sisal plantation.

43

working with chili; wash hands immediately after preparing chili.) Place ancho chili and water in blender container; cover. Puree until smooth.

4.   Sauté pureed chili mixture, onion, green chili pepper, garlic, salt and epazote in lard in small skillet over medium heat until golden, about 3 minutes. Stir into pureed beans. Heat, stirring constantly, until hot. (Add water if mixture becomes dry while heating.) Remove green chili pepper halves before serving.

*TIPS: *Black beans are small flat charcoal-colored beans. They can be purchased in Latin American grocery stores and supermarket specialty sections.*

**One tablespoon ancho powder can be substituted for the ancho pepper. Omit step 3.

***Epazote leaves are strongly flavored crumbled dried herb leaves. They can be purchased in Latin American grocery stores and supermarket specialty sections.

SQUASH WITH PEPITAS (Chayote con Pepitas)   *Makes 3 cups*

3	chayote squash (6 to 7 inches long each), pared, seeded, chopped*
½	cup coarsely chopped salted pepitas**
2	tablespoons butter or margarine
¼	cup butter or margarine
1	teaspoon salt
¼	teaspoon white pepper

Heat chayote squash in water to cover in 2-quart saucepan over medium heat until tender, about 20 minutes. Meanwhile, sauté pepitas in 2 tablespoons butter, stirring occasionally, until golden, about 5 minutes. Drain chayote squash; stir in pepitas, ¼ cup butter, the salt and white pepper.

*TIPS: *Chayote squash is a round or pear-shaped, mild-flavored squash with 1 seed. It can be purchased in Latin American grocery stores. Summer squash can be substituted for the chayote.*

**Pepitas are small light green shelled seeds toasted in oil for delicate flavor. They can be purchased in Latin American grocery stores and supermarket gourmet sections. Salted toasted squash or domestic pumpkin seeds can be substituted for the pepitas.

CORN PUDDING (Atole)   *Makes 3⅓ cups*

2	cups half-and-half
⅓	cup yellow cornmeal
1	package (10 ounces) frozen whole-kernel corn, thawed
1½	teaspoons salt
1	jar (4 ounces) chopped pimientos, drained
2	tablespoons butter or margarine

Heat half-and-half in 2-quart saucepan over low heat; add cornmeal. Cook over medium heat, stirring constantly, until thick, about 10 minutes. Add corn and salt. Cook until corn is tender, about 10 minutes. Stir in pimientos and butter.

Caramel Custard is a spectacular dessert originally from Spain.

CARAMEL CUSTARD (Flan)   *Makes 8 servings*

¾ cup sugar
⅓ cup water

1 cup milk, scalded
2 cups half-and-half
6 eggs, slightly beaten
⅔ cup sugar
1 teaspoon vanilla
⅛ teaspoon salt

1 cup water
½ cup raisins

Heat oven to 350°

1. Heat ¾ cup sugar and ⅓ cup water in small saucepan over low heat, stirring occasionally, until syrup turns light golden, about 15 minutes. Pour syrup into 1½-quart baking dish; coat sides. Set dish aside.

2. Mix milk, half-and-half, eggs, ⅔ cup sugar, the vanilla and salt; pour mixture into prepared baking dish. Place baking dish in shallow baking pan on oven rack; pour ½ inch hot water into pan. Bake until knife inserted 1 inch from edge of custard comes out clean, 55 to 60 minutes. Remove baking dish from water. Cool custard to lukewarm; refrigerate covered until cold.

3. Meanwhile, heat 1 cup water and the raisins in 1-quart saucepan over low heat to boiling; remove from heat. Let stand 15 minutes; drain raisins.

4. Loosen edges of custard with spatula. Invert onto rimmed serving plate. Sprinkle with raisins.

Alsatian Fare

A cobblestone Alsatian square is bordered by tiled-roof buildings.

CHOUCROUTE DINNER MENU

- **ALSATIAN SAUERKRAUT WITH
  MEATS AND SAUSAGES
  TOSSED GREENS WITH
  VINAIGRETTE
  FRENCH BREAD**

- **ANISE COOKIES
  COFFEE OR TEA**

- Recipes included

Pork is plentiful in the rich French farm country of provincial Alsace. The inhabitants there prepare the meat with legendary Gallic style and panache. One of their most famous pork dishes, *choucroute garnie à l'Alsacienne*, is a meal in itself that makes a robust introduction to country French cookery.

The *choucroute* recipe here bakes pork, bacon and sauerkraut — cabbage is a mainstay of Alsatian cuisine — in an aromatic spice and white wine broth. A mélange of four kinds of sausages is heaped onto the pork, and served with boiled potatoes and Poached Liver Dumplings. Such a formidable entrée requires the subtlest accompaniments. Tossed greens with vinaigrette and crisp French bread complement the *choucroute* fittingly.

Pâtisserie is a source of justifiable pride for the Alsatians. Choose one of their irresistible, but light, baked desserts, Anise Cookies, to conclude the hearty dinner. Serves 8.

Wine Suggestion: For an Alsatian dinner, wine from the region, like a Trimbach Sylvaner or Dopff Riesling, should be the perfect accompaniment.

The charm of Alsace includes antiques, inns and historical architecture, in addition to Alsatian Sauerkraut with Meats and Sausages (top right) and Anise Cookies (bottom left).

1 Week Before:	Make Anise Cookies.
4 Hours 30 Minutes Before Serving:	Make Alsatian Sauerkraut with Meats and Sausages. Prepare greens for salad; refrigerate. Make vinaigrette dressing; refrigerate covered.
At Serving Time:	Toss salad.

ALSATIAN SAUERKRAUT WITH MEATS AND SAUSAGES (Choucroute Garnie à l'Alsacienne) *Makes 8 servings*

2 **medium onions (about 12 ounces), sliced**
3 **tablespoons goose fat or lard**
4 **smoked pork hocks (about 12 ounces each), or 2 pounds pork spareribs, cut into 3-rib portions**
1 **smoked pork shoulder roll (about 2 pounds), cut crosswise into ¾-inch slices, or 6 to 8 smoked pork loin chops, ¾ inch thick each**
1 **pound smoked slab bacon, rind removed, cut lengthwise into ½-inch slices**
6 **pounds fresh or canned sauerkraut, rinsed, drained**
3 **cloves garlic, crushed**
8 **juniper berries**
3 **whole cloves**
1 **bay leaf**
½ **teaspoon salt**
¼ **teaspoon freshly ground black pepper**
2 **cups Riesling wine or Sylvaner wine**
1 **cup beef broth**

   Poached Liver Dumplings (recipe follows)

2 **knockwurst or frankfurters***
2 **Thuringer sausages***
2 **bratwurst or bockwurst***
2 **blood sausage links (about 8 ounces), if desired***

   Parslied boiled potatoes

1.   Sauté onions in goose fat in 6- to 8-quart Dutch oven until golden, about 5 minutes. Arrange pork hocks, pork shoulder slices and bacon over onions. Combine sauerkraut, garlic, juniper berries, cloves, bay leaf, salt and pepper; arrange over meats. Pour in wine and broth; heat to boiling and cover. Heat oven to 375°. Bake until meats are tender and liquid is absorbed, 2½ to 3 hours.

2.   Prepare Poached Liver Dumplings through step 1 in recipe; cover and refrigerate.

3.   Remove sauerkraut mixture from oven; keep warm over low heat on top of stove. Increase oven temperature to broil and/or 550°. Cook knockwurst and Thuringer uncovered in simmering water until tender, about 10 minutes; keep warm. Broil bratwurst and blood sausages 3 inches from heat source until brown, about 5 minutes on each side; keep warm. Complete liver dumplings.

4.   Arrange sauerkraut in mound on deep wide serving platter. Place all meats and sausages around and leaning against sauerkraut. Serve with liver dumplings and parslied potatoes.

*TIP: *Any number and/or combination of these sausages can be used as desired.*

Pork liver dumplings are a hearty accompaniment to the sauerkraut and meats.

POACHED LIVER DUMPLINGS (Quenelles de Foie)   *Makes 8*

⅓   cup chopped onion
2   tablespoons chopped shallots
1   tablespoon vegetable oil
8   ounces fresh pork liver, cut into small pieces
4   ounces fresh pork fatback or cold lard, cut into small pieces
¼   cup snipped fresh parsley
1   egg
½   cup all-purpose flour
2   tablespoons semolina or farina
2   teaspoons seasoned salt
¼   teaspoon freshly ground black pepper

3   quarts water
4   peppercorns
2   whole cloves
1   bay leaf
1   teaspoon salt
     Snipped fresh parsley

1. Sauté onion and shallots in oil in small skillet until tender, about 5 minutes. Combine with liver, fatback and ¼ cup parsley in medium-size bowl. Pass mixture through fine blade of meat grinder twice. Stir egg, flour, semolina, seasoned salt and pepper into liver mixture until smooth.

2. Fifteen to 20 minutes before serving, heat remaining ingredients except snipped parsley in Dutch oven to boiling. Measure liver mixture by scant ¼ cupfuls and push into boiling liquid using rubber spatula; cover. Cook until dumplings rise to surface and become firm throughout, about 10 minutes. Lift dumplings with slotted spoon to heated serving dish. Sprinkle with snipped parsley. Serve immediately.

TIP: Poached Liver Dumplings can serve 4 as an entrée. Serve with parslied boiled potatoes or buttered egg noodles, tossed salad and French bread.

ANISE COOKIES (Biscuits à l'Anis)   *Makes about 5 dozen*

3   eggs
1½   cups sugar
2   cups all-purpose flour
1   tablespoon anise seeds

1. Beat eggs and sugar in large mixer bowl on medium speed, scraping bowl frequently, 5 minutes. Combine flour and anise seeds; stir into egg-sugar mixture, a few tablespoons at a time, scraping bowl constantly. Beat 3 minutes on medium speed after last addition.

2. Attach a ⅜-inch-diameter plain writing tip to pastry bag. Pipe dough through bag onto greased baking sheets, forming 1½-inch circles. Refrigerate uncovered to dry dough at least 6 hours, no longer than 24 hours.

3. Heat oven to 300°. Bake cookies until firm, about 20 minutes. (Cookies will separate into 2 layers when baking.) Cool on wire racks.

4. Store cookies in airtight container with slice of bread (change bread often) at room temperature no longer than 1 month. Flavor mellows after 1 week.

Alsatian Riesling wine accents the chicken and mushroom entrée.

ALSATIAN CHICKEN MENU

- **ALSATIAN ONION TART**

- **CHICKEN WITH RIESLING WINE
  BUTTERED ASPARAGUS
  HEARTS OF PALM SALAD WITH
      HERB DRESSING**

- **YEAST COFFEE CAKE
  COFFEE OR TEA**

- Recipes included

Elegant French cooking isn't produced only in Parisian kitchens. Some of the most exquisite chapters in France's culinary history were written in provinces like Alsace. From this historic region of orchards and vineyards, wedged next to Germany, comes an array of glorious gastronomy ideal for a special dinner party.

Open the meal with élan — with a sumptuous onion tart. Since dairy products are abundant there, the tables of Alsace often hold delicate egg and cream creations such as this. World-famous Alsatian vineyards contribute an accent for the entrée, Chicken with Riesling Wine. A bouquet of the subtle white wine and shallots simmers the poultry to mouth-watering tenderness, then becomes the base for a creamy mushroom sauce. Understated side dishes — buttered asparagus and hearts of palm salad with herb dressing — complement the chicken best.

For dessert, present a showpiece of Alsatian pastry chefs, *kougelhopf*. This rich brioche with raisins and almonds is said to have been a favorite of Marie Antoinette. And your guests may feel like monarchs as they sample the sweet with coffee or tea. Serves 6.

Wine Suggestion: The best selection would be the same wine used in cooking. So open a bottle of Alsatian Riesling, either from Hügel or Trimbach.

A golden onion tart is rich with eggs and cream.

51

The region's famous vineyards surround a charming village in Alsace.

PARTY PLAN FOR ALSATIAN CHICKEN MENU

2 Days Before: Make Yeast Coffee Cake.

That Afternoon: Prepare Alsatian Onion Tart through step 2 in recipe; refrigerate onions and Pastry, separately, covered.
Prepare salad and dressing ingredients; refrigerate separately.
Prepare asparagus; refrigerate.

1 Hour 30 Minutes Before Serving: Complete Alsatian Onion Tart.
Make Chicken with Riesling Wine.

15 Minutes Before Serving: Cook asparagus.
Complete salad.

20 Minutes Before Dessert: Heat Yeast Coffee Cake loosely wrapped in aluminum foil at 350° 15 minutes, if desired.

ALSATIAN ONION TART (Quiche aux Oignons à l'Alsacienne)

Makes 6 appetizer servings

¼ cup butter or margarine
3 large onions (about 1½ pounds), thinly sliced

   Pastry (recipe follows)

2 tablespoons flour
3 eggs plus 2 egg yolks, beaten
1 cup milk
1 cup whipping cream
¾ teaspoon salt
⅛ teaspoon ground nutmeg
⅛ teaspoon cayenne pepper
⅛ teaspoon freshly ground black pepper

1¼ cups all-purpose flour
½ teaspoon salt
½ cup cold butter or margarine
1 egg, beaten
2 tablespoons cold water

1. Melt butter in 10-inch skillet over low heat. Stir in onions; cover. Cook until soft and golden, about 20 minutes.

2. Make Pastry.

3. Heat oven to 425°. Stir flour into onions until evenly coated. Arrange onions in pastry-lined pie plate. Mix remaining ingredients; pour over onions.

4. Bake tart 15 minutes. Reduce oven temperature to 350°. Bake until filling is set and top is brown, 30 to 35 minutes. Let stand 15 minutes before cutting.

TIP: Serve Alsatian Onion Tart as a luncheon entrée with tossed salad, French bread and fruit.

PASTRY   *Makes one 9-inch crust*

1. Measure flour and salt into small bowl. Cut in cold butter. Mix egg and cold water; stir into dry ingredients until dough almost cleans side of bowl. Gather dough into ball.

2. Roll dough on lightly floured cloth-covered surface into 11-inch circle. Fold pastry into quarters; unfold and ease into 9-inch pie plate. Trim and fold pastry into high rim; flute.

53

CHICKEN WITH RIESLING WINE (Poularde au Riesling) *Makes 6 servings*

1   broiler-fryer chicken (about 3½
        pounds), cut up
1   whole chicken breast (about 12
        ounces), split
¼   cup butter or margarine
⅓   cup minced shallots
1   tablespoon flour
1   cup Riesling wine
½   cup chicken broth
½   teaspoon salt
⅛   teaspoon freshly ground black
        pepper

8   ounces fresh mushrooms,
        cut into quarters
2   tablespoons butter or margarine

1   cup whipping cream
1   teaspoon fresh lemon juice
     Snipped fresh parsley

1.   Cook chicken, a few pieces at a time, in ¼ cup butter in large skillet until brown, about 20 minutes; remove. Sauté shallots in pan drippings until soft, about 3 minutes. Stir in flour, scraping up brown particles. Return chicken to skillet. Stir in wine, broth, salt and pepper. Heat to boiling; reduce heat and cover. Simmer until chicken is tender, about 30 minutes.

2.   Sauté mushrooms in 2 tablespoons butter in small skillet until tender, about 5 minutes; reserve.

3.   Remove chicken to serving platter; keep warm. Strain pan juices through sieve into saucepan. Heat to boiling; boil until liquid is reduced to 1 cup, 3 to 5 minutes. Reduce heat; stir in reserved mushrooms, the cream and lemon juice. Cook and stir until thickened, about 2 minutes. Pour sauce over chicken. Sprinkle with parsley.

YEAST COFFEE CAKE (Kougelhopf) *Makes one 9-inch cake*

1   package active dry yeast
¾   cup warm milk (105° to 115°)

½   cup granulated sugar
½   cup butter or margarine, softened
1   teaspoon salt
1½   teaspoons grated lemon peel
1   teaspoon almond extract
4   eggs, at room temperature
3   cups all-purpose flour

1   cup golden raisins
¼   cup cherry-flavored liqueur
     Whole natural almonds

     Powdered sugar

1.   Dissolve yeast in ¼ cup of the warm milk; let stand 10 minutes.

2.   Measure granulated sugar, butter, salt, lemon peel and extract into large mixer bowl. Beat on medium speed, scraping bowl occasionally, until smooth, about 3 minutes. Add eggs, 1 at a time, beating well after each addition. Beat in yeast mixture; beat in flour alternately with remaining warm milk. Beat on medium speed 2 minutes after last addition; cover. Let rise in warm place until double, about 2 hours.

3.   Cook raisins and liqueur in covered saucepan over low heat until liqueur is absorbed, about 10 minutes; cool. Butter an 8-cup kougelhopf mold or other decorative tube mold. Arrange almonds in bottom of mold.

4.   Stir raisins into batter. Spoon batter into prepared mold; cover with greased waxed paper. Let stand in warm place until batter rises just to top of mold, about 1 hour 20 minutes; remove paper.

5.   Heat oven to 425°. Bake cake 10 minutes. Reduce oven temperature to 350°. Bake until top is brown and cake pulls slightly from side of mold, about 30 minutes. Cool in mold 10 minutes; invert onto wire rack. Serve warm or at room temperature sprinkled with powdered sugar.

TIP: Store cooled Kougelhopf in airtight plastic bag at room temperature no longer than 2 days or in freezer no longer than 4 months.

Kougelhopf makes an elegant dessert offering.

An Indian Buffet

The sights of India: An elephant in festive dress; a woman with *puja*, a religious offering of fresh fruit and flowers.

INDIAN BUFFET MENU

- **DEEP-FRIED FILLED PASTRIES**
- **MULLIGATAWNY SOUP**

- **CURRIED LAMB**
- **SHRIMP AND RICE**
- **ROAST SPICED CHICKEN**
- **SPICY RICE**
- **FRIED LENTILS**
- **GREEN BEANS WITH COCONUT**
- **CHUTNEY**
- **SIDE DISHES**
- **BREAD**
  BEER

- **CARROT PUDDING**
  TEA

- Recipes included

India boasts an inexhaustible number of native foods based on racial, religious and tribal traditions. Curry and chutney merely scratch the surface of a cuisine that ranges from the lavish lamb and poultry dishes of the North to the rich rice, fish and coconut specialties of the South. Our menu offers a panorama of the diverse flavors in Indian cookery.

Samosas — tiny pastry triangles stuffed with lamb or shrimp — begin the buffet. Hot and pungent Mulligatawny Soup derives its name from a southern Indian word meaning "pepper water."

The main dishes of the authentic meal include neither beef, since the cow is sacred to the Hindus, nor pork, prohibited by Muslim law. Curried Lamb, cooked in yogurt and aromatic spices, originated in the Kashmir region of northern India. Also from the North, our chicken entrée demonstrates a classic *tandoori* delicacy, prepared in a special pit-type clay oven in its native land.

The Spicy Rice and Shrimp and Rice recipes show off the widely grown Indian grain at its savory best. Fried Lentils and green beans flecked with coconut are tasty vegetable accompaniments from the South. To complement these foods, serve a mixed fruit chutney, *pappadams* — thin lentil-flour breads — and bowls of side dishes such as egg, nuts, onion and toasted coconut. For a sweet finale to the feast, set out Carrot Pudding, adorned with edible silver leaf when served in India. Serves 16 to 20.

Wine Suggestion: We often revert to a thirst-quenching beer to match the spiciness of Indian foods. But a Hungarian Lake Balaton Cabernet or young Zinfandel from California would also go well with the menu.

Curries are made from countless blends of herbs and spices.

Lemon decorates both the Shrimp and Rice and Curried Lamb dishes.

PARTY PLAN FOR INDIAN BUFFET MENU

2 Weeks Before:

Make Clarified Butter; cover and refrigerate.
Make Chutney.
Make Deep-fried Filled Pastries.

2 Days Before:

Make Mulligatawny Soup, except do not garnish.
Complete Curried Lamb, except do not garnish.

1 Day Before:

Prepare Carrot Pudding through step 2 in recipe.
Fry Bread; cover tightly.
Prepare Roast Spiced Chicken through step 1 in recipe.

That Afternoon:

Cut fresh green beans, if used, for Green Beans with Coconut and prepare through step 1 in recipe; cover and refrigerate.

Shown are Spicy Rice, side dishes, lentils, Roast Spiced Chicken, Shrimp and Rice, Curried Lamb, green beans, and Mulligatawny Soup.

Prepare garnishes and Side Dishes for menu; cover and refrigerate.
Complete step 2 of Fried Lentils recipe.
Cook rice for Shrimp and Rice; cover and refrigerate.

2 Hours Before Serving: Complete Roast Spiced Chicken.

1 Hour 15 Minutes Before Serving: Make Spicy Rice.

45 Minutes Before Serving: Complete Shrimp and Rice.
Complete Fried Lentils.
Complete Green Beans with Coconut.
Heat Deep-fried Filled Pastries.
Heat Mulligatawny Soup; garnish.
Heat Curried Lamb; garnish.

15 Minutes Before Dessert: Complete Carrot Pudding.

2 cups all-purpose flour
¾ teaspoon salt
¼ cup butter or margarine
¾ cup unflavored yogurt

Lamb or Shrimp Filling
(recipes follow)

4 cups vegetable oil
*Ti leaf, if desired
Lemon wedges,
if desired
Parsley, if desired

1. Mix flour and salt; cut in butter thoroughly. Stir in yogurt. Shape dough into ball; cover with damp cloth. Refrigerate 2 hours.

2. Make either Lamb or Shrimp Filling.

3. Roll ¼ of the dough ¹/₁₆ inch thick on lightly floured cloth-covered surface. Cut into 4-inch circles. Cut each circle in half. Moisten edges with water. (Cover remaining dough with damp cloth until needed.)

4. Place 1 teaspoonful of the filling on each half circle. Fold dough over filling forming triangle. Press edges together securely; place on baking sheet and cover. Refrigerate while preparing remaining pastries. (Pastries can be stored in refrigerator up to 24 hours before frying.)

5. Heat oven to 225°. Heat oil in deep-fat fryer or kettle to 375°. Fry about 5 pastries at a time until light brown on both sides, about 4 minutes. Keep warm in oven while frying remaining pastries.** Arrange pastries on ti leaf on platter. Garnish with lemon wedges and parsley.

TIPS: *Ti leaves can be purchased in florist shops.

**Pastries can be stored tightly wrapped in aluminum foil in freezer for 2 weeks. To serve, heat oven to 375°. Place pastries on ungreased baking sheet. Bake until hot, about 10 minutes.

LAMB FILLING
Makes about 2 cups

½ cup minced onion
2 cloves garlic, minced
2 tablespoons vegetable oil
¾ pound ground lamb*
1 tablespoon curry powder
1 teaspoon salt
1 teaspoon crushed coriander seeds
1 teaspoon crushed cumin seeds
½ teaspoon freshly ground
    black pepper
3 tablespoons unflavored yogurt

Sauté onion and garlic in oil over medium heat 8 minutes. Mix in remaining ingredients except yogurt. Cook, stirring constantly, until meat loses red color. Mix in yogurt; reduce heat. Cook over low heat, stirring occasionally, 15 minutes. Cool slightly; cover and refrigerate.

TIP: *¾ pound ground beef can be substituted for the ground lamb.

SHRIMP FILLING
Makes about 2 cups

½ cup minced onion
1 clove garlic, minced
2 tablespoons butter or
    margarine
¾ pound shrimp, shells removed,
    deveined, chopped
¼ cup diced peeled tomatoes
1 teaspoon salt
1 teaspoon crushed coriander
    seeds
1 teaspoon crushed cumin seeds
⅛ teaspoon crushed
    red pepper
2 hard-cooked eggs, finely
    chopped

Sauté onion and garlic in butter over medium heat 8 minutes. Mix in remaining ingredients except eggs. Cook, stirring frequently, 5 minutes. Cool slightly; stir in eggs. Cover and refrigerate.

MULLIGATAWNY SOUP (Murghi Shoorva)

Makes 16 servings (about ½ cup each)

2   quarts water
1   tablespoon salt
6   peppercorns
2   broiler-fryer chickens,
      (2 pounds each), cut up

2   teaspoons ground coriander
1   teaspoon ground turmeric
½   teaspoon ground ginger
¼   teaspoon crushed red pepper
1½   teaspoons vinegar
½   cup thinly sliced onion
2   tablespoons butter or
      margarine

Snipped fresh parsley,
    if desired

1. Combine water, salt, peppercorns and chicken pieces in Dutch oven. Heat to boiling; reduce heat and cover loosely. Simmer until thickest chicken pieces are tender, about 45 minutes. Skim fat from broth.

2. Mix coriander, turmeric, ginger, red pepper and vinegar into paste. Sauté onion in butter over very low heat until onion is tender but not brown, about 10 minutes. Stir spice paste into onion. Cook and stir 5 minutes.

3. Stir onion mixture into chicken soup. Cook 10 minutes. Remove meat from bones and cut up. Return meat to soup.* Garnish with snipped parsley.

TIP: *Mulligatawny Soup can be made 2 days in advance; cover and refrigerate. To serve, heat until hot.*

CURRIED LAMB (Rogan Josh)

Makes 6 to 8 servings

¼   cup Clarified Butter
      (recipe follows)

1   cup unflavored yogurt
1½   teaspoons salt
¼   teaspoon crushed
      red pepper
3   pounds boneless lamb, cut
      into 1-inch cubes

2   cups chopped onions
1   tablespoon minced gingerroot
2   cloves garlic, minced
2   teaspoons crushed
      coriander seeds
1   teaspoon ground turmeric
1   teaspoon crushed cumin seeds
½   teaspoon ground cinnamon
½   teaspoon freshly ground
      black pepper
⅛   teaspoon crushed cardamom
      seeds
¼   cup unflavored yogurt
1   cup chicken broth
      Lemon wedges
      Onion rings

1. Make Clarified Butter.

2. Mix 1 cup yogurt, the salt and red pepper; pour over lamb. Stir until lamb is coated with yogurt mixture; cover. Refrigerate, stirring meat occasionally, at least 3 hours, no longer than 12 hours.

3. Melt Clarified Butter in Dutch oven; cook and stir remaining ingredients except ¼ cup yogurt, the chicken broth, lemon wedges and onion rings in Clarified Butter over medium heat 7 minutes. Stir in lamb, ¼ cup yogurt and the chicken broth. Heat to boiling; reduce heat and cover. Simmer until lamb is tender, about 1¼ hours.* Garnish with lemon wedges and onion rings.

TIP: *Curried Lamb can be made 2 days in advance. Cool slightly; cover and refrigerate. To serve, skim layer of fat from lamb mixture, if desired. Heat until hot.*

CLARIFIED BUTTER (Ghee)   *Makes about 2 cups*

1. Cut 1½ pounds unsalted butter into 10 pieces; place in saucepan. Heat over medium heat, stirring frequently, until butter is melted. Heat over high heat to boiling, until butter foams; reduce heat. Cook over low heat 30 minutes.

2. Line strainer with several layers of damp cheesecloth. Pour butter slowly through cheesecloth into dry jar; cover. (If any solids go through, strain until Ghee is completely clear.) Refrigerate until needed. Just before using, let stand at room temperature about 30 minutes.

TIP: Ghee is traditionally preferred in many Indian recipes. Butter can be used but it has a much lower burning point, due to the milk solids. The milk solids are discarded when Ghee is prepared.

SHRIMP AND RICE (Jhinga Pilau)   *Makes 6 to 8 servings*

¼ cup Clarified Butter
    (see recipe above)

1½ cups uncooked long grain
    rice

2 pounds unshelled deveined
    shrimp
2 cups minced onions
1 cup ground blanched almonds
½ cup unflavored yogurt
2 cloves garlic, minced
2 teaspoons ground coriander
2 teaspoons salt
½ teaspoon ground turmeric
½ teaspoon ground cumin
½ teaspoon freshly ground
    pepper
¾ cup water

½ teaspoon ground cinnamon

    *Lemon peel rose

1. Make Clarified Butter.

2. Cook rice according to package directions; reserve.

3. Combine remaining ingredients except water, cinnamon and lemon peel. Cook and stir shrimp mixture in Clarified Butter in large skillet over high heat 2 minutes. Stir in water and cover. Cook 2 minutes.

4. Heat oven to 300°. Spread half the reserved rice in greased 2½-quart casserole. Remove shrimp from skillet with fork, and arrange on rice. Reserve several shrimp for garnish, if desired. Cover with remaining rice. Pour onion sauce over top layer of rice. Garnish with reserved shrimp. Sprinkle with cinnamon and cover.

5. Bake until hot, about 25 minutes. Garnish with lemon peel rose.

*TIP: *To make lemon peel rose, carefully cut continuous strip of peel from lemon. Wind peel into rose shape; fasten with wooden pick.*

ROAST SPICED CHICKEN (Tandoori Murghi)   *Makes 6 to 8 servings*

1 cup unflavored yogurt
2 tablespoons minced gingerroot
1 tablespoon salt
2 teaspoons ground cumin
2 teaspoons paprika
1 teaspoon ground coriander
1 teaspoon ground cinnamon
½ teaspoon ground cardamom
½ teaspoon ground nutmeg
½ teaspoon freshly ground
    black pepper
    Dash cayenne pepper,
    if desired
4 drops red food color

1. Mix all ingredients except chickens, butter, lemons and parsley. Spread yogurt mixture on chickens, including inside cavities; cover. Refrigerate at least 4 hours, no longer than 24 hours.

2. Heat oven to 375°. Place chickens in greased roasting pan, 15½ x 10½ x 2¼ inches. Pour butter over chickens.

3. Roast chickens, spooning butter over frequently, until drumstick meat feels very soft when pressed between fingers, 1¼ to 1½ hours. Garnish with lemon wedges and parsley. To serve, carve or cut chickens into eighths.

TIP: In India a special pit-type clay oven, called a tandoor oven, is used for cooking the chicken.

2   broiler-fryer chickens
      (about 2½ pounds each)

¼   cup butter or margarine,
      melted

2   lemons, cut into wedges
      Parsley sprigs

SPICY RICE (Massale Dar Pilau)   *Makes 16 servings*

¾   cup Clarified Butter
      (see recipe, page 62)

4   cups uncooked long grain
      rice

4   onions, thinly sliced
2   cups unflavored yogurt
3   teaspoons salt
4   cloves garlic, minced
6   cardamom seeds, crushed
1   teaspoon ground turmeric
1   teaspoon ground ginger
½   teaspoon crushed red pepper
6   cups hot chicken broth

    Green pepper rings,
      if desired
    Tomato wedges, if desired

1. Make Clarified Butter.

2. Cover rice with water; let soak 30 minutes.

3. Sauté onions in Clarified Butter in Dutch oven until onions are brown. Drain rice. Cook and stir rice in onion mixture 5 minutes. Stir in remaining ingredients except broth, green peppers and tomatoes. Cook over high heat 5 minutes. Stir in broth; cover.

4. Heat rice mixture to boiling; reduce heat. Cook over low heat until rice is tender, about 25 minutes. Garnish with pepper rings and tomato wedges.

FRIED LENTILS (Dal)   *Makes 16 servings*

½   cup Clarified Butter
      (see recipe, page 62)

3   cups lentils

2   cups chopped onions
3   teaspoons salt
2   teaspoons ground turmeric
2   teaspoons crushed cumin seeds
½   teaspoon crushed red pepper

¾   cup snipped fresh coriander
      leaves or parsley
    Lemon peel, if desired

1. Make Clarified Butter.

2. Cover lentils with water; let soak 1 hour. Heat lentils and water to boiling. Cook 45 minutes. Drain well.

3. Melt Clarified Butter in 12-inch skillet or Dutch oven. Sauté onions, salt, turmeric, cumin and pepper in Clarified Butter over low heat until onions are tender; reserve some onion for garnish, if desired.

4. Stir in lentils. Cook over low heat, stirring frequently, 20 minutes. (Watch carefully to prevent burning.) Stir in coriander leaves; sprinkle with reserved onion. Garnish with strip of lemon peel.

GREEN BEANS WITH COCONUT (Same ki Bhaji)   *Makes 16 servings*

2   cups flaked coconut
2   cups water

2   cups chopped onions
½   teaspoon mustard seeds
2   cloves garlic, minced
4   tablespoons vegetable oil

1. Measure half the coconut and water into blender; cover. Blend on medium speed, scraping sides of container, if necessary, 3 minutes; reserve. Repeat procedure with remaining coconut and water.

2. Sauté onions, mustard seeds and garlic in oil in Dutch oven over medium heat 5 minutes. Mix in remaining ingredients and reserved coconut mixture; cover.

4	pounds fresh green beans, cut into 2-inch pieces*
2	tablespoons crushed coriander seeds
3	teaspoons salt
2	teaspoons ground turmeric

3. Heat to boiling; reduce heat. Simmer, stirring occasionally, 15 minutes.

*TIP: *6 packages (9 ounces each) frozen cut green beans, thawed, can be substituted for the fresh green beans.*

CHUTNEY (Chatni)   *Makes about 4 cups*

1	pound apples, chopped (about 5 cups)
½	pound dried apricots or peaches, chopped (about 2 cups)
3	limes or lemons, cut into thin wedges, seeds removed
1½	cups packed brown sugar
1	cup cider vinegar
2	cloves garlic, minced
2	teaspoons ground ginger
1½	teaspoons salt
1	teaspoon ground cinnamon
1	teaspoon chili powder
½	teaspoon ground coriander
½	teaspoon ground cloves
½	teaspoon freshly ground black pepper
¼	teaspoon crushed red pepper

Combine all ingredients in large saucepan. Heat to boiling; reduce heat. Cook over low heat, stirring frequently, until soft and brown, about 1 hour. Cool slightly and cover. Serve at room temperature.

TIP: Chutney can be stored covered in refrigerator 2 weeks.

SIDE DISHES

Side dishes are often served with an Indian meal. They are passed and eaten with all the foods for texture and flavor contrast. Side dishes can include:

Hard-cooked egg — chopped.
Nuts — chopped.
Coconut — toasted.
Onion — chopped and mixed with yogurt.
Cucumber — chopped and mixed with yogurt.
Chutney — see recipe above.

BREAD (Pappadams)   *Makes about 30*

| | Vegetable oil |
| 1 | package pappadams (about 30)* |

Heat oil (2 inches) to 375°. Fry bread in oil until brown, about 30 seconds on each side. Drain on paper toweling.**

*TIPS: *Pappadams can be purchased at specialty and gourmet shops.*

**Bread can be fried 2 days in advance; cover tightly and store at room temperature.*

Carrot Pudding flecked with pistachios and served with tea completes the buffet.

CARROT PUDDING (Gajar Halva) *Makes 16 servings*

2   **pounds carrots, pared, grated (about 10 cups)**
3   **cups milk**
1   **cup heavy cream**

2   **cups ground blanched almonds**
1   **cup packed brown sugar**
½   **cup butter or margarine**
½   **teaspoon ground nutmeg**
¼   **teaspoon ground saffron**

½   **cup unsalted pistachio or pine nuts**

1. Combine carrots, milk and cream in Dutch oven. Heat, stirring constantly, to boiling; reduce heat. Cook over medium heat, stirring frequently, until milk and cream are absorbed, about 45 minutes.

2. Stir in almonds, brown sugar, butter, nutmeg and saffron. Cook over low heat, stirring frequently, 20 minutes.*

3. Spoon Carrot Pudding on serving dish, mounding it in center. Garnish with pistachio nuts. Serve warm.

*TIP: *Carrot Pudding can be prepared to this point 24 hours in advance. Cool slightly; cover and refrigerate. To serve, heat over low heat, stirring frequently, until warm. Proceed with step 3.*

A Finnish Coffee Table

Finland's fresh colors are both natural and man-made.

Even the plainest coffee table occupies a place of distinction in Finnish homes. For it is there that family and friends gather to sample the special brand of hospitality known as coffee-table entertaining. To accompany their highly savored cups of coffee, Finns often set out a lavish spread of breads, cookies and cakes.

Customarily, the coffee table (like the one we photographed in the city of Lahti) begins with *pulla*. This cardamom-flavored coffee bread perfectly complements that first cup of robust brew. After the second is poured, guests proceed to a rich Cream Pound Cake, and a choice of three kinds of cookies — rye, almond or ginger.

The showpiece is left until last. A magnificent three-layer Strawberry Cake spread with whipped cream and sprinkled with almonds is meant for the third cup of coffee. And after that, it's only polite to try any of the treats one might have missed before. Serves 18.

Wine Suggestion: In between bites of cake and cookies, sip a glass of fabulous late-harvest Johannisberg Riesling from Joseph Phelps Vineyard, or Hungary's famous Tokaji Aszú.

FINNISH COFFEE-TABLE MENU

- **CARDAMOM COFFEE BREAD**
- **RYE COOKIES**
- **FINNISH COOKIE S'S**
- **FINNISH GINGER COOKIES**
- **CREAM POUND CAKE**
- **STRAWBERRY CAKE**
  COFFEE

• Recipes included

1 Week Before:	Make Rye Cookies; store in airtight container.
	Make Finnish Ginger Cookies; store in airtight container.
	Make Finnish Cookie S's; store in airtight container.
1 Day Before:	Make Cardamom Coffee Bread; wrap in aluminum foil and store at room temperature. Second loaf can be frozen up to 2 months, if desired.
	Prepare Strawberry Cake through step 2 in recipe.
3 Hours Before Serving:	Make Cream Pound Cake.
	Complete Strawberry Cake; refrigerate uncovered until served.

CARDAMOM COFFEE BREAD (Pulla)

Makes 2 loaves

1	package active dry yeast
¼	cup warm water (105° to 115°) ·
1	cup evaporated milk
½	cup sugar
½	teaspoon salt
½	teaspoon ground cardamom
2	eggs, slightly beaten
4	to 4½ cups all-purpose flour
¼	cup butter or margarine, melted
1	egg yolk
2	tablespoons whole milk
¼	cup sliced blanched almonds
	Sugar

1. Dissolve yeast in warm water in large bowl. Stir in evaporated milk, ½ cup sugar, the salt, cardamom, 2 eggs and 2 cups of the flour. Beat in butter until mixture is smooth and glossy. Stir in enough of the remaining flour to make dough easy to handle; cover. Let rest 15 minutes.

2. Turn dough onto lightly floured surface. Knead until smooth and elastic, about 10 minutes. Place in greased bowl. Turn greased side up; cover. Let rise in warm place until double, about 1 hour. Punch down dough; cover. Let rise again until double, about 1 hour. (Dough is ready if impression remains.)

3. Divide dough in half. Divide each half into 3 parts. Roll each part into strand, 1 inch in diameter. Braid 3 strands together to make straight loaf. Pinch ends; fold under. Repeat procedure with remaining 3 strands. Place each loaf on lightly greased baking sheet; cover. Let rise until double, 30 to 45 minutes.

4. Heat oven to 375°. Mix egg yolk and whole milk. Brush loaves with mixture; sprinkle with almonds and sugar. Bake until loaves are light brown and sound hollow when tapped, 20 to 25 minutes. Cool on wire racks.

RYE COOKIES (Ruiskakut)

Makes about 3½ dozen

½	cup butter or margarine, softened
⅓	cup sugar
1	to 1½ cups rye flour
½	cup all-purpose flour
1	egg, slightly beaten
	Heat oven to 400°

1. Beat butter and sugar in medium-size bowl until light and fluffy. Stir in rye and all-purpose flours. Mix in egg. Work dough with hands until smooth. Roll dough ⅛ inch thick on lightly floured cloth-covered surface. Cut into 2-inch circles.

2. Place cookies 1 inch apart on greased baking sheets. Cut hole slightly off center in each cookie with cap of small bottle. Pierce entire cookie with fork. Bake until light brown, 5 to 7 minutes. Cool on wire racks.

On next pages: Cream Pound Cake, Cardamom Coffee Bread, Strawberry Cake, and rye, ginger, and S-shaped cookies.

FINNISH COOKIE S'S (Suomalaiset Pikkuleivät)

Makes about 3½ dozen

½ cup butter or margarine, softened
¼ cup sugar
1 egg
½ teaspoon almond extract
Dash salt
1½ to 1¾ cups all-purpose flour

1 egg, beaten
Sugar
¼ cup finely chopped toasted
    almonds

1. Beat butter, ¼ cup sugar, 1 egg, the almond extract and salt in small mixer bowl until light and fluffy. Stir in enough of the flour to make dough easy to handle. Work dough with hands until smooth.

2. Heat oven to 375°. Shape dough into long strands, ½-inch thick each. Cut strands into 2½-inch lengths. Dip into beaten egg; roll in sugar, then in almonds. Arrange in S shapes on greased baking sheets. Bake just until golden, about 8 minutes. Cool on wire racks.

FINNISH GINGER COOKIES (Inkiväärileivät)

Makes about 3½ dozen

¼ cup butter or margarine, softened
¼ cup packed dark brown sugar
¼ cup whipping cream
¼ cup light molasses or dark
    corn syrup
1½ teaspoons ground ginger
1½ teaspoons ground cinnamon
½ teaspoon baking powder
¼ teaspoon salt
1½ to 1¾ cups all-purpose flour

1. Mix butter, sugar, cream and molasses in medium-size bowl. Stir in remaining ingredients; cover. Refrigerate at least 3 hours.

2. Heat oven to 375°. Divide dough into 4 parts. Roll each part ⅛ inch thick on lightly floured cloth-covered surface. Cut into 2½-inch circles with scalloped cookie cutter. Place 1 inch apart on greased baking sheets.

3. Bake cookies until light brown, about 8 minutes. Cool on wire racks.

CREAM POUND CAKE (Kermakakku)

Makes 12 servings

1 cup whipping cream
2 eggs
1 teaspoon vanilla
1½ cups all-purpose flour
1 cup granulated sugar
2 teaspoons baking powder
½ teaspoon salt

Powdered sugar, if desired

Heat oven to 350°

1. Beat whipping cream in chilled medium-size bowl until stiff peaks form. Beat eggs and vanilla in small bowl until light and fluffy; fold into whipped cream. Mix remaining ingredients except powdered sugar. Fold into cream mixture.

2. Pour batter into greased 9-cup Bundt cake pan. Bake until cake pulls away from sides of pan, 50 to 60 minutes. Cool in pan 10 minutes. Invert onto wire rack; cool completely. Sprinkle with powdered sugar.

STRAWBERRY CAKE (Mansikkakakku)

4   eggs
1   cup sugar
2   tablespoons water
½   teaspoon vanilla
1   cup all-purpose flour
2   teaspoons cornstarch
1   teaspoon baking powder
¼   teaspoon salt

½   cup orange-flavored liqueur
2   tablespoons lemon juice
1½   cups whipping cream
2   tablespoons sugar

1   teaspoon unflavored gelatin
½   cup water
1   tablespoon sugar

1   cup halved strawberries
     Ground toasted almonds

     Heat oven to 375°

1.   Beat eggs in large mixer bowl until foamy, about 3 minutes. Beat in 1 cup sugar until thick and lemon colored; mix in 2 tablespoons water and the vanilla. Mix flour, cornstarch, baking powder and salt. Fold into egg mixture.

2.   Divide batter among 3 greased and floured layer pans, 8 x 1½ inches each. Bake until wooden pick inserted in center comes out clean, 10 to 15 minutes. Cool in pans 10 minutes; remove from pans. Cool completely on wire racks.*

3.   Mix liqueur and lemon juice. Brush bottom side of each cake layer generously with liqueur mixture. Beat whipping cream and 2 tablespoons sugar in chilled small bowl until stiff peaks form.

4.   Place 1 cake layer liqueur side up on serving plate; spread with thin layer of whipped cream. Place second layer liqueur side up over first; spread with thin layer of whipped cream. Top with third cake layer liqueur side up. Refrigerate remaining whipped cream.

5.   Soften gelatin in ¼ cup of the water. Heat remaining water to boiling. Stir in softened gelatin and 1 tablespoon sugar until dissolved. Refrigerate until mixture is consistency of unbeaten egg whites.

6.   Arrange strawberries on top of cake. Spoon gelatin over strawberries. Spread remaining whipped cream on side of cake; pipe rim of whipped cream around top edge. Sprinkle ground almonds around bottom layer. Refrigerate.

TIP: *Cake can be prepared to this point up to 24 hours in advance. Cover and refrigerate. Proceed with step 3.

A sampling of Finnish arts, crafts and sights.

An Eastern Finnish Offering

Marinated Mushroom Salad features a favorite vegetable of Finns.

KARELIAN DINNER MENU

- BORSCHT

- KARELIAN RAGOUT
  BOILED POTATOES WITH DILL
- MARINATED MUSHROOM SALAD
  SALTED CUCUMBERS
- KARELIAN RICE PASTIES
  WITH EGG BUTTER

- CRANBERRY FRUIT SOUP
  HOMEMADE BEER

• Recipes included

On Finland's eastern fringe — facing the Soviet Union — lies Karelia. This lake-studded region is renowned for its cooking, which combines typically Finnish foods with those reflecting a Russian influence.

Steaming Borscht afloat with thin sausage slices looks eastward for its origins. The soup is a hearty opening course served with sour cream and lemon slices. Beef, lamb and pork blend their flavors into robust Karelian Ragout, popular throughout Finland. Favorite Finnish vegetables star in several of the dinner's accompaniments: Marinated Mushroom Salad, boiled potatoes sprinkled with ever-present dill, and cucumbers.

Piirakat, rye-flour pasties stuffed with rice, are Karelian specialties that appear in bakeries, coffee shops and open markets all over Finland. A traditional side dish to meat, the pasties are offered with Egg Butter.

Like the *piirakat*, dessert displays a Russian accent. Cranberry soup, made from one of the best-loved of Finnish fruits, is topped with whipped cream and fresh berries. Serves 8.

Wine Suggestion: Begin with a vodka to warm body and soul. Then enjoy a mellow red wine with your dinner. Stag's Leap Merlot or a lovely Saint-Émilion, Château Figeac, would be just right.

Karelian dinner specialties are rice pasties with Egg Butter, a three-meat ragout, Borscht and Cranberry Fruit Soup.

PARTY PLAN FOR KARELIAN DINNER MENU

1 Day Before:
Prepare Karelian Rice Pasties with Egg Butter through step 5 in recipe; refrigerate covered.
Prepare Cranberry Fruit Soup through step 1 in recipe; refrigerate covered.

5 Hours 30 Minutes Before Serving:
Make Karelian Ragout.

4 Hours Before Serving:
Prepare Marinated Mushroom Salad through step 1 in recipe.
Make salted cucumbers.
Measure and label ingredients for remaining recipes;
refrigerate perishables.
Prepare garnishes for menu; refrigerate.

1 Hour Before Serving:
Make Borscht.
Make boiled potatoes.
Remove Egg Butter from refrigerator.
Bake rice pasties uncovered at 350° 20 minutes, if serving hot.
Remove Cranberry Fruit Soup from refrigerator.
Complete Marinated Mushroom Salad.

15 Minutes Before Dessert:
Complete Cranberry Fruit Soup.

BORSCHT (Borschkeitto)

4	medium beets, tops removed, pared, cut into julienne strips
2	tablespoons butter or margarine
6	cups beef broth
1	small head red cabbage (about 2 pounds), shredded
2	carrots, pared, cut into julienne strips
1	clove garlic, crushed
1	bay leaf
1	tablespoon sugar
2	tablespoons cider vinegar
1	teaspoon salt
8	ounces Polish sausage
	Dairy sour cream, if desired
	Lemon slices, if desired

1. Sauté beets in butter in Dutch oven about 3 minutes. Stir in remaining ingredients except sausage, sour cream and lemon slices. Heat to boiling; reduce heat. Simmer uncovered until vegetables are tender, about 30 minutes.

2. Cut sausage diagonally into ¼-inch slices. Stir sausage into vegetable mixture; heat until hot. Serve with dollops of sour cream and lemon slices.

KARELIAN RAGOUT (Karjalanpaisti)

1	pound beef for stew, cut into 1-inch cubes
1	pound lamb for stew, cut into 1-inch cubes
1	pound pork shoulder blade steak, cut into 1-inch cubes
5	medium onions, sliced
1	tablespoon salt
1	teaspoon ground allspice
6	whole allspice
1	to 2 bay leaves
1	quart beef broth or water

Layer meat cubes and onions in Dutch oven, sprinkling each layer with salt, ground allspice and whole allspice. Top with bay leaves. Heat broth to boiling. Pour over meat; cover. Heat oven to 275°. Bake meat, stirring occasionally, until tender, about 5 hours. Remove bay leaves.

MARINATED MUSHROOM SALAD (Marinoitu Sienisalaatti)

1	pound fresh mushrooms, coarsely chopped
2	tablespoons grated onion
2	tablespoons lemon juice
2	teaspoons sugar
½	teaspoon freshly ground pepper
½	cup whipping cream
¼	cup dairy sour cream
1	teaspoon salt
⅛	teaspoon dry mustard
	Romaine
	Tomato wedges
	Parsley sprigs

1. Toss mushrooms, onion, lemon juice, sugar and pepper in medium-size bowl; cover. Refrigerate at least 30 minutes, no longer than 4 hours.

2. Beat whipping cream in chilled small bowl until stiff peaks form; fold in sour cream, salt and mustard. Stir into mushroom mixture. Line serving bowl with romaine; mound mushroom mixture in center. Garnish with tomato wedges and parsley sprigs.

KARELIAN RICE PASTIES WITH EGG BUTTER (Karjalanpiirakat ja Munavoi)   *Makes 8 servings (16 pasties)*

Egg Butter (recipe follows)

1   **cup uncooked regular rice**
1   **can (13 ounces) evaporated milk**
2   **tablespoons butter or margarine**
     Salt

1   **cup water**
2   **tablespoons butter or margarine, melted**
1   **teaspoon salt**
1½   **cups all-purpose flour**
1½   **cups rye flour, rye meal or pumpernickel rye flour**

½   **cup butter or margarine, melted**
½   **cup hot milk**

1.   Make Egg Butter.

2.   Cook rice according to package directions. Stir evaporated milk into cooked rice. Cook and stir over medium heat until mixture is thick and bubbly, about 10 minutes. Stir in 2 tablespoons butter. Season with salt. Remove from heat. Cool to consistency of mashed potatoes. (Thin mixture with ½ to 1 cup milk, if necessary.)

3.   Mix 1 cup water, 2 tablespoons butter and 1 teaspoon salt in medium-size bowl. Stir in all-purpose flour. Stir in rye flour gradually to make stiff dough. Turn dough onto board dusted with rye flour. Knead until smooth, 2 to 3 minutes.

4.   Heat oven to 450°. Shape dough into roll 2 inches in diameter. Cut roll into 16 equal pieces. Shape each piece into ball. Roll each ball into 6-inch circle. Spread ¼ cup of the rice filling in 3-inch strip across center of each circle, almost to edge. Fold opposite sides over filling, leaving 1 inch of filling exposed in center. Crimp each edge. Pinch ends to form oval and seal in filling.

5.   Place pasties 3 inches apart on greased baking sheets. Mix ½ cup butter and ½ cup hot milk; brush lightly over pasties. Bake, brushing once with milk mixture, until light brown, about 15 minutes. Remove from oven; brush again with milk mixture.

6.   Serve pasties hot or cold with Egg Butter.

TIP: Leftover pasties can be refrigerated well wrapped up to 2 days.

EGG BUTTER   *Makes 2 cups*

1   **cup butter or margarine, softened**
¼   **teaspoon salt**
⅛   **teaspoon ground ginger**
4   **hard-cooked eggs, finely chopped**
     Parsley, if desired

Beat butter, salt and ginger in small bowl until light and fluffy. Stir in eggs; cover and refrigerate. Remove from refrigerator 30 minutes before serving. Garnish with parsley.

CRANBERRY FRUIT SOUP (Karpalakiisseli)   *Makes 8 servings*

1   **cup sugar**
¼   **cup potato starch or cornstarch**
1   **quart cranberry juice cocktail**

1   **cup whipping cream**
     Chopped fresh cranberries

1.   Mix sugar and potato starch in 2-quart saucepan. Stir in cranberry juice cocktail. Cook over medium heat, stirring constantly, until mixture thickens and boils. Boil and stir 1 minute. Remove from heat; cover. Cool to room temperature.

2.   Beat whipping cream in chilled small bowl until stiff peaks form. Serve soup in sherbet or dessert dishes. Top with whipped cream and cranberries.

A French Supper

- FRENCH ONION SOUP
- TARRAGON SALAD
- CRUSTY RYE BREAD

- FRESH PEACH TART
  COFFEE OR TEA

• Recipes included

Cheese and crusty bread change a simple broth into that continental specialty French Onion Soup. Laden with melted Gruyère, the beef-base potage is the focal point for a light supper or after-theater collation.

Match the thick and flavorful soup with greens and mushrooms tossed in a tarragon dressing, and loaves of Crusty Rye Bread.

From the pastry chefs of France comes an elegant dessert to complete the repast. In our tart recipe, luscious fresh peach slices are baked with apricot preserves in a pastry rich with cream cheese. Serves 6.

Wine Suggestion: This meal deserves a warm and pleasant wine, like a Château des Tours Beaujolais, or a young Bully Hill wine from Walter Taylor.

PARTY PLAN FOR FRENCH ONION SOUP SUPPER MENU

1 Day Before: Make Crusty Rye Bread; wrap in aluminum foil and store at room temperature.

That Afternoon: Prepare French Onion Soup through step 2 in recipe.
Prepare Fresh Peach Tart through step 3 in recipe.
Prepare ingredients for Tarragon Salad; refrigerate dressing, greens and mushrooms, separately, covered.

30 Minutes Before Serving: Complete French Onion Soup.
Complete Tarragon Salad.

10 Minutes Before Dessert: Complete Fresh Peach Tart.

FRENCH ONION SOUP

Makes 6 servings (about 2¼ cups each)

⅓	cup butter
¼	cup vegetable oil
3	pounds yellow onions, thinly sliced
¼	cup all-purpose flour
3	quarts beef stock or canned beef bouillon
	Salt
	Freshly ground pepper
6	slices French bread
	Butter
1	cup grated Gruyère cheese
	Butter
	Freshly grated nutmeg

1. Melt ⅓ cup butter with the oil in Dutch oven; stir in onions. Cook covered over medium heat, stirring occasionally, just until onions begin to turn golden, 20 to 25 minutes.

2. Sprinkle flour over onions; stir until smooth. Stir beef stock into onions; simmer covered 15 minutes. Season to taste with salt and pepper.*

3. Set oven control to broil and/or 550°. Spread both sides of bread slices lightly with butter. Toast bread slices 4 inches from heat, about 3 minutes on each side. Sprinkle bread with ⅔ cup of the cheese; top each slice with small pat of butter and sprinkle with nutmeg.

4. Pour soup into oven-proof tureen; place bread slices on top. Broil 4 inches from heat until cheese has melted and is light brown, 1 to 2 minutes. Ladle soup into individual soup bowls. Top each serving with slice of bread. Sprinkle with remaining cheese.

*TIP: *Soup can be prepared to this point 1 day in advance. Cool and refrigerate covered. Heat to simmering and proceed with step 3.*

TARRAGON SALAD

Makes 6 servings

6	tablespoons olive oil
3	tablespoons red wine vinegar
2½	teaspoons dried tarragon leaves

Combine oil, vinegar, tarragon, garlic salt, mustard, black pepper and cayenne pepper in jar with tight-fitting lid; cover and shake. Pour over greens and mushrooms; toss. Serve immediately.

Our French supper fare includes a full-bodied onion soup and Crusty Rye Bread.

or 1 tablespoon plus 2 teaspoons
snipped fresh tarragon leaves
¼ teaspoon garlic salt
⅛ teaspoon dry mustard
Dash black pepper
Dash cayenne pepper
1 quart torn romaine leaves
1 quart torn fresh spinach
8 ounces fresh mushrooms, sliced

CRUSTY RYE BREAD
Makes 2 loaves

2 packages active dry yeast
¼ cup warm water (105° to 115°)
2 cups lukewarm potato water*
2 tablespoons butter or margarine, melted
1½ teaspoons salt
1½ teaspoons caraway seeds
1½ cups rye flour, rye meal or pumpernickel rye flour
1½ cups graham flour
3 to 3½ cups all-purpose flour

Butter or margarine, melted

1. Dissolve yeast in warm water in large bowl. Stir in potato water, 2 tablespoons butter, the salt and caraway. Beat in rye flour and graham flour until smooth. Stir in 2½ cups of the all-purpose flour. Stir in enough of the remaining flour to make dough easy to handle; cover. Let rest 10 minutes.

2. Turn dough onto lightly floured surface. Knead until smooth and elastic, about 10 minutes. Shape into ball. Place in greased bowl; turn greased side up and cover. Let rise in warm place until double, about 1 hour. (Dough is ready if impression remains.)

3. Divide dough in half. Shape each half into long loaf on greased baking sheet; cover. Let rise in warm place until double, 1 hour.

4. Heat oven to 375°. Pierce entire loaves with fork. Bake loaves until light brown, 35 to 45 minutes. Brush with melted butter while hot. Cool on wire racks.

TIP: *Plain water can be substituted for the potato water.*

FRESH PEACH TART
Makes 6 servings

Rich Tart Pastry (recipe follows)

3 tablespoons apricot preserves
3 tablespoons flour
6 fresh peaches, peeled, pitted, sliced*
2 tablespoons apricot preserves
1 teaspoon hot water

2 tablespoons apricot preserves

1. Make Rich Tart Pastry.

2. Heat oven to 375°. Mix 3 tablespoons apricot preserves and the flour in small bowl; spread on bottom of prepared pastry. Arrange peach slices in circular pattern on apricot mixture. Thin 2 tablespoons apricot preserves with 1 teaspoon hot water; brush on peaches. Bake tart until peaches are tender and pastry is brown, 30 to 45 minutes; cool.

3. Melt 2 tablespoons apricot preserves in small saucepan. Brush over baked tart. Cool tart in pan on wire rack.

4. To serve tart, remove rim of pan; cut tart into wedges.

TIP: *Any fresh fruit in season can be substituted for the peaches.*

RICH TART PASTRY

1 cup all-purpose flour
2 teaspoons sugar
⅛ teaspoon salt
½ cup butter
4 ounces cream cheese

1. Mix flour, sugar and salt in medium-size bowl. Cut in butter until mixture resembles marbles; cut in cream cheese until mixture resembles coarse crumbs. Press dough into ball; refrigerate, wrapped in waxed paper, at least 1 hour.

2. Roll dough on lightly floured surface into 10-inch circle. Fold pastry into quarters; unfold and ease into 8-inch tart pan with removable bottom. Press pastry against bottom and side of pan.

An elegant peach tart is filled with fresh fruit and apricot preserves.

A St. Augustine Fiesta

Walnut Pancakes claim a Spanish heritage, as does an old St. Augustine inn.

STUFFED TURKEY BUFFET MENU

• **MEAT-CHEESE STUFFED PEPPERS**

• **FISH SOUP**

• **STUFFED TURKEY**
• **RICE WITH PINE NUTS**
• **TOMATO-ONION SALAD**
• **DATIL PEPPER JELLY**

• **WALNUT PANCAKES**

• Recipes included

The Hispanic heritage of St. Augustine proudly appears in the cookery of that venerable American city. But old-world culinary traditions carried there by conquistadores were transformed by the nature of the new land. This happy fusion of Old and New Spain is evident in our gala St. Augustine dinner.

Peppers stuffed with meat and cheese are an example of *tapas*. Pre-dinner treats inspired by Spain's late luncheon and dinner hours, *tapas* helped stave off between-meal hunger. With a scarcity of cookware, early St. Augustine settlers treasured their kettles and developed soups, stews and endless variations of the one-pot meal. A homemaker of New Spain might have stirred a hearty *sopa*, such as our Fish Soup, created from an ocean or river catch.

Turkey, the dinner's main course, mingles the seasonings of Spain and a specialty of America. Indians originally taught the conquistadores about the wild fowl. In the recipe here, the bird is marinated in red wine and spices, then stuffed with traditional Spanish favorites — sausage, green pepper, raisins and nuts. Rice with Pine Nuts, an accompaniment to the turkey, displays the colonists' ingenuity for changing a plain grain with unusual tastes and textures. And the onion and tomato salad is a gift of the gardens planted in Florida.

Datil Pepper Jelly is a St. Augustine "original." Introduced there by Minorcans from the Balearic isles off Spain, the concoction makes a fiery meat garnish. The dessert is pancakes — with walnuts in the batter and in the accompanying sour cream. Serves 12.

Wine Suggestion: Sangría, a wine-fruit punch, would be served by Spaniards. For an American alternate, try a rosé from Paul Masson.

Stuffed Turkey is offered with pepper jelly, Fish Soup, tomato and onion salad, Rice with Pine Nuts, and peppers filled with meat and cheese.

PARTY PLAN FOR STUFFED TURKEY BUFFET MENU

1 Week Before:	Make Datil Pepper Jelly.
2 Days Before:	Make Tomato-Onion Salad.
1 Day Before:	Prepare Stuffed Turkey through step 1 in recipe. Prepare Meat-Cheese Stuffed Peppers through step 3 in recipe.
5 Hours Before Serving:	Complete Stuffed Turkey. Measure and label ingredients for remaining recipes; refrigerate perishables.
1 Hour 30 Minutes Before Serving:	Make Fish Soup.
45 Minutes Before Serving:	Make Rice with Pine Nuts.
20 Minutes Before Serving:	Complete Meat-Cheese Stuffed Peppers.
20 Minutes Before Dessert:	Make Walnut Pancakes.

MEAT-CHEESE STUFFED PEPPERS (Pimientos Rellenos con Carne y Queso)   *Makes 12 servings*

6   **red or green peppers,
      cut lengthwise in half**

1   **pound ground beef**
½   **cup shredded mozzarella cheese**
1   **clove garlic, minced**
2   **teaspoons snipped fresh parsley**
¼   **teaspoon black pepper**
1   **egg**
½   **cup all-purpose flour**
2   **eggs, beaten**
1   **cup olive or vegetable oil**

¾   **cup beef broth**
½   **cup tomato sauce**
1   **bay leaf**

Parsley sprigs

Heat oven to 400°

1.   Bake pepper halves in jelly-roll pan, 15½ x 10½ x 1 inch, 10 minutes; drain.

2.   Combine beef, cheese, garlic, 2 teaspoons parsley, the black pepper and 1 egg. Divide beef mixture evenly among pepper halves. Dip bottoms of peppers into flour, then into beaten eggs. Coat with flour. Fry peppers on both sides in oil in 12-inch skillet until brown. Remove peppers and pour off oil. Return peppers to skillet.

3.   Combine broth, tomato sauce and bay leaf. Pour broth mixture over peppers. Heat to boiling; reduce heat and cover. Simmer 40 minutes.*

4.   Arrange peppers on serving platter. Spoon additional sauce on peppers, if desired. Garnish with parsley sprigs.

TIP: *Stuffed peppers can be stored covered in refrigerator 24 hours. To serve, heat until hot.*

FISH SOUP (Sopa de Pescado)

Makes 12 servings (about 1 cup each)

1 cup minced onion
⅓ cup butter or margarine
3 cups water
3 cups clam juice
2 cups dry white wine
½ cup ground almonds
½ teaspoon white pepper
½ teaspoon paprika
⅛ teaspoon crushed chili peppers
Dash ground cumin

2 slices white bread, crusts removed, cubed (about 1 cup)
1 cup milk

2 pounds halibut or sole, cut into 1-inch cubes
2 hard-cooked egg yolks, finely chopped

1 cup whipping cream
Lemon slices
Snipped fresh parsley

1. Sauté onion in butter in Dutch oven until tender and light brown. Stir in water, clam juice, wine, almonds, white pepper, paprika, chili peppers and cumin. Heat to boiling; reduce heat. Simmer uncovered 30 minutes.

2. Soak bread in milk; mash until smooth. Stir bread mixture into soup. Heat to boiling; reduce heat. Simmer 10 minutes.*

3. Stir fish and egg yolks into soup; reduce heat. Simmer until fish flakes, about 5 minutes.

4. Pour cream gradually into soup, stirring constantly. Heat until hot. Garnish with lemon slices and snipped parsley.

TIP: *Fish Soup can be prepared to this point up to 24 hours in advance. Store covered in refrigerator. To serve, heat until hot; proceed with step 3.

STUFFED TURKEY (Pavo Relleno)

Makes 12 servings

1 turkey (10 to 12 pounds)
2 cups dry red wine
1 cup minced onion
2 cloves garlic, minced
1 tablespoon salt
1 teaspoon freshly ground black pepper
1 bay leaf

½ pound pork sausage
1½ cups chopped onions
¾ cup chopped green pepper
⅓ cup olive or vegetable oil
2 cups ground almonds
1 cup golden raisins
1 cup sliced pimiento-stuffed olives
4 slices bread, cubed (about 3 cups)
3 hard-cooked eggs, diced
½ cup chopped prunes
1 teaspoon salt
½ teaspoon ground thyme

Tomato slices, if desired
Green pepper slices, if desired

1. Place turkey in large plastic bag. Combine wine, 1 cup onion, the garlic, 1 tablespoon salt, the black pepper and bay leaf. Pour marinade over turkey in bag; close tightly. Place bag in baking dish, 13½ x 8¾ x 1¾ inches. Refrigerate turkey, turning frequently, up to 24 hours.

2. Sauté sausage, 1½ cups onions and the chopped green pepper in oil until sausage is brown and onions are tender; remove from heat. Stir in remaining ingredients except tomato slices and green pepper slices.

3. Heat oven to 325°. Drain turkey, reserving marinade. Fill neck cavity with stuffing. Fasten neck skin to back with skewer. Fold wings across back with tips touching. Fill body cavity loosely with stuffing.* Tuck drumsticks under band of skin at tail, or tie together with heavy string, then tie to tail.

4. Place turkey breast side up on rack in open shallow roasting pan. Insert meat thermometer so tip is in thickest part of inside thigh muscle, away from bone.

5. Roast turkey uncovered until thermometer registers 185°, 3½ to 4½ hours. After 1 hour of baking, pour reserved marinade into roasting pan. Spoon marinade frequently over turkey. When ⅔ done, cut band of skin or string holding legs. Let turkey stand about 20 minutes before carving. (Remove all stuffing from turkey before carving.) Garnish with tomato and green pepper slices.

TIP: *Place any leftover stuffing in covered casserole in refrigerator. To heat, bake in 325° oven until hot, 30 to 40 minutes.

RICE WITH PINE NUTS (Arroz con Piñones)

Makes 12 servings

¾ **cup chopped onion**
3 **tablespoons butter or margarine**
2 **cups uncooked regular rice**

1½ **teaspoons salt**
¼ **teaspoon ground saffron**
1 **tablespoon dry sherry**
4 **cups chicken broth**
1 **cup pine nuts**
3 **tablespoons butter or margarine, melted**
  Pimiento, if desired

1. Sauté onion in 3 tablespoons butter in 3-quart saucepan over medium heat until tender; stir in rice.

2. Stir salt, saffron, sherry and chicken broth into rice mixture. Cook rice according to package directions. Stir in pine nuts and melted butter. Garnish with pimiento.

TOMATO-ONION SALAD (Ensalada de Tomates y Cebollas)

Makes 12 servings

5 **medium tomatoes, cubed (about 4 cups)**
4 **medium red onions, chopped (about 3 cups)**
¾ **cup olive oil**
¼ **cup red wine vinegar**
1½ **teaspoons salt**
½ **teaspoon dried basil leaves**
¼ **teaspoon crushed red pepper**
  Lettuce leaves

Toss tomatoes and onions in large glass bowl. Mix oil, vinegar, salt, basil and red pepper; stir into tomato mixture and cover. Refrigerate at least 3 hours, no longer than 2 days. Serve on lettuce leaves.

DATIL PEPPER JELLY (Jalea de Pimiento de Dátil)

Makes four 8-ounce glasses

1 **cup datil peppers or small hot green peppers***
1 **medium green pepper**
¾ **cup white wine vinegar**
¾ **cup water**
1 **package (1¾ ounces) fruit pectin**
3 **drops green food color**
5 **cups sugar**

  Paraffin, melted

1. Check jelly glasses for nicks, cracks or sharp edges on sealing surfaces. Wash glasses in hot soapy water; rinse well. Place in pan with folded cloth or rack on bottom. Cover glasses with hot water. Heat to boiling; boil gently 15 minutes. Keep glasses in hot water until ready to use. About 5 minutes before the end of jelly's cooking time, remove glasses from water and invert on clean folded towel out of draft to drain.

2. Remove stems and seeds from peppers. Pass peppers through food grinder using fine blade. Combine peppers, vinegar, water, fruit pectin and food color in Dutch oven. Heat to boiling. Stir in sugar. Heat to boiling; boil 1 minute. Remove from heat; immediately skim off foam.

3. Ladle hot jelly into 1 hot sterilized glass at a time to within ½ inch of top. Hold ladle close to top of glass to prevent air bubbles from forming.

4. Cover hot jelly immediately with a ⅛-inch layer of hot paraffin. To ensure a good seal, paraffin must touch side of glass and be even. Pierce any bubbles that appear on paraffin as they can allow spoilage. When paraffin is hard, check seal. Cover glasses with metal or glass lids. Store in dark dry place. Once opened, store glasses covered in refrigerator.

TIP: *Datil peppers are grown only in Florida, but other hot peppers can be substituted. Datil peppers are extremely hot. Rubber gloves should be worn when working with them.

Castillo de San Marcos in St. Augustine is a moated fortress built in the 17th century.

WALNUT PANCAKES (Panqueques de Nueces)   *Makes 12*

6	eggs
⅓	cup sugar
¼	cup brandy
3	tablespoons flour
¾	cup ground walnuts
1	teaspoon grated lemon peel
¼	cup butter or margarine, melted

Whole strawberries, if desired
Mint leaves, if desired
Dairy sour cream
Chopped walnuts

1. Place all ingredients except strawberries, mint, sour cream and chopped walnuts in blender container; cover. Blend on high speed until thick and smooth.

2. Butter 6-inch skillet lightly for each pancake. Pour a scant ¼ cup batter into pan, tilting pan quickly so that batter covers pan. Cook pancakes until light brown, about 2 minutes on each side. Fold into quarters; keep warm. Repeat procedure with remaining batter. Arrange folded pancakes on serving platter. Garnish with whole strawberries and mint leaves. Serve with sour cream sprinkled with chopped walnuts.

A Russian Easter

Russian masterpieces: A basket of Easter eggs and the tsar's palace estate at Petrodvorets.

RUSSIAN EASTER MENU

• **FLAVORED VODKA**
  DRY RED WINE
  DRY WHITE WINE

• **RUSSIAN EASTER HAM**
  ROAST TURKEY
  ROAST LEG OF LAMB
• **RUSSIAN MUSTARD**
• **LIVER PATE**
• **POACHED HALIBUT WITH**
  PICKLED CARROTS
• **HERRING PLATTER**
• **RED CAVIAR CHEESE BALL**
• **VEGETABLE VINAIGRETTE**
• **EGGPLANT CAVIAR**
• **CUCUMBERS IN SOUR CREAM**
• **RADISHES AND SOUR CREAM**
• **MUSHROOM PICKLES**
  BLACK BREAD AND RYE BREAD

• **KULICH**
• **PASKHA**
• **ALMOND MAZURKA**
• **MERINGUE CONFECTIONS**
  RUSSIAN TEA

• Recipes included

After a long Lenten fast, Orthodox Russians greet the feast of Easter with age-old ritual and a bountiful repast. From midnight services, families return home to tables set with all the ingredients for the traditional three-day celebration.

The first foods sampled are *zakuska*, or appetizers, accompanied by vodka. One might begin with Liver Pâté, the platter of herring, or poached halibut squares topped with Pickled Carrots. A ball of cheese studded with that Russian delicacy, caviar, is served with thin slices of rye bread.

Magnificent roasts — ham, turkey and lamb — are the meat of the menu. The ham, baked in a tangy-sweet mustard paste, is then chilled and spread with a smooth cheese mixture. And savory Russian Mustard accents the ham, or any of the cold meat offerings.

Vegetables in many forms play a prominent role in the Easter feasting. Vegetable Vinaigrette is a piquant medley of cooked potatoes, beets, beans, peas and carrots. Cucumbers and radishes are each tossed in their own special sour cream blend. Mushroom Pickles and a "caviar" of eggplant provide lively complements for the spread of foods.

Russian Easter is unthinkable without two particular sweets, Kulich and Paskha. Kulich, a tall cylindrical yeast bread rich with fruit and nuts, is adorned with icing, candies and flowers. Traditionally paired with the Kulich, Paskha is a creamy cheese blend formed in a pyramidal mold. Leaf-shaped Almond Mazurka cake and Meringue Confections also grace the gala banquet which rejoices in the season of rebirth. Serves 24.

Wine Suggestion: From the well-chilled vodka, proceed to dry wines with the Easter foods. The red — a Bordeaux, Château Beychevelle, or a Stag's Leap Cabernet. And for the white — a Chablis Grand Cru, Vaudésir Pic, or the Fumé Blanc of Robert Mondavi.

Flavored Vodka begins the Easter dinner.

PARTY PLAN FOR RUSSIAN EASTER MENU

1 Month Before: Prepare Kulich through step 7 in recipe.

3 Weeks Before: Make Eggplant Caviar.
Prepare Almond Mazurka through step 3 in recipe.

2 Weeks Before: Make Flavored Vodka; refrigerate.
Make Russian Mustard.
Prepare Mushroom Pickles through step 1 in recipe.
Make Meringue Confections.

1 Week Before: Prepare Liver Pâté through step 4 in recipe.
Prepare Poached Halibut with Pickled Carrots through step 1 in recipe.
Prepare Paskha through step 3 in recipe.

2 Days Before: Prepare Red Caviar Cheese Ball through step 1 in recipe.
Prepare Vegetable Vinaigrette through step 2 in recipe.
Complete Almond Mazurka.

1 Day Before: Prepare Russian Easter Ham through step 1 in recipe.

4 Hours Before Serving: Complete Russian Easter Ham.
Complete step 2 of Poached Halibut with Pickled Carrots recipe.
Make Cucumbers in Sour Cream.
Complete steps 8 and 9 of Kulich recipe.
Prepare garnishes for menu; refrigerate.

1 Hour 30 Minutes Before Serving:	Make Radishes and Sour Cream.
	Complete Liver Pâté.
	Complete Red Caviar Cheese Ball.
	Complete Paskha.
	Complete Poached Halibut with Pickled Carrots.
	Complete Kulich.
30 Minutes Before Serving:	Make Herring Platter.
	Complete Mushroom Pickles.
	Complete Vegetable Vinaigrette.

FLAVORED VODKA

Makes ⁴/₅ quart

2 teaspoons lemon peel strips
    or ¼ teaspoon peppercorns
    or 5 blades zubrovka (buffalo
    grass)*
1 bottle (⁴/₅ quart) vodka

Place 1 of the flavoring agents in vodka bottle; let stand covered at room temperature at least 2 days. To serve, refrigerate vodka until cold; pour into decanter. Remove flavoring agent, if desired.

*TIP: *Buffalo grass can be purchased in health food stores.*

RUSSIAN EASTER HAM

Makes 12 to 18 servings

1 whole smoked ham (about 12
    pounds)
½ cup sugar
1 teaspoon dry mustard
3 tablespoons mayonnaise or
    salad dressing

1 package (8 ounces) cream
    cheese, softened
½ cup cottage cheese
4 teaspoons prepared mustard
7 hard-cooked egg whites
    Green pepper strips
    Pitted ripe olives, sliced
    Lemon leaves, if desired

Heat oven to 350°

1. Trim rind and all but ¼ inch of fat from ham. Place ham fat side up on rack in shallow roasting pan. Mix sugar and dry mustard in small bowl; blend with mayonnaise to make a thick paste. Spread paste on top and sides of ham. Bake ham 1 hour. Increase oven temperature to 400°; bake until brown, about 30 minutes. Remove ham from oven; cool slightly. Refrigerate covered until cold.

2. Beat cheeses and prepared mustard in small mixer bowl until smooth; spread cheese mixture on top and sides of chilled ham. Press egg whites through sieve; sprinkle on cheese mixture. Garnish with green pepper strips, olives and lemon leaves. Refrigerate ham at least 1 hour before serving.

RUSSIAN MUSTARD

Makes 1 cup

1 can (2 ounces) dry mustard
½ cup sugar
½ teaspoon salt
2 tablespoons honey
1 tablespoon distilled white vinegar
2 tablespoons boiling water
2 tablespoons apple butter

Mix mustard, sugar and salt. Stir in honey and vinegar. Add boiling water; stir until sugar is dissolved. Stir in apple butter. Refrigerate covered.

TIP: Russian Mustard can be stored covered in refrigerator up to 1 month.

LIVER PATE

Makes about 4½ cups

1 cup minced onion
2 tablespoons rendered chicken fat*
4 ounces mushrooms, minced (about
    1 cup)

1. Sauté onion in 2 tablespoons hot chicken fat in medium-size skillet over medium heat until onion is transparent, about 10 minutes. Add mushrooms. Cook and stir 3 minutes; do not brown mushrooms. Transfer onion and mushrooms to large bowl.

A magnificent fountain at Petrodvorets.

6	tablespoons rendered chicken fat
3	tablespoons flour
½	cup milk
½	pound chicken livers, trimmed, rinsed, drained
¼	pound ground round steak
1	egg
1½	teaspoons salt
½	teaspoon pepper
2	hard-cooked eggs, finely chopped
2	tablespoons sweet Italian vermouth
2	tablespoons chopped ripe olives
1	teaspoon distilled white vinegar
¼	cup snipped fresh parsley

2.   Melt 6 tablespoons chicken fat in medium-size skillet over low heat. Add flour; cook and stir 2 minutes. Add milk all at once; cook and stir over medium heat until mixture thickens and separates, about 3 minutes. Stir flour mixture into onion and mushrooms.

3.   Place chicken livers, ground round steak, 1 egg, the salt and pepper in blender container; cover. Blend, scraping sides of blender container, until smooth, about 15 seconds. Stir liver mixture, chopped eggs and vermouth into mushroom mixture.

4.   Heat oven to 350°. Pour liver mixture into ungreased 1½-quart baking dish suitable for serving. Cover baking dish tightly with double-thickness aluminum foil. Place dish in larger shallow pan. Pour 1 inch boiling water into shallow pan. Bake pâté 45 minutes; remove foil. Bake uncovered 1 hour. Refrigerate covered at least 6 hours.

5.   Toss chopped olives with vinegar and parsley. Garnish pâté with olive mixture. Serve pâté at room temperature.

TIPS: *The use of chicken fat is particularly important in this recipe and accounts for the pâté's unique flavor. Rendered chicken fat is available in many meat departments, or can be prepared by frying chicken fat in skillet over medium heat until fat melts; remove cracklings and use rendered fat.*

Liver Pâté can be stored covered in refrigerator up to 1 week.

POACHED HALIBUT WITH PICKLED CARROTS

Makes about 3 dozen appetizers

	Pickled Carrots (recipe follows)
1	cup water
3	tablespoons lemon juice

1.   Make Pickled Carrots.

2.   Heat water, lemon juice, peppercorns, salt and bay leaves in 10-inch skillet to boiling; arrange fish in single layer in boiling liquid. Reduce heat; simmer covered, turning once, until fish flakes with fork, about 3 minutes

On next pages: A sumptuous spread of traditional foods is a focal point of the Russian Easter festival.

1	teaspoon peppercorns
2	teaspoons salt
2	bay leaves
2	pounds halibut fillets
	Lemon slices, if desired
	Watercress, if desired
2	cups shredded carrots
⅔	cup green pepper julienne strips, 1 x ⅛ inch each
⅓	cup minced celery
¼	cup water
2	tablespoons vegetable oil
1	teaspoon sugar
1	teaspoon salt
1	cup minced onion
¼	teaspoon sugar
1	tablespoon vegetable oil
¼	cup tomato catsup
2	tablespoons lemon juice

on each side. Remove from heat. Refrigerate covered until firm, about 3 hours.

3. Cut fish into 1½-inch squares. Top each square with about 1 tablespoon of the Pickled Carrots. Garnish with lemon slices and watercress.

PICKLED CARROTS *Makes about 2½ cups*

1. Heat carrots, green pepper, celery, water, 2 tablespoons oil, 1 teaspoon sugar and the salt in medium-size saucepan over medium heat to boiling; reduce heat. Simmer uncovered, stirring occasionally, just until vegetables are tender, 5 to 10 minutes. Remove from heat.

2. Sauté onion with ¼ teaspoon sugar in 1 tablespoon oil over low heat until onion is transparent, about 10 minutes; do not brown. Stir onion, catsup and lemon juice into carrot mixture. Simmer uncovered over medium heat 5 minutes. Refrigerate covered until cold.

TIP: Pickled Carrots can be stored covered in refrigerator up to 1 week.

HERRING PLATTER
Makes 12 to 16 appetizer servings

1	jar (12 ounces) herring in wine sauce, drained
4	hard-cooked eggs, finely chopped
1	bunch green onions with tops, thinly sliced (about ¾ cup)
	Onion rings, if desired
	Carrot curls, if desired
1	cup dairy sour cream

Arrange herring attractively on serving platter with eggs and green onions; garnish with onion rings and carrot curls. Serve with sour cream.

RED CAVIAR CHEESE BALL
Makes 12 to 16 appetizer servings

1	package (8 ounces) cream cheese, softened
¼	cup cottage cheese
2	tablespoons dairy sour cream
1	jar (4 ounces) red caviar, drained
	Thinly sliced rye bread

1. Beat cheeses in small mixer bowl until smooth. Refrigerate covered until firm, at least 2 hours.*

2. Form cheese mixture into ball. Place on serving plate with rim. Coat cheese ball with sour cream. Press caviar onto surface of ball. (Do not break grain of caviar.) Serve with thinly sliced rye bread.

*TIP: *Red Caviar Cheese Ball can be prepared to this point up to 2 days in advance.*

VEGETABLE VINAIGRETTE
Makes 12 to 16 servings

1	pound red potatoes (about 3 medium), cooked, pared
⅓	cup olive or vegetable oil
2	large cloves garlic, crushed
½	teaspoon sugar
1	can (16 ounces) red kidney beans, rinsed, drained

1. Cut potatoes into 1-inch pieces. Toss potatoes with oil, garlic and sugar in large bowl. Let stand 30 minutes.

2. Add remaining ingredients except peas and carrots to potato mixture. Refrigerate covered at least 24 hours.*

3. Just before serving, stir peas and carrots into salad.

1 can (16 ounces) diced beets,
    drained
1 package (10 ounces) frozen lima
    beans, cooked, drained
1½ cups chopped dill pickles
3 tablespoons dill pickle juice
1½ teaspoons salt
½ teaspoon pepper

1 package (10 ounces) frozen peas
    and carrots, cooked, drained

*TIP: *Vegetable Vinaigrette can be prepared to this point and stored covered in refrigerator up to 3 days.*

EGGPLANT CAVIAR
Makes about 3 cups

---

1 large eggplant (about 2 pounds),
    unpared, minced
½ cup water
¼ cup vegetable oil
1 teaspoon sugar

1 cup minced onion
¼ teaspoon sugar
¼ cup vegetable oil
⅓ cup tomato paste
3 tablespoons lemon juice
1½ teaspoons salt
½ teaspoon pepper
¼ cup mayonnaise or salad dressing

1. Cook eggplant, water, ¼ cup vegetable oil and 1 teaspoon sugar uncovered in Dutch oven over low heat, stirring occasionally, 30 minutes. Cook over medium heat, stirring occasionally, until mixture sticks to Dutch oven, about 40 minutes.

2. Meanwhile, heat onion and ¼ teaspoon sugar in ¼ cup vegetable oil in small skillet over low heat until onion is transparent, about 15 minutes; do not brown. Add tomato paste; cook, stirring frequently, 5 minutes. Add onion mixture to eggplant mixture; simmer uncovered over low heat, stirring occasionally, until mixture sticks to Dutch oven and holds shape on spoon, about 30 minutes. Remove from heat; stir in lemon juice, salt and pepper. Refrigerate covered until cold; stir in mayonnaise.

TIP: Eggplant Caviar can be stored covered in refrigerator up to 3 weeks.

CUCUMBERS IN SOUR CREAM
Makes about 3 cups

---

3 cucumbers (about 10 ounces each)
2½ teaspoons salt
1 cup dairy sour cream
2 green onions with tops,
    thinly sliced
2 tablespoons drained capers
1½ teaspoons snipped fresh dill
1 teaspoon sugar
½ teaspoon pepper
½ teaspoon snipped fresh dill,
    if desired

Pare thin lengthwise strips from cucumbers at ½-inch intervals. Cut cucumbers crosswise into thin slices. Sprinkle with salt; let stand 1 hour. Drain; pat dry on paper toweling. Combine sour cream, green onions, capers, 1½ teaspoons dill, the sugar and pepper. Toss cucumbers with sour cream mixture. Refrigerate covered 1 hour. Garnish with ½ teaspoon dill.

RADISHES AND SOUR CREAM
Makes about 2 cups

---

2 bunches radishes, thinly sliced
    (about 2 cups)
½ teaspoon salt

⅔ cup dairy sour cream
1 tablespoon prepared horseradish
½ teaspoon sugar
    Radish roses, if desired

1. Place sliced radishes and salt in water to cover; let stand at room temperature 1 hour. Drain. Rinse radishes; pat dry on paper toweling.

2. Mix remaining ingredients except radish roses in small bowl. Just before serving, toss sliced radishes with sour cream mixture. Garnish with radish roses.

MUSHROOM PICKLES

Makes about 3 cups

1   cup distilled white vinegar
½   cup water
2   teaspoons salt
½   teaspoon sugar
½   teaspoon snipped fresh dill
¼   cup peppercorns
1   bay leaf
1   clove garlic, crushed
1   pound fresh small mushrooms
1   carrot, pared, cut into julienne
       strips, 2 x ¼ inch each
1   stalk celery, cut into julienne
       strips, 2 x ¼ inch each

1.   Heat all ingredients except mushrooms, carrot and celery in 2-quart saucepan over high heat to boiling. Add mushrooms, carrot and celery. Heat to boiling; reduce heat. Simmer uncovered over medium heat, stirring occasionally, 10 minutes. Cool to lukewarm. Refrigerate covered at least 2 days.

2.   Drain mixture before serving. Arrange in serving bowl.

TIP: Mushroom Pickles can be stored covered in refrigerator up to 2 weeks.

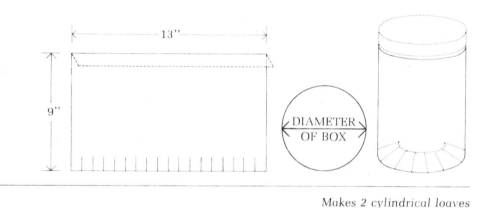

KULICH

Makes 2 cylindrical loaves

¼   cup milk
2   tablespoons butter or margarine
¼   cup all-purpose flour
1   egg

1   package active dry yeast
1   teaspoon sugar
¼   cup warm water (105° to 115°)

1   cup sugar
¾   cup butter or margarine
½   teaspoon salt
8   egg yolks

1   vanilla bean (6 to 8 inches long)
¼   cup chopped candied citron
¼   cup slivered blanched almonds,
       toasted
¼   cup golden raisins
¼   cup currants
¼   cup milk
1   tablespoon vodka
⅛   teaspoon ground cardamom
⅛   teaspoon ground nutmeg
⅛   teaspoon ground saffron
3   to 4 cups all-purpose flour

1.   Heat ¼ cup milk and 2 tablespoons butter in small saucepan, stirring constantly, to boiling. Stir in ¼ cup flour; remove from heat. Stir until mixture forms ball. Stir in egg. Cool to lukewarm.

2.   Dissolve yeast and 1 teaspoon sugar in ¼ cup warm water in small bowl. Let stand at room temperature 5 minutes. Stir yeast mixture into flour mixture. Cover; let rise in warm place until double, about 30 minutes.

3.   Cream 1 cup sugar, ¾ cup butter and the salt in large mixer bowl until light and fluffy. Beat in egg yolks, 2 at a time, beating well after each addition.

4.   Split vanilla bean. Remove seeds; mince pod. Combine seeds and pod, citron, almonds, raisins, currants, ¼ cup milk, the vodka, cardamom, nutmeg and saffron in small bowl. Beat fruit mixture into egg mixture gradually. Stir yeast mixture into egg mixture. Mix in enough of the 3 to 4 cups flour to make dough easy to handle. Turn dough onto floured surface. Knead until smooth and elastic, about 20 minutes. Place in well-buttered bowl; turn buttered side up. Cover; let rise in warm place until double, about 3 hours. (Dough is ready if impression remains.)

5.   Meanwhile, prepare baking forms. Use two 1-pound cylindrical oatmeal boxes. Grease insides of boxes with shortening; line with parchment paper (see diagram above). Extend paper 2 inches above tops of boxes. Fold extension down to form double-thickness paper collar, 1 inch high. Grease paper linings; sprinkle with bread crumbs. Shake out excess crumbs.

95

Kulich, Pashka, leaf-shaped Almond Mazurka and Meringue Confections highlight the Easter sweet table.

Dry bread crumbs

Icing (recipe follows)

Colored candy sprinkles
Fresh or confection flowers,
  if desired
Lemon leaves, if desired

6. Break off portion of dough with oiled hands; ease dough into prepared boxes gently, using both hands, until about half full. Cover; let rise until double, 3 to 4 hours.

7. Remove all but bottom shelf in oven. Heat oven to 300°. Bake breads until tops are light brown, about 1 hour. Remove breads from oven. Lay boxes on their sides; roll boxes ¼ turn every 2 minutes for 10 minutes. Remove breads from boxes by grasping paper collars. Remove paper linings. Cool breads completely on wire racks.*

8. Make Icing.

9. Ice bread tops, letting Icing drip down sides. Decorate with candy sprinkles, flowers and lemon leaves.

10. To serve, cut ½-inch slices from bottoms of loaves; cut slices in half. Place uncut decorated tops in center of serving plates; surround with halved slices.

TIP: *Kulich can be frozen, securely wrapped, at this point up to 6 weeks.

ICING

1	egg white
2½	cups powdered sugar
½	teaspoon vanilla
2	to 3 tablespoons water

Beat egg white in small mixer bowl on high speed until soft peaks form. Beat in sugar at medium speed gradually; beat in vanilla. Add water, a few drops at a time, until icing is of spreading consistency.

PASKHA   *Makes 2½ quarts*

1	pound unsalted butter
1½	cups sugar
1	vanilla bean (5 to 8 inches long)
7	hard-cooked egg yolks, sieved
4⅔	cups large-curd cottage cheese
3	tablespoons chopped blanched almonds, toasted
3	tablespoons chopped candied citron
2	teaspoons lemon juice
1	teaspoon vanilla extract
¼	teaspoon grated lemon peel
⅛	teaspoon salt
⅔	cup whipping cream
⅔	cup dairy sour cream
½	cup unblanched whole almonds

Fresh or confection flowers,
  if desired
Lemon leaves, if desired

1. Line 2½-quart paskha mold* with double-thickness damp cheesecloth, letting cheesecloth hang over edge 3 inches.

2. Cream butter and sugar in large mixer bowl until light and fluffy. Split vanilla bean. Remove seeds; mince pod. Stir seeds and pod into butter mixture; beat at medium speed 1 minute.

3. Beat egg yolks and cottage cheese into butter mixture. Stir in toasted almonds, citron, lemon juice, vanilla extract, lemon peel and salt. Whip cream in chilled small bowl. Fold whipped cream and sour cream into cottage cheese mixture; spoon into prepared mold. Fold overhanging cheesecloth over cheese mixture; cover with lid. Elevate mold for drainage in shallow pan. Place weight on lid; refrigerate until firm, at least 24 hours.**

4. Unmold cheese mixture onto serving platter; remove cheesecloth. Decorate with whole almonds, flowers and lemon leaves. Serve with Kulich or fresh fruit.

TIPS: *A 2½-quart plastic container with drainage holes or a clean clay flowerpot with drainage can be substituted for the paskha mold.

**Paskha can be refrigerated covered up to 1 week.

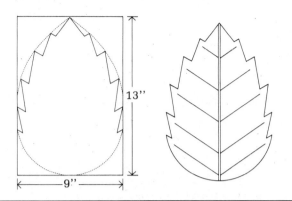

13"

9"

ALMOND MAZURKA
Makes 16 to 20 servings

1 cup (8 ounces) almond paste
3 eggs, separated
2 tablespoons lemon juice
1 tablespoon vegetable oil
½ teaspoon almond extract
1 cup sugar
1½ cups all-purpose flour
1½ teaspoons baking powder
½ teaspoon salt

2 tablespoons fine dry bread crumbs

Almond Icing (recipe follows)

1. Break up almond paste in large mixer bowl. Add egg yolks. Add lemon juice, oil and almond extract; beat on low speed, scraping bowl frequently, until smooth, about 2 minutes. Add sugar gradually, beating well after each addition. Beat in ½ cup of the flour, the baking powder and salt. Stir in remaining flour.

2. Heat oven to 350°. Beat egg whites in small mixer bowl until stiff but not dry. Stir half the egg whites into almond mixture; fold in remaining egg whites. Butter baking pan, 13 x 9 x 2 inches; sprinkle with bread crumbs. Shake out excess crumbs. Spread batter evenly in pan. Bake until golden, about 30 minutes.

3. Cool cake in pan 30 minutes. Loosen cake from pan; invert onto baking sheet covered with waxed paper. Cut into leaf shape (see diagram) with sharp knife.*

4. Make Almond Icing.

5. Invert cake onto serving plate. Frost half the top and sides of cake with dark green Almond Icing, and half with light green icing, leaving ⅛-inch center strip uniced. Let stand until icing sets. Outline "veins" with tip of knife. Store cake securely wrapped in aluminum foil up to 2 days.

*TIP: *Almond Mazurka can be frozen, securely wrapped in aluminum foil, at this point up to 1 month.*

ALMOND ICING

1 egg white
2½ cups powdered sugar
½ teaspoon almond extract
2 to 3 tablespoons water
1 drop red food color

5 drops green food color

1. Beat egg white in small mixer bowl on high speed until soft peaks form. Beat in sugar at medium speed gradually; beat in almond extract. Add water, a few drops at a time, until icing is of spreading consistency. Mix in red food color.

2. Spoon half the icing into small bowl; mix in 1 drop of the green food color. Mix 4 drops of the green food color into remaining icing.

MERINGUE CONFECTIONS
Makes about 6 dozen

1 cup egg whites (about 7)
⅛ teaspoon cream of tartar
⅛ teaspoon salt
2¼ cups sugar
1 teaspoon vanilla
1 teaspoon instant coffee powder
Dash freshly ground nutmeg
¼ cup finely chopped walnuts
¼ teaspoon grated lemon peel

Heat oven to 300°

Beat egg whites, cream of tartar and salt until mixture forms soft peaks. Beat in sugar, 2 tablespoons at a time, beating until stiff and glossy. Beat in vanilla. Place half the mixture in medium-size bowl; fold in coffee powder and nutmeg. Fold walnuts and lemon peel into remaining mixture. Drop by tablespoonfuls 1 inch apart onto buttered baking sheets.* Bake until meringues are set and just begin to turn brown at edges, about 1 hour. Cool on wire racks.

*TIPS: *Meringues can be piped through pastry tube using large star tip.*

Meringues can be stored in airtight container at room temperature up to 2 weeks.

An English Pub Party

PUB PARTY MENU

COLD FOODS:
• PICKLED EGGS
• PICKLED ONIONS
• CHEESE AND ONION ROLLS
• OLD ENGLISH HERB CHEESE

HOT FOODS:
• SHEPHERD'S PIE
• CORNISH PASTIES
• SAUSAGE ROLLS

RELISHES:
• APPLE AND TOMATO CHUTNEY
PICKLED BEETS

DESSERT:
• MARMALADE PUDDING

BEVERAGES:
BEER
• SHANDY

• Recipes included

English pubs range in style from simple to sophisticated. But the atmosphere is always the same. Pubs are warm comfortable places to meet friends, engage in lively discussions and, most of all, enjoy hearty food and drink. For a relaxing evening at home, recreate this convivial scene with your own pub party.

Guests can begin by sampling savory cold foods, such as Cheese and Onion Rolls, or a Cheddary herb spread on English crackers. Our hot dishes include pub "regulars" like Shepherd's Pie, a robust ground beef mixture covered with whipped potatoes. Golden brown Cornish Pasties — originally made for farm workers' lunches in the fields — and Sausage Rolls are other favorites that will tantalize partygoers. Accompany all these foods with tangy Pickled Eggs and Pickled Onions, beets and a homemade chutney of apples, onions, tomatoes and raisins.

The beverages should flow like the conversation. Beer and sherry are traditional, but try Shandy, a refreshing blend of chilled beer and sparkling lemonade. And even the most satisfied pub patron won't pass up a classic Marmalade Pudding for dessert. Serves 12.

PARTY PLAN FOR PUB PARTY MENU

1 Week Before:	Make Pickled Onions. Make Pickled Eggs.
2 Days Before:	Make Apple and Tomato Chutney. Prepare Old English Herb Cheese through step 1 in recipe.
1 Day Before:	Prepare Cornish Pasties through step 2 in recipe.
That Afternoon:	Complete step 3 of Cornish Pasties recipe. Make Cheese and Onion Rolls; refrigerate covered. Measure and label ingredients for remaining recipes; refrigerate perishables.
3 Hours Before Serving:	Make Marmalade Pudding.
1 Hour Before Serving:	Make Shepherd's Pie. Complete Cornish Pasties. Make Sausage Rolls. Complete Old English Herb Cheese. Make Shandy.

The profusion of foods found in English pubs and stores tempts even the most indifferent palates.

PICKLED EGGS

16   hard-cooked eggs, peeled
4   cups malt or cider vinegar
½   cup sugar
1   tablespoon salt
2   teaspoons chopped fresh
    gingerroot
2   teaspoons whole allspice
2   teaspoons peppercorns

Pack eggs snugly in clean wide-necked jars. Combine remaining ingredients in large saucepan. Heat to boiling; boil uncovered 10 minutes. Pour hot vinegar mixture over eggs; cool. Screw lids in place. Refrigerate at least 5 days before serving.

TIP: Eggs can be stored covered in refrigerator up to 2 weeks without change in flavor or texture.

PICKLED ONIONS

4   cups tiny white boiling
    onions, peeled (about 1½ pounds)
¼   cup salt

3   cups malt or cider vinegar
¼   cup plus 2 tablespoons sugar
4   whole cloves
2   bay leaves
1   dried red pepper
1   small piece cinnamon stick
1   small slice fresh gingerroot
2   teaspoons mustard seeds
1   teaspoon peppercorns

1.   Wash onions in cold water; drain and pat dry. Place in large glass bowl; stir in salt. Let stand covered at room temperature overnight.

2.   Rinse onions under cold running water; drain thoroughly. Combine remaining ingredients in large saucepan. Heat to boiling; boil uncovered 5 minutes. Add onions; boil uncovered 5 minutes. Do not overcook; onions should be crisp.

3.   Pack onions in clean 1-quart glass jar. Pour hot vinegar mixture over onions, filling to 1 inch from top; cool. Screw lid in place. Refrigerate at least 1 week before serving.

TIP: Leftover onions can be stored covered in refrigerator up to 3 weeks without change in flavor or texture.

CHEESE AND ONION ROLLS

6   hamburger or sandwich buns
    Softened butter or margarine
    Prepared domestic or English
    hot-style mustard*
6   slices natural Cheddar cheese,
    about ¼ inch thick each
6   thin slices onion

Slice buns horizontally in half. Spread butter liberally on top and bottom halves of buns. Spread mustard to taste on top halves of buns. Place cheese slice on each bottom half; top with onion slice and top half of bun.

*TIP: *English mustard is hotter in flavor than domestic varieties; use with caution.*

OLD ENGLISH HERB CHEESE

4   ounces sharp Cheddar cheese,
    shredded
3   tablespoons dry sherry
2   tablespoons whipping cream
½   teaspoon salt
½   teaspoon parsley flakes
½   teaspoon minced chives or
    green onion tops
⅛   teaspoon white pepper
⅛   teaspoon dried sage leaves
⅛   teaspoon dried tarragon leaves
⅛   teaspoon dried thyme leaves
⅛   teaspoon dried chervil leaves
¼   teaspoon prepared mustard

    *Assorted English crackers

1.   Combine all ingredients except crackers in top of double boiler. Heat over simmering water, stirring constantly, until cheese melts and mixture is smooth. Pour into 2 small decorative pots or custard cups; cool. Refrigerate covered until serving.

2.   Serve cheese at room temperature with assorted crackers or English biscuits.

*TIPS: *English crackers can be purchased in specialty stores.*

Old English Herb Cheese tastes best when made 1 to 2 days before serving to blend flavors.

Bottom: Pasties, Shepherd's Pie. Center: Cheese and Onion Rolls, chutney, onions, eggs, Sausage Rolls, herb cheese. Top: Pudding.

SHEPHERD'S PIE

Makes 6 servings

2	medium onions, minced
2	tablespoons butter or margarine
1	pound lean ground beef
½	cup beef broth
1	tablespoon catsup
¼	teaspoon Worcestershire sauce
¼	teaspoon prepared mustard
1½	teaspoons salt
¼	teaspoon pepper
4	to 6 medium red potatoes, pared, cooked, mashed (3 cups)
¼	cup warm milk
3	tablespoons butter or margarine
1	teaspoon salt

Heat oven to 425°

1. Sauté onions in 2 tablespoons butter in 10-inch skillet over medium heat until tender, about 5 minutes. Stir in ground beef; sauté until brown. Mix in broth, catsup. Worcestershire sauce, mustard, 1½ teaspoons salt and the pepper. Pour mixture into buttered 8- or 9-inch-square baking dish.

2. Beat mashed potatoes, warm milk, 3 tablespoons butter and 1 teaspoon salt until light and fluffy. Spread over meat mixture, sealing to edge of dish. Run fork over potatoes for a rippled surface. Bake until potatoes are brown, about 30 minutes. Cut into squares; serve piping hot.

CORNISH PASTIES

Makes 15 to 18

2	cups all-purpose flour
1	teaspoon salt
⅔	cup cold shortening
3	to 4 tablespoons cold water
8	ounces lean ground beef
1	medium potato, pared, shredded
1	medium onion, minced
2	tablespoons butter or margarine, softened
¾	teaspoon salt
¼	teaspoon pepper
⅛	teaspoon dry mustard
	Butter or margarine
1	egg, slightly beaten

1. Mix flour and 1 teaspoon salt in medium-size bowl. Cut in cold shortening thoroughly. Sprinkle in cold water, 1 tablespoon at a time, mixing until dough almost cleans side of bowl. Gather dough into ball; cover with plastic wrap.

2. Combine ground beef, potato, onion, 2 tablespoons butter, ¾ teaspoon salt, the pepper and mustard thoroughly in medium-size bowl.*

3. Divide dough in half. Roll half the dough on lightly floured cloth-covered surface into circle about ¼-inch thick. Cut into 4-inch circles. Spoon about 1 tablespoon of the filling onto half of each circle; dot with butter. Dampen edges of dough with water. Fold dough over filling, pressing edges together firmly; crimp with fork. Repeat procedure with remaining dough and filling.**

4. Heat oven to 400°. Place pasties on lightly greased baking sheet. Cut slits for steam in top of each; brush with beaten egg. Bake until light brown, 20 to 25 minutes. Serve hot.

*TIPS: *Pasties can be prepared to this point in advance. Store dough and filling, separately, covered in refrigerator overnight. Proceed with step 3.*

***Pasties can be prepared to this point in advance. Store covered in refrigerator no longer than 6 hours. Proceed with step 4.*

SAUSAGE ROLLS

Makes 6 servings

6   small hot dog buns or finger
     rolls, about 3 inches long each*
6   fresh pork sausage links
     English mustard
     Chutney

     Heat oven to 250°

Slash each bun vertically from top, down to ¼ inch from bottom crust. Wrap in aluminum foil; place in oven until warm. Fry pork sausages in small skillet until fully cooked; drain on paper toweling. Place 1 sausage in each bun. Serve with mustard and chutney on the side.

*TIP: *If 3-inch buns are not available, slice 3 regular hot dog buns crosswise in half.*

APPLE AND TOMATO CHUTNEY

Makes about 1 quart

1   tablespoon mixed pickling spice
4½   cups minced onions (1 pound)
3½   cups diced pared tart apples
     (about 4)
3   medium tomatoes, peeled, sliced
4   ounces dark or golden raisins
     (about ¾ cup)
1   cup malt or cider vinegar
1   cup packed dark brown sugar
1   teaspoon salt

Tie pickling spice in cheesecloth bag. Combine remaining ingredients in Dutch oven; add spice bag and cover. Heat to boiling; reduce heat. Simmer uncovered, stirring occasionally, until mixture thickens, about 2 hours. Spoon hot chutney into clean glass jars; screw lids in place and refrigerate.

TIP: Chutney tastes best when made 2 to 3 days before serving. Store leftover chutney covered in refrigerator up to 2 months.

MARMALADE PUDDING

See recipe on page 109 in Sweet Trolley Menu.

SHANDY

Makes 12 servings (about 1 cup each)

2   quarts chilled beer
1   quart chilled carbonated
     lemon-lime beverage

Pour beer and lemon-lime beverage into large glass pitcher; stir. Do not add ice. Serve in chilled beer mugs or glasses.

A British Sweet Trolley

The love of sweets is a passion of national proportion in Britain. Smart hostesses there indulge the sweet tooth, never settling for one dessert when they can serve many. Since it's often rolled in on a tea cart, the glorious assortment of treats is called a "sweet trolley."

A proper sweet trolley is laden with delicacies guaranteed to satisfy everyone's cravings. Coffee Gateau is a glamorous cake of ladyfingers wrapped around a whipped cream and coffee-flavored interior. Traditional British favorites include Crème Caramel, a delicate custard, and orange-accented Marmalade Pudding. For creamy, not-too-filling delectables, sample Raspberry Fool or a cool fluffy Syllabub with a dash of brandy and nutmeg.

Make-ahead jam tarts and Brandy Snaps — an unlikely name for these light cream-filled cylinders — are especially convenient for the busy host. The sweet trolley won't even pass by those more or less counting calories. Baked apples stuffed with dried fruits can be eaten with or without a Custard Sauce. And fresh strawberries or a medley of seasonal fruits both come with cream optional.

Our Sweet Trolley Menu has many possibilities. The ambitious entertainer would set out the entire selection with hot tea for a smashing dessert party. Or you might want to choose just a few special offerings for lunch, dinner or at coffee time. Serves 30.

Wine Suggestion: Serve a refreshing fruit punch, or a not-too-dry sparkling wine, like an Italian Asti Spumante, with your sweets.

PARTY PLAN FOR SWEET TROLLEY MENU

2 Days Before:
Prepare Brandy Snaps through step 3 in recipe.
Make Custard Sauce for apples; refrigerate covered.

1 Day Before:
Prepare Coffee Gateau through step 2 in recipe.
Prepare Fresh Fruit Salad with Cream through step 1 in recipe.
Prepare Crème Caramel through step 2 in recipe.
Prepare Raspberry Fool through step 1 in recipe.
Make English Jam Tarts; store lightly covered at room temperature.

That Morning:
Prepare Fresh Strawberries with Mock Devonshire Cream through step 1 in recipe; refrigerate berries and cream mixture in separate covered containers.
Prepare Baked Stuffed Apples with Custard Sauce through step 2 in recipe.
Prepare Syllabub through step 1 in recipe.

3 Hours Before Serving:
Make Marmalade Pudding.
Complete Coffee Gateau.
Complete Crème Caramel; refrigerate uncovered.
Complete step 2 of Fresh Fruit Salad with Cream recipe.
Complete Brandy Snaps.

45 Minutes Before Serving:
Complete Raspberry Fool.
Complete Syllabub.
Complete Fresh Fruit Salad with Cream.
Complete Fresh Strawberries with Mock Devonshire Cream.
Heat Custard Sauce over low heat, if serving warm.

British desserts: Syllabub, Coffee Gateau, fresh fruit salad, Crème Caramel, Brandy Snaps, strawberries with cream, jam tarts, and Raspberry Fool.

COFFEE GATEAU

Makes 6 to 8 servings

12 ladyfingers (one 3-ounce
    package)
2 tablespoons rum

1¼ cups whipping cream
¾ cup powdered sugar
¾ cup butter or margarine,
    softened
2 eggs
1 tablespoon instant coffee
    powder

¾ cup whipping cream
2 tablespoons powdered sugar
½ teaspoon vanilla
    Grated chocolate, if desired

1. Split ladyfingers lengthwise in half; sprinkle cut surfaces with rum. Stand 16 ladyfinger halves upright around inside of 1-quart soufflé dish or glass bowl.

2. Beat 1¼ cups whipping cream in chilled small bowl until stiff peaks form. Cream ¾ cup powdered sugar and the butter in small mixer bowl until light and fluffy. Add eggs, 1 at a time, beating well after each addition. Fold in coffee powder. Fold coffee mixture into beaten cream until smooth. Pour mixture into prepared mold; top with remaining 8 ladyfinger halves. Cover with plastic wrap; refrigerate at least 3 hours.

3. Forty-five minutes before serving, run knife around edge of dish. Invert gateau onto serving platter. Beat ¾ cup whipping cream and 2 tablespoons powdered sugar in chilled small bowl until stiff peaks form; beat in vanilla. Spread about ¼ cup of the cream mixture over top of gateau. Pipe remaining cream mixture through pastry tube around top and sides to decorate. Sprinkle with grated chocolate; refrigerate. To serve, cut into wedges.

TIP: Gateau in photograph was made in a 9-inch springform pan using double the recipe.

FRESH FRUIT SALAD WITH CREAM

Makes 8 to 10 dessert servings

¾ cup sugar
1½ cups water
    Juice of 1 lemon, strained

1 cantaloupe or other seasonal
    melon (about 1½ pounds)
3 navel oranges, peeled,
    sectioned
3 bananas, sliced
2 red apples, unpared,
    cored, diced
2 green apples, unpared, cored,
    diced
8 ounces seedless green grapes
    (about 1½ cups)
8 ounces purple or red grapes,
    halved, seeded (about 1½ cups)

¼ cup sherry (optional)
    Heavy cream

1. Dissolve sugar in water in 1-quart saucepan. Heat to boiling; reduce heat. Simmer uncovered until light syrup is formed, about 10 minutes; remove from heat. Stir in lemon juice; refrigerate syrup covered until cold.

2. Halve cantaloupe; remove seeds and scoop out pulp with melon ball cutter. Combine melon balls, orange sections, sliced bananas, diced apples and grapes in large bowl. Pour lemon syrup over fruit; toss gently until evenly coated. Cover and refrigerate.

3. Just before serving, stir in sherry. Pass cream in separate pitcher to pour over fruit.

CREME CARAMEL

Makes 8 servings

¾ cup sugar
¾ cup water

6 eggs
¼ cup sugar
1½ teaspoons vanilla
4 cups milk, scalded, cooled

1. Heat oven to 325°. Dissolve ¾ cup sugar and ¾ cup water in 1-quart saucepan. Heat to boiling; reduce heat. Simmer gently until caramel-colored syrup forms, 18 to 20 minutes; do not overcook. Meanwhile, heat 2-quart soufflé dish in oven until hot, about 3 minutes.* Pour syrup immediately into soufflé dish; tilt and rotate dish to coat bottom and side.

2. Beat eggs, ¼ cup sugar and the vanilla in large bowl until smooth. Stir in milk gradually; cool. Pour into prepared soufflé dish. Place dish on rack in large pan filled with hot water coming ⅔ up side of soufflé dish; cover with aluminum foil. Bake until knife inserted halfway between center and edge comes out clean, about 1½ hours. Remove dish from water; cool slightly. Refrigerate covered until cold, at least 4 hours or overnight.

3. To serve, run knife around edge of dish. Invert custard onto serving dish with rim. Caramel sauce will drizzle down sides of custard.

TIP: *Crème Caramels can be prepared individually. Divide hot caramel syrup among 9 heated 6-ounce custard cups. Proceed with step 2, except bake at 350° 45 minutes.

BRANDY SNAPS *Makes about 30*

¾   **cup molasses**
¾   **cup butter or margarine,
      softened**
½   **cup granulated sugar**
1   **cup all-purpose flour**
1   **teaspoon ground ginger**
2   **teaspoons brandy**

1½ **cups whipping cream**
½   **cup powdered sugar**
3   **tablespoons brandy**

     Heat oven to 350°

1. Mix molasses, butter and granulated sugar in top of double boiler. Heat over simmering water, stirring constantly, until sugar dissolves and mixture is smooth; remove from heat. Mix flour and ginger; beat into molasses mixture gradually. Beat in 2 teaspoons brandy until smooth.

2. Drop batter by teaspoonfuls about 4 inches apart on well-greased baking sheet. Bake until cookies spread into 3- to 4-inch circles and turn golden, 6 to 8 minutes. Coat handle of long wooden spoon with butter.

3. Let cookies cool slightly; loosen from sheet with metal spatula. Working quickly, wrap each cookie around spoon handle to form cylinder with 2 open ends. If cookies become too stiff to roll, return sheet to oven a moment to soften. Slide cylinders onto wire rack; cool completely. Repeat procedure with remaining batter.*

4. One hour before serving, beat whipping cream in chilled small bowl until thickened; beat in powdered sugar until stiff peaks form. Fold in 3 tablespoons brandy. Pipe cream mixture through pastry tube into cookie cylinders. Arrange on serving plate; refrigerate until served.**

TIPS: *Cookies can be prepared to this point up to 2 days in advance. Store in airtight container at room temperature. Proceed with step 4.

**Leftover filled Brandy Snaps can be refrigerated lightly covered overnight.

FRESH STRAWBERRIES WITH MOCK DEVONSHIRE CREAM *Makes 8 servings*

3   **pints fresh strawberries,
      hulled**
½   **cup whipping cream**
     Powdered sugar
1   **cup dairy sour cream**

     Brown sugar, if desired

1. Arrange berries in large glass serving bowl; cover and refrigerate. Beat whipping cream and powdered sugar to taste in chilled small bowl until stiff peaks form. Fold into sour cream until blended.

2. Serve cream mixture over berries. Sprinkle with brown sugar.

ENGLISH JAM TARTS *Makes 15 to 18 3-inch tarts*

2   cups all-purpose flour
⅛   teaspoon salt
½   cup cold butter or margarine
4   to 5 tablespoons
     cold water

     *Assorted English jams
       (strawberry, raspberry,
       apricot, etc.)
     Powdered sugar, if desired

1.   Mix flour and salt in medium-size bowl. Cut in cold butter thoroughly. Sprinkle in cold water, 1 tablespoon at a time, mixing until dough almost cleans side of bowl. Form dough into ball; divide in half.

2.   Heat oven to 400°. Roll half the dough on lightly floured cloth-covered surface into circle about ¼ inch thick. Cut into 4-inch circles; fit into 3-inch tart pans, crimping to edge.** Pierce bottoms and sides thoroughly with fork. Arrange pans on baking sheet. Repeat procedure with remaining dough.

3.   Bake shells 10 minutes; remove from oven. Fill with desired jam, no more than ⅔ full. Bake until brown and bubbly, 7 to 10 minutes; cool on wire rack. Sprinkle lightly with powdered sugar. Remove tarts from pans. Serve at room temperature.

TIPS: *English jams are less sweet and richer in fruit flavor than our domestic varieties. Domestic jams can be substituted, however.*

**If tart pans are not available, pastry circles can be fitted over backs of muffin cups or small custard cups, pleating so pastry fits closely. Pierce and bake 12 minutes. Cool; remove from cups. Fill and continue baking according to directions in step 3.*

RASPBERRY FOOL *Makes 6 to 8 servings (about ¾ cup each)*

4   cups fresh raspberries
       or strawberries, hulled*
½   to ¾ cup sugar
1   teaspoon vanilla

2   cups whipping cream

1.   Rinse raspberries; do not dry. Cook raspberries in 2-quart saucepan over low heat, stirring occasionally, until berries are softened and juices flow, 20 to 30 minutes. Mash berries slightly with back of spoon. Add sugar and vanilla; stir until sugar is dissolved. Cover and refrigerate.

2.   Thirty minutes before serving, beat whipping cream in chilled large bowl until stiff peaks form. Fold berry mixture into cream gradually. Do not overmix; berries should form a marbled effect in cream. Refrigerate. Serve in iced parfait glasses or sherbet dishes.

TIP: *1 package (32 ounces) frozen unsweetened whole raspberries or strawberries can be substituted for the fresh berries. Partially thaw; do not rinse or dry. Proceed with step 1.*

SYLLABUB *Makes 8 servings*

½   cup sugar
¼   cup plus 2 tablespoons brandy
       or sherry*
     Grated peel of 1 lemon
     Juice of 1 lemon, strained

2   cups whipping cream
     Freshly grated nutmeg

1.   Stir sugar, brandy, lemon peel and lemon juice in small bowl until sugar is dissolved. Let stand covered at room temperature to blend flavors, at least 1 hour; refrigerate.

2.   Thirty minutes before serving, beat whipping cream in chilled large bowl until stiff peaks form. Fold brandy mixture into cream gradually, until soft and fluffy; refrigerate. Serve in individual iced parfait glasses or sherbet dishes. Sprinkle with nutmeg.

TIP: *½ cup dry white wine such as Chablis can be substituted for the brandy. Resulting Syllabub will be softer in consistency.*

BAKED STUFFED APPLES WITH CUSTARD SAUCE

Makes 6 servings

6 medium baking apples
      (Rome Beauty, McIntosh,
      Jonathan)
¾ cup chopped mixed dried fruits
      or raisins (about 4 ounces)
¼ cup sugar
¼ cup butter or margarine, softened
      Dash ground ginger
      Dash ground cinnamon

      Custard Sauce (recipe follows)

      Heat oven to 350°

2 egg yolks
2 tablespoons sugar
      Dash salt
1 cup milk, scalded,
      cooled
½ teaspoon vanilla

1. Core apples; pare 1 inch skin off stem end of each. Arrange apples upright in baking pan large enough to fit apples snugly.

2. Combine dried fruits, sugar, butter and spices; stuff centers of apples with mixture. Pour small amount of water into bottom of pan; cover with aluminum foil. Bake until apples are tender, 35 to 40 minutes. Do not overbake. Remove from oven; uncover. Cool apples to room temperature.

3. Make Custard Sauce. Serve sauce hot or cold over apples.

CUSTARD SAUCE
Makes 1¼ cups

Beat egg yolks, sugar and salt in top of double boiler until smooth. Stir in milk gradually. Heat over simmering water, stirring constantly, until mixture thickens and coats a metal spoon; remove from heat. Stir in vanilla.

MARMALADE PUDDING

Makes 8 servings

½ cup sugar
½ cup butter or margarine,
      softened
2 eggs, slightly beaten
1⅓ cups all-purpose flour
1½ teaspoons baking powder
2 tablespoons milk

¾ cup orange marmalade

      Sweetened whipped cream,
      if desired

1. Cream sugar and butter in large mixer bowl until light and fluffy. Beat in eggs gradually. Mix flour and baking powder; stir into butter mixture. Stir in milk.

2. Spread marmalade in bottom of buttered 1-quart English pudding basin, soufflé dish or plain mold. Spread batter over marmalade, spreading to side of mold. Cover with greased aluminum foil; tie securely with string.

3. Place mold on rack in Dutch oven. Pour boiling water into pot coming about ⅔ up side of mold; cover pot tightly. Heat water to boiling; reduce heat. Simmer gently until wooden pick inserted in center of pudding comes out clean, 1½ hours.

4. Remove mold from water; remove foil. Cool pudding on wire rack about 30 minutes. Run knife around edge of mold; invert pudding onto serving platter. Serve immediately. Pass sweetened whipped cream.

A Haitian Collation

The foods of Haiti are as lush and inviting as the island itself. In this country that was controlled by France until 1804, French cuisine is still served in elegant homes and restaurants. But the Haitian people, most of whom are of African descent, delight in Creole cookery. It's hot, sweet and piquant, and it glories in the abundant tropical fruits and vegetables available on the island.

Rum and rum drinks are popular beverages in Haiti, and our punch mixes gold rum and fruit juices into a refreshing aperitif. Accompany it with an appetizer of savory Meat Pies.

Chicken Haitian Style thrills the taste buds with curry powder, saffron and red pepper, plus a soupçon of rum and a sprinkling of lime. Leeks, sweet pepper and tomato turn plain rice into a truly Creole creation.

Haitian cooking often features plantains — banana-like fruit growing plentifully on the island. In our recipe, the plantains are lightly glazed and topped with a rum-lime sauce. Brilliantly hued Fresh Tomato Relish sparkles with a wealth of vegetables. To crown the fascinating flavors of dinner, and cool diners' palates, offer Lime Ice served on pineapple slices. Serves 4.

Wine Suggestion: Go with a light red wine to accompany these lively Haitian dishes. A good Beaujolais, Château des Tours, or Walter Taylor's Bully Hill Red will do nicely.

Still lifes of Haiti — its people, flora and architecture. Opposite: plantains, chicken and rice highlight our Haitian dinner.

HAITIAN DINNER MENU

- **RUM FRUIT PUNCH**
- **MEAT PIES**

- **CHICKEN HAITIAN STYLE**
- **CREOLE RICE**
- **GLAZED RIPE PLANTAINS**
- **FRESH TOMATO RELISH**

- **LIME ICE**

- Recipes included

Serve the Meat Pies appetizer with refreshing Rum Fruit Punch.

PARTY PLAN FOR HAITIAN DINNER MENU

1 Day Before: Prepare Lime Ice through step 3 in recipe.

That Afternoon: Prepare Fresh Tomato Relish through step 2 in recipe.
Prepare Meat Pies through step 2 in recipe; refrigerate covered.
Measure and label ingredients for remaining recipes; refrigerate perishables.
Prepare garnishes for menu; refrigerate.
If serving Rum Fruit Punch in coconuts, prepare coconuts.

1 Hour 15 Minutes Before Serving: Make Glazed Ripe Plantains.
Make Chicken Haitian Style.
Make Creole Rice.
Complete Meat Pies.
Complete Fresh Tomato Relish.
Make Rum Fruit Punch.

10 Minutes Before Dessert: Complete Lime Ice.

RUM FRUIT PUNCH (Cocktail de Fruits au Rhum)

Makes 4 servings (1½ cups each)

1½ cups gold rum
1½ cups lime juice
1½ cups orange juice
¾   to 1 cup grenadine syrup
    Ice
    Lime slices

Mix rum, juices and syrup in pitcher; add ice. Pour into tall glasses. Garnish with lime slices. Serve with straws.

TIP: Rum Fruit Punch can be served in green or brown coconuts, if desired. For green coconuts: Remove husk from top third of each. Cut across top to make hole in top center about 2 inches in diameter. For brown coconuts: Remove outer husk of each. Make opening in 2 of the 3 eyes of each with ice pick. Pour out coconut "milk"; refrigerate covered for later use. Add punch to each coconut. Serve with long straws.

MEAT PIES (Pâté de Viande)

Makes 14 appetizers

⅓   pound lean ground beef
1   medium clove garlic, crushed
2   tablespoons minced green onion
2   tablespoons minced green
      pepper
1½ tablespoons butter or
      margarine
2   tablespoons minced tomato
2   tablespoons snipped fresh
      parsley
½   teaspoon curry powder
¼   to ½ teaspoon red
      pepper sauce
¼   teaspoon salt

1   tablespoon gold rum

1   package (11 ounces) piecrust mix

1. Sauté beef, garlic, onion and pepper in butter in skillet over medium heat until beef loses pink color. Stir in tomato, parsley, curry powder, red pepper sauce and salt. Cook and stir 3 to 4 minutes.

2. Stir rum into beef mixture. Cook until most of liquid is evaporated, about 1 minute.

3. Heat oven to 425°. Make piecrust dough according to package directions. Divide dough in half. Roll each half ¹/₁₆-inch thick on well-floured surface. Cut each half into seven 4-inch circles. Top half of each circle with 2 teaspoons of the meat mixture. Moisten edges of circles with water. Fold circles in half, sealing edges with tines of fork. Place on ungreased baking sheets.

4. Bake pies until golden, 12 to 15 minutes. Serve hot or at room temperature.

CHICKEN HAITIAN STYLE (Poulet à l'Haitienne)

Makes 4 servings

1   broiler-fryer chicken
      (3 to 3½ pounds),
      cut up
¼   cup olive or vegetable oil
2   tablespoons butter or margarine
4   medium onions, sliced
3   cloves garlic, minced
2   teaspoons curry powder
⅛   teaspoon crushed saffron
1½ teaspoons salt
1   to 1½ teaspoons crushed red
      pepper flakes

1   cup chicken broth
2   tablespoons gold rum
    Lime juice
    Watercress, if desired

1. Dust chicken pieces with flour. Cook chicken pieces in oil and butter in 12-inch skillet until brown, about 20 minutes; remove from skillet. Sauté onions and garlic in pan drippings until golden, about 5 minutes. Stir in curry powder, saffron, salt and red pepper flakes.

2. Return chicken to skillet. Stir in chicken broth. Heat to boiling; reduce heat and cover. Simmer 10 minutes; uncover. Simmer until chicken is tender, about 10 minutes. Stir in rum; simmer 1 minute. Sprinkle chicken lightly with lime juice. Garnish with watercress.

CREOLE RICE (Riz Créole) *Makes 4 servings*

2	tablespoons butter or margarine
¼	cup minced leeks or green onions
3	tablespoons minced sweet red pepper
1	small tomato, minced
1	teaspoon salt
½	teaspoon paprika
	Dash white pepper
	Dash ground turmeric
2	cups water
1	cup uncooked regular rice

1. Heat butter in medium-size saucepan. Sauté leeks and red pepper in butter 2 to 3 minutes. Add tomato, salt, paprika, white pepper and turmeric. Sauté 1 minute.

2. Add water and rice to mixture in saucepan. Heat to boiling; reduce heat and cover. Simmer, stirring twice during cooking time, until rice is tender, about 15 minutes. Remove from heat. Let stand covered 5 minutes.

GLAZED RIPE PLANTAINS (Bananes Jeunes Glacées) *Makes 4 servings*

2	medium ripe plantains, peeled, cut lengthwise in half*
¼	cup plus 2 tablespoons butter or margarine
1	cup water
1	cup sugar
¼	teaspoon ground cinnamon
¼	cup gold rum
1	tablespoon lime juice

1. Soak plantains in salted water to cover (2 teaspoons salt to 3 cups water) 30 minutes. Drain on paper toweling.

2. Heat half the butter in large skillet. Cook plantains in butter over medium heat until golden. Add 1 cup water and the sugar. Heat to boiling; reduce heat and cover. Simmer 15 minutes; uncover. Simmer until water and sugar form light syrup and plantains are tender, 10 to 15 minutes. Add remaining butter and the cinnamon.

3. Heat rum in small saucepan; ignite. Pour over plantains in skillet. Stir in lime juice. Place plantains on serving platter; pour sauce over top. Serve immediately.

*TIP: *Plantains can be purchased in Latin American grocery stores. Firm, slightly underripe bananas can be substituted for the plantains. Omit step 1. Cook bananas in butter until golden; remove from skillet. Proceed with remainder of step 2. Return bananas to skillet. Proceed with step 3.*

FRESH TOMATO RELISH (Condiment de Tomates) *Makes about 2 cups*

2	medium tomatoes, chopped
1	medium onion, chopped
2	green onions, chopped (use 2 inches of green tops)
3	shallots or green onions, minced
2	medium cloves garlic, minced
1	tablespoon grated fresh gingerroot
1	small sweet red pepper, minced
1	teaspoon salt
⅛	teaspoon white pepper
2	tablespoons lime juice
1	tablespoon olive oil
2	teaspoons snipped fresh parsley

1. Combine tomatoes, onions, shallots, garlic, gingerroot, red pepper, salt and white pepper. Let stand 15 minutes.

2. Stir lime juice and olive oil into tomato mixture. Refrigerate covered 3 to 4 hours.

3. Just before serving, stir relish. Sprinkle with parsley.

Voodoo dancers wear white dresses that symbolize purity.

LIME ICE (Fresco de Citron)

Makes 4 to 6 servings

1	cup sugar
3	cups water
½	cup light corn syrup
⅛	teaspoon salt
1½	teaspoons unflavored gelatin
¼	cup cold water
¾	cup lime juice
¾	teaspoon grated lime peel
2	egg whites
1	tablespoon sugar
4	to 6 fresh or canned unsweetened pineapple slices

1.   Mix 1 cup sugar, 3 cups water, the corn syrup and salt in medium-size saucepan. Heat to boiling; boil 5 minutes. Remove from heat. Dissolve gelatin in ¼ cup cold water. Stir into sugar syrup. Add lime juice and peel; cool.

2.   Pour cooled mixture into baking pan, 9 x 9 x 2 inches. Freeze uncovered until slushy, 2 to 3 hours.

3.   Beat egg whites and 1 tablespoon sugar until stiff peaks form. Place lime mixture in large bowl; beat with rotary beater until smooth. Fold egg whites into lime mixture. Pour mixture into baking pan. Freeze uncovered, stirring frequently, 1 hour. Cover with aluminum foil; freeze until firm.

4.   To serve, scoop Lime Ice onto pineapple slices.

An Indonesian Banquet

Rijsttafel — the Dutch word that means simply "rice table" belies the fabulous richness of this Indonesian invention. Dutch explorers who came to the archipelago in the 1600s eagerly took to Indonesian cuisine with its unusual spices and new ways of preparing fruits and vegetables. Later settlers adopted the native *nasi ramas* — rice served with a variety of delicacies to enhance the abundant grain. They turned the meal into a formal feast with dozens of fiery, cool and pungent dishes, and renamed it *rijsttafel*.

The rice table is uniquely suited for buffet-style entertaining. But even the most industrious host will probably need two ovens and some assistance in the kitchen to manage the preparation. Or you might want to ask friends to pitch in for a potluck-type endeavor.

Rice is at the center of the banquet — not only white but the famous *nasi goreng*, or fried rice, and Yellow Rice tinged with coriander and turmeric. Surrounding this "staple" are foods brilliant in flavor and color. Shrimp and chicken in a sassy sauce; cubes of beef cooked in a blend of coconut, gingerroot and chili peppers; and beef slices browned in an aromatic broth are some of the standard fare.

Marinate bits of pork in sherry and soy, skewer, then barbecue them, or wrap fish fillets in cabbage leaves before steaming for attractively authentic *rijsttafel* dishes. Hot Chicken, accented with chili peppers, is one of the renowned *pedis* (dragon mouth) items of Indonesia. A platter of succulent fresh vegetables is set out with a creamy Peanut Dip, and shallots spark a cool Cucumber Salad. Golden Corn Fritters, Stewed Cabbage with Eggs and shrimp chips are all welcome complements to the spicier foods.

Mouth-watering tropical fruits are a perfect ending to the evening's parade of tastes and textures. Serves 12.

Wine Suggestion: With so great a variety of flavors here, I suggest a simple rosé, such as Almadén's Grenache Rosé, or a good Tavel from France.

PARTY PLAN FOR RICE TABLE MENU

2 Days Before:

Prepare Fresh Fried Shrimps in Spicy Sauce through step 1 in recipe.
Prepare Yellow Rice through step 1 in recipe.
Prepare Barbecued Pork on Bamboo Skewers through step 1 in recipe.
Prepare Meat Main Dish in Hot Sauce through step 1 in recipe.
Prepare Fried Chicken Pieces in Spicy Sauce through step 1 in recipe.
Make Cucumber Salad.

1 Day Before:

Prepare Vegetable Salad with Peanut Dip through step 2 in recipe.
Complete steps 2, 3 and 4 of Meat Main Dish in Hot Sauce recipe.
Complete steps 2 and 3 of Fried Chicken Pieces in Spicy Sauce recipe.
Prepare Fried Rice with Garnishes through step 2 in recipe; refrigerate Omelet Strips covered.

That Afternoon:

Prepare Barbecued Fish Rolled in Banana Leaves through step 3 in recipe; refrigerate covered.
Complete Vegetable Salad with Peanut Dip; refrigerate covered.
Measure and label ingredients for remaining recipes; refrigerate perishables.
Arrange fruits for dessert on platter or in bowl; refrigerate.

2 Hours Before Serving:

Complete Barbecued Pork on Bamboo Skewers. Heat in oven 15 minutes before serving.
Fresh Fried Shrimps in Spicy Sauce is dotted with tomato and green onion bits.

1 Hour Before Serving:

Heat oven to 200°. As following recipes are completed, place in oven to keep warm.

Make Fried Shrimp Chips.

Make Corn Fritters.

Complete Yellow Rice.

Complete Fried Rice with Garnishes.

Complete Barbecued Fish Rolled in Banana Leaves.

Make Simmered Beef Slices.

Make Hot Chicken.

Complete Fried Chicken Pieces in Spicy Sauce.

Complete Meat Main Dish in Hot Sauce.

Make Stewed Cabbage with Eggs.

Complete Fresh Fried Shrimps in Spicy Sauce.

Regale your guests with *rijsttafel* — a feast of exotic flavors with rice at its center.

FRIED RICE WITH GARNISHES (Nasi Goreng)

Makes 4 to 6 servings

Fried Onions (recipe follows)

1. Make Fried Onions.

Omelet Strips (recipe follows)

2. Make Omelet Strips.

¼ cup vegetable oil
1 egg, beaten
10 green onions with tops, chopped
1 clove garlic, crushed
1 cup chopped cooked
    chicken, meat or seafood

3. Heat oil in large skillet or *wok*. Scramble egg in oil. Add onions, garlic and chicken. Sauté about 2 minutes. Stir in rice, catsup and soy sauce. Season with salt and pepper. Cook until hot. Garnish with Fried Onions and Omelet Strips.

4	cups hot cooked rice
2	tablespoons catsup
2	tablespoons soy sauce
	Salt
	Pepper

FRIED ONIONS

2	medium onions, sliced
	Vegetable oil

Arrange onions on paper toweling. Let stand at room temperature overnight. Heat oil (1 inch) in small saucepan to 365°. Fry onions until golden. Drain on paper toweling. Store onions in covered container.

OMELET STRIPS

1	egg
1	teaspoon water
	Butter or margarine

Beat egg and water in small bowl. Butter small omelet pan or skillet. Pour egg mixture into pan. Tilt pan from side so that entire bottom is covered. Cook egg mixture over medium heat, lifting sides of omelet with spatula to allow uncooked portion to run underneath, if necessary, until set. Slide omelet out of pan and onto plate. Cut into ¼-inch strips.

YELLOW RICE (Nasi Kuning)   *Makes 4 to 6 servings*

2	cups Coconut Milk (recipe follows)
1	cup uncooked regular rice
½	teaspoon salt
1	bay leaf
¼	teaspoon ground turmeric
¼	teaspoon ground coriander
¼	teaspoon pepper
	*Chili flower, if desired

1. Make Coconut Milk.

2. Heat Coconut Milk in medium-size saucepan to boiling. Stir in rice and remaining ingredients except chili flower; reduce heat and cover. Simmer until rice is tender, 15 to 20 minutes. Arrange rice in bowl; garnish with chili flower.

*TIP: *To make chili flower, trim stem end from red or green chili pepper. With scissors or sharp knife, make cuts through chili to opposite end, being careful to keep point intact. Soak in ice water.*

1	cup chopped fresh coconut*
1	cup hot water

COCONUT MILK   *Makes 1 cup*

Place coconut and hot water in blender container; cover. Blend on high speed until coconut is finely chopped. Cool to room temperature. Squeeze coconut through several layers of cheesecloth to obtain milk. Store in refrigerator up to 2 days.

*TIPS: *To open coconut: Puncture eyes of coconut with ice pick; drain liquid. Heat oven to 375°. Bake coconut 12 to 15 minutes. Remove from oven. Tap shell with hammer to open. Pare brown skin from coconut meat. A 1½-pound coconut will yield 3 to 4 cups coconut meat.*

Coconut Milk can also be made from grated dried unsweetened coconut (available at health food stores or gourmet food shops). Place 1 cup coconut and 1 cup hot water in blender container; cover. Blend on high speed 1 minute. Cool to room temperature. Squeeze coconut through several layers of cheesecloth to obtain milk.

VEGETABLE SALAD WITH PEANUT DIP (Gado-Gado)   *Makes 6 to 8 servings*

	Peanut Dip (recipe follows)
2	carrots, pared, cut into thin slices
8	ounces fresh green beans, cut into 2-inch pieces or 8 ounces fresh pea pods
1	small head cauliflower, trimmed, cut into pieces

1. Make Peanut Dip.

2. Cook carrots, beans, cauliflower, broccoli and potatoes in boiling water until crisp-tender; drain. Refrigerate until cold.

3. Pare and slice potatoes. Mound bean sprouts in center of large serving platter. Arrange vegetables attractively around bean sprouts. Garnish with egg slices. Serve with Peanut Dip.

120

8   ounces broccoli, stems
       trimmed, cut into pieces
2   medium potatoes with skins

12 ounces fresh bean sprouts or
       1 can (16 ounces) bean
       sprouts, drained, soaked
       in ice water
1   cucumber, unpared, sliced
4   to 6 white radishes, pared
8   ounces fresh spinach, trimmed
2   hard-cooked eggs, sliced

1¼ to 1½ cups Coconut Milk
      (see recipe, page 120)

¼   cup minced onion
6   to 8 cloves garlic, crushed
1½ teaspoons crushed red pepper
½   teaspoon ground coriander
1   tablespoon brown sugar
½   cup chunk-style peanut butter

PEANUT DIP   *Makes 1⅔ cups*

1. Make Coconut Milk.

2. Place onion, garlic, pepper and coriander in blender container; cover. Blend until paste is formed, about 1 minute. Place mixture in medium-size skillet. Cook over low heat, stirring constantly, 3 to 4 minutes. Stir in Coconut Milk gradually. Stir in brown sugar and peanut butter. Simmer 5 minutes. Add more Coconut Milk, if thinner consistency is desired. Store covered at room temperature up to 3 days.

CUCUMBER SALAD (Acar Ketimun)   *Makes 2 or 3 servings*

½   cup distilled white
      vinegar
2   tablespoons water
2   small red or green chili peppers,
      seeded, thinly sliced
3   shallots or green onions,
      white part only,
      thinly sliced
1   large cucumber, unpared,
      thinly sliced
3   tablespoons sugar

Combine vinegar, water, chilies and shallots. Let stand 30 minutes. Add cucumber and sugar. Cover and refrigerate up to 2 days.

CORN FRITTERS (Saté Jagung)   *Makes 12*

    Vegetable oil
1   can (17 ounces) corn, drained
3   eggs
6   green onions with tops,
      minced
1   clove garlic, crushed
¼   teaspoon salt
    Freshly ground pepper

Heat oil (1 inch) in 10-inch skillet to 365°. Combine remaining ingredients. Drop corn mixture by tablespoonfuls into hot oil. Fry until golden, 2 to 3 minutes. Drain on paper toweling. Serve warm.

FRESH FRIED SHRIMPS IN SPICY SAUCE (Sambal Goreng Udang)   *Makes 4 servings*

    Coconut Milk (see recipe,
      page 120)

⅓   cup vegetable oil
1   pound medium raw shrimp,
      shells removed
2   medium onions, sliced

1. Make Coconut Milk.

2. Heat oil in skillet or *wok* until hot. Sauté shrimp, onions, garlic and red pepper until shrimp start to turn pink, 2 to 3 minutes. Stir in tomato, green onions, brown sugar and Coconut Milk. Simmer uncovered until shrimp are tender, about 5 minutes. Season with salt and black pepper.

3   cloves garlic, minced
¾   to 1 teaspoon crushed
       red pepper
1   large tomato, chopped
1   cup sliced green onions with tops
1   tablespoon brown sugar
    Salt
    Black pepper

BARBECUED PORK ON BAMBOO SKEWERS (Saté)   *Makes 4 servings*

Peanut Dip (see recipe,
    page 121)

½   cup soy sauce
2   tablespoons dry sherry
1   tablespoon brown sugar
2   cloves garlic, crushed
1   pound lean boneless pork,
       beef or chicken, cut into
       ¾-inch cubes

Coriander or parsley sprigs

1. Make Peanut Dip.

2. Mix soy sauce, sherry, brown sugar and garlic in medium-size bowl. Add meat and toss to coat pieces. Marinate at room temperature 30 minutes.

3. Remove meat from marinade. Thread 4 pieces of meat on each of 10 to 12 bamboo skewers. Broil meat or grill over charcoal, turning occasionally, 15 to 20 minutes. Garnish with coriander. Serve with Peanut Dip.

HOT CHICKEN (Ajam Pedis)   *Makes 4 servings*

¼   cup vegetable oil
1¼ pounds boneless chicken
       breast, diced
1   medium onion, chopped
5   cloves garlic, minced
5   dried red chili peppers, seeds
       removed, crushed
2   tablespoons fresh lime juice
½   teaspoon salt
    Freshly ground black pepper
    Lime wedges

Heat oil in skillet or *wok*. Sauté chicken quickly in oil over medium-high heat until light brown, about 2 minutes. Stir in remaining ingredients except lime wedges. Cook until onion is tender, 2 to 3 minutes. Garnish with lime wedges.

BARBECUED FISH ROLLED IN BANANA LEAVES (Pepes Ikan)   *Makes 6 servings*

1   large head cabbage, with outer
       leaves if possible*

¼   cup butter or margarine,
       softened
1   large onion, minced
3   thin slices fresh gingerroot,
       minced
½   teaspoon crushed red pepper
1   teaspoon ground turmeric

1. Remove core and damaged leaves from cabbage; place cabbage in boiling water to cover in Dutch oven. Simmer, removing outer leaves as they become tender; drain.

2. Place butter, onion, gingerroot, pepper and turmeric in blender container; cover. Blend until paste is formed, about 1 minute. (Mixture will appear curdled.)

3. Cut fish into 12 pieces. Place 1 piece of fish in center of each cabbage leaf. Top with scant 1 tablespoon of the butter mixture. Top with several coriander sprigs. Fold ends in and roll up.

Barbecued fish enveloped in cabbage
leaves appears with crisp Fried Shrimp
Chips.

1½ pounds fish fillets (red
   snapper, whitefish,
   perch)
Coriander, mint or parsley
   sprigs

4. Place rolls in steamer.** Steam until fish is tender, 20 to 25 minutes.

TIPS: *Steamed fish is authentically prepared in banana leaves.

**A rack or colander with legs set in a Dutch oven with small amount of boiling water can be used in place of the steamer.

STEWED CABBAGE WITH EGGS (Ora Arik Kool)   *Makes 3 or 4 servings*

¼   cup vegetable oil
1   medium onion, thinly sliced
2   cloves garlic, crushed
3   cups shredded cabbage
    (about 8 ounces)
4   eggs, scrambled
1½ tablespoons soy sauce
⅛   teaspoon pepper

Heat oil in large skillet or wok until hot. Sauté onion and garlic in oil until tender, 2 to 3 minutes. Stir in cabbage. Cook, stirring constantly, until cabbage is crisp-tender, 2 to 3 minutes. Stir in remaining ingredients. Cook 1 minute.

FRIED CHICKEN PIECES IN SPICY SAUCE (Opor Ajam)   *Makes 4 servings*

1¾ cups Coconut Milk
    (see recipe, page 120)

1   broiler-fryer chicken
    (3 to 3½ pounds), cut up
¼   cup vegetable oil
1½ cups sliced onions
3   cloves garlic, crushed
1   tablespoon flour
1   tablespoon minced fresh
    gingerroot or 1
    teaspoon ground ginger
½   teaspoon ground turmeric
1   bay leaf

1½ tablespoons distilled
    white vinegar
    Salt

    Green onion tassels or
    parsley sprigs*

1. Make Coconut Milk.

2. Brown chicken pieces in oil in large skillet, about 20 minutes; remove from skillet. Sauté onions and garlic in pan drippings until golden, 3 to 4 minutes. Stir in flour, gingerroot, turmeric and bay leaf.

3. Return chicken to skillet. Stir in Coconut Milk and vinegar. Heat to boiling; reduce heat and cover. Simmer 15 minutes; uncover. Simmer until chicken is tender, about 10 minutes. Season to taste with salt.**

4. Arrange chicken on platter. Garnish with green onion tassels.

TIPS: *To make onion tassels, trim root end and green top from green onions, leaving white and some green (about three inches long). With sharp small knife, slit green end 5 or 6 times, leaving 1 inch at end intact. Drop into bowl of ice water for at least 2 hours; ends will curl slightly.

**Fried Chicken Pieces in Spicy Sauce can be prepared to this point 24 hours in advance; refrigerate covered. Heat covered until hot, 10 to 15 minutes.

124

MEAT MAIN DISH IN HOT SAUCE (Rendang)   *Makes 6 to 8 servings*

2½ cups Coconut Milk
     (see recipe, page 120)

¼   cup grated fresh coconut or
     dried unsweetened coconut*
4   thin slices fresh gingerroot,
     peeled, minced
2   to 3 dried chili peppers,
     seeds removed, crushed
3   cloves garlic, minced
1   tablespoon ground coriander

2   tablespoons vegetable oil
2   pounds beef loin sirloin
     steak, boneless, cut into
     ¾-inch cubes
2   tablespoons vegetable oil
1   medium onion, chopped

1   medium tomato, chopped
1   tablespoon brown sugar
1   small bay leaf
     Salt
     Pepper

     Tomato wedges

1. Make Coconut Milk.

2. Toast coconut in large skillet over low heat, stirring occasionally. Place coconut, gingerroot, chili peppers, garlic and coriander in blender container; cover. Blend until paste is formed, about 1 minute.

3. Heat 2 tablespoons oil in large skillet. Add coconut mixture. Cook mixture over low heat, stirring constantly; remove from skillet. Brown meat, half at a time, in 2 tablespoons oil in same skillet. Add onion; cook until tender, about 2 minutes.

4. Stir in coconut mixture, chopped tomato, brown sugar, bay leaf, Coconut Milk, salt and pepper. Cook uncovered over medium heat until most of liquid is evaporated, about 45 minutes.**

5. Arrange meat mixture on platter. Garnish with tomato wedges.

*TIPS: *Dried unsweetened coconut can be purchased at health food stores or gourmet food shops.*

***Meat Main Dish in Hot Sauce can be prepared to this point 24 hours in advance; refrigerate covered. Heat over medium heat 10 to 15 minutes before serving.*

SIMMERED BEEF SLICES (Semur Daging)   *Makes 3 or 4 servings*

¼   cup vegetable oil
1   pound beef loin sirloin steak,
     boneless, thinly sliced*
2   cups thinly sliced onions
1   cup beef bouillon or stock
3   tablespoons soy sauce
1   teaspoon ground allspice
1   teaspoon sugar

Heat oil in skillet or wok. Brown meat quickly in oil over high heat, about 3 minutes. Stir in onions. Cook and stir until onions are tender, 2 to 3 minutes. Stir in remaining ingredients. Cook 2 to 3 minutes.

*TIP: *Chicken or pork can be substituted for the beef.*

FRIED SHRIMP CHIPS (Krupuk)   *Makes 12 servings*

     Vegetable oil
1   package (8 ounces) shrimp
     wafers*

Heat oil (1 to 2 inches) in skillet to 350°. Fry wafers in oil about 30 seconds or until they have expanded to 3 to 4 times their original size. Drain wafers on paper toweling.

*TIP: *Shrimp wafers can be purchased at Oriental markets and gourmet food shops.*

A Newfoundland Dinner

NEWFOUNDLAND DINNER MENU

- **NEWFIE PEA SOUP**

- **BOILED DINNER**
- **OAT BREAD**

- **DUFF PUDDING**
  COFFEE OR TEA

- Recipes included

The sea surrounds the rugged cliffs and virgin forests that cover New-foundland. Charming cities and villages dot the terrain, testimony to the human element amid the vastness of nature there. And Newfoundlanders' hearty fare is meant to match their rigorous out-of-doors life.

A robust opener for any meal, thick Newfie Pea Soup is an island tradition guaranteed to keep cold weather at bay. Corned beef brisket and vegetables make a popular dinner-in-a-pot, much like the New England variety.

That Newfoundland staple, home-baked bread, enlivens the kitchen with warmth and fragrance. Our menu offers an Oat Bread recipe for two golden brown loaves — best spread with fresh butter.

Sweet steamed Duff Pudding claims an English heritage, and is accompanied by tart egg-based Lemon Sauce. Serves 8.

Wine Suggestion: Light, young and fruity red wines go well with this type of fare. My choice is a Moulin-à-Vent by Maufoux or Sebastiani's Gamay Beaujolais.

Hearty Newfoundland foods include a corned beef-and-vegetables Boiled Dinner, Oat Bread and steamed pudding with Lemon Sauce.

PARTY PLAN FOR NEWFOUNDLAND DINNER MENU

1 Day Before:	Make Newfie Pea Soup; refrigerate covered. Make Oat Bread; wrap in aluminum foil and store at room temperature. Second loaf can be frozen up to 2 months, if desired.
4 Hours Before Serving:	Make Boiled Dinner.
2 Hours Before Serving:	Prepare Duff Pudding through step 1 in recipe.
20 Minutes Before Serving:	Heat Newfie Pea Soup over low heat.
20 Minutes Before Dessert:	Complete Duff Pudding.

The sea is the dominant theme in views of Newfoundland's harbors, beaches and coastal towns.

NEWFIE PEA SOUP

Makes 8 servings (about 1 cup each)

1 pound dried split peas
2 quarts water
1 ham bone
⅓ cup chopped carrot
½ cup chopped onion
½ cup chopped turnip
 Salt
 Pepper

Heat peas and water in Dutch oven over medium heat to boiling. Boil 2 minutes; remove from heat. Cover; let stand 1 hour. Add remaining ingredients except salt and pepper to peas. Heat to boiling; reduce heat. Simmer uncovered, stirring occasionally, until mixture is thick, about 2 hours. Season with salt and pepper.

BOILED DINNER

Makes 8 servings

1 corned beef brisket (about 5 pounds)
1 medium onion, cut into quarters
10 peppercorns
1 bay leaf

4 medium potatoes, pared, cut into quarters
3 turnips, pared, cut into 8 wedges
6 carrots, pared, cut into 3-inch pieces
4 small onions
1 small head cabbage, cut into 8 wedges

1. Place corned beef, onion quarters, peppercorns and bay leaf in Dutch oven. Add water to cover. Heat over medium heat to boiling; reduce heat. Simmer covered over low heat until meat is tender, 3 to 4 hours.

2. About 30 minutes before end of cooking time, add potatoes, turnips, carrots and small onions. Simmer covered 20 minutes; add cabbage. Simmer covered until vegetables are tender, about 10 minutes.

OAT BREAD

Makes 2 loaves

1 package active dry yeast
½ cup warm water (105° to 115°)
1 teaspoon sugar
2 cups milk, scalded
2 cups uncooked rolled oats
⅓ cup dark molasses
2 tablespoons butter or margarine, softened
1 teaspoon salt
4 to 4½ cups all-purpose flour

 Butter or margarine, softened

1. Dissolve yeast in warm water in large bowl; stir in sugar. Let stand at room temperature until bubbly, about 10 minutes. Stir milk, oats, molasses, 2 tablespoons butter and the salt into yeast mixture. Stir in enough of the flour to make dough easy to handle. Turn dough onto lightly floured surface. Knead until smooth and elastic, about 10 minutes. Place in well-buttered bowl; turn buttered side up. Cover; let rise in warm place until double, about 1 hour 30 minutes. (Dough is ready if impression remains.)

2. Butter 2 loaf pans, 8½ x 4½ x 2½ inches each. Punch down dough; shape into 2 loaves. Place in pans; brush with softened butter. Cover; let dough rise in warm place until double, about 30 minutes.

3. Heat oven to 375°. Bake bread until loaves are light brown and sound hollow when tapped, 30 to 35 minutes. Remove from pans; cool on wire rack.

DUFF PUDDING   *Makes 8 servings*

1   **cup all-purpose flour**
1   **cup dry bread crumbs**
1   **cup packed brown sugar**
1   **cup dark raisins**
¼   **pound minced beef kidney suet,**
    membrane trimmed (about 1 cup)
1   **teaspoon grated lemon peel**
⅛   **teaspoon salt**
1   **teaspoon baking soda**
¼   **cup milk, scalded**
½   **cup milk**
1   **egg, slightly beaten**

    Lemon Sauce (recipe follows)

1   **lemon**
2   **cups water**
1   **egg**
1   **egg yolk**
3   **tablespoons lemon juice**
1½ **tablespoons sugar**

1.   Combine flour, bread crumbs, sugar, raisins, suet, lemon peel and salt in medium-size bowl. Stir baking soda into ¼ cup scalded milk in small bowl; add ½ cup milk and the egg. Stir into dry mixture. Spoon batter into well-buttered 1-quart mold. Cover tightly with aluminum foil. Place mold on rack in deep kettle; add 1 inch water. Heat water to boiling; reduce heat and cover kettle. Steam until wooden pick inserted in center of pudding comes out clean, about 2½ hours. (Add boiling water to kettle, if necessary.)

2.   Meanwhile, make Lemon Sauce.

3.   Remove mold from kettle; cool slightly. Unmold onto serving platter. Serve with Lemon Sauce.

LEMON SAUCE
Cut thin yellow peel from lemon; cut into narrow strips. Heat 2 cups water in 1-quart saucepan over medium heat to boiling; add lemon strips. Boil 1 minute. Drain; rinse with cold water. Pat dry on paper toweling. Combine egg, egg yolk, lemon juice, sugar and lemon strips in top of 2-quart double boiler. Cook over hot water, stirring constantly, until thick and foamy. Serve warm or cold.

A fisherman in the old harbor village of Bay Bulls.

A Turkish Gourmet Gala

The domes of a mosque and gleaming street wares are familiar sights in Istanbul.

TURKISH GOURMET DINNER MENU

- **MINIATURE FILLO PASTRIES**
- **STUFFED GRAPEVINE LEAVES**
- **BEET SALAD**
- **CHICK-PEA DIP**
- **APPETIZER MEATBALLS**
- **TOASTED PITA BREAD WEDGES**
  TOMATOES WITH HOT PEPPER GARNISH
  CALAMATA OLIVES
  SLICED MELONS
  FETA CHEESE WITH OLIVE OIL SHRIMP

- **CHICKEN AND YOGURT SOUP**

- **SPIT-ROASTED LAMB AND BEEF ROLL**
- **RICE PILAF**
  STEAMED ZUCCHINI SLICES
- **SPINACH SALAD**

- **GOLDEN DOMES**
- **BIRDS' NESTS**
  ASSORTED FRUIT
- **TURKISH COFFEE**

• Recipes included

Like a vision of Byzantine splendor, a table of Turkish delicacies startles the eye with myriad colors and shapes. For an opulent dinner offering, let your guests partake of this dream, and set before them the magnificent foods of Turkey.

The junction of Europe and Asia, and touched by numerous cultures throughout history, Turkey boasts a wonderfully cosmopolitan cuisine. The first course of our gourmet menu — a table of hors d'oeuvres called *mezes* — symbolizes the richness of this heritage. The sampling includes crisp fillo pastries filled with meat or cheese, and little packets of pine nuts and rice wrapped in grapevine leaves. Tiny lamb meatballs grace the spread, along with grated beets tossed with the ever-present yogurt. And *humus*, or Chick-pea Dip, stands ready to be scooped onto wedges of that Turkish staple, Pita Bread. Pepper-splashed tomatoes, dark olives, feta cheese, shrimp and melon add to the wealth of appetizers.

To continue the glorious banquet, serve creamy Chicken and Yogurt Soup. Then follow with a succulent roll of marinated lamb and beef roasted on a spit. With the flavorful meats, the pride of Turkish cooking — Rice Pilaf — is fitting. Steamed slices of zucchini, and a fresh spinach and orange salad with yogurt dressing round out the main courses.

Two luxurious desserts seem like the sweets of a sultan. Golden Domes are apricots stuffed with whipped cream and whole almonds. Rings of fillo leaves filled with a walnut mixture, and topped with Lemon Peel Syrup are called Birds' Nests. Incredibly dark and rich Turkish Coffee should accompany the desserts. Traditionally, the brew is made in a small cylindrical copper pot, with a long handle, known as a *jezve*, then poured into tiny cups. Serves 10.

Wine Suggestion: The Turks offer an anise-flavored liquor called *raki* with their hors d'oeuvres. With the entrée, present a Cabernet Sauvignon by Robert Mondavi or Louis M. Martini, or one from Spain's Rioja district.

Istanbul's markets abound with foodstuffs — such as fresh produce and fish hauled from the Bosphorus.

Spit-Roasted Lamb and Beef Roll is surrounded by traditional Turkish side dish

Coffeepots and pulverizers help prepare the Turkish brew, which is served on a three-wire tray.

PARTY PLAN FOR TURKISH GOURMET DINNER MENU

2 Weeks Before:	Make Pita Bread.
1 Week Before:	Make Yogurt. Make Miniature Fillo Pastries.
3 Days Before:	Prepare Spit-Roasted Lamb and Beef Roll through step 1 in recipe.
2 Days Before:	Prepare Stuffed Grapevine Leaves through step 3 in recipe.
1 Day Before:	Prepare Chick-pea Dip through step 1 in recipe; refrigerate covered. Make Appetizer Meatballs. Prepare Rice Pilaf through step 2 in recipe; refrigerate covered. Prepare Golden Domes through step 1 in recipe.
6 Hours Before Serving:	Complete Spit-Roasted Lamb and Beef Roll. Make Birds' Nests. Complete Golden Domes.
4 Hours 30 Minutes Before Serving:	Complete step 2 of Beet Salad recipe. Refrigerate beets and yogurt mixture, separately, covered. Complete step 2 of Spinach Salad recipe. Refrigerate salad and dressing, separately, covered.
2 Hours Before Serving:	Complete steps 2, 3 and 4 of Chicken and Yogurt Soup recipe. Refrigerate yogurt mixture only.
1 Hour Before Guests Arrive:	Complete Chick-pea Dip.
30 Minutes Before Guests Arrive:	Heat Miniature Fillo Pastries. Heat Appetizer Meatballs. Complete Beet Salad. Toast Pita Bread. Reserve 8 Pita Breads for entrée; cut remaining Pita Breads into wedges. Complete Stuffed Grapevine Leaves.
30 Minutes Before Serving:	Complete Chicken and Yogurt Soup.
15 Minutes Before Serving:	Steam zucchini slices. Complete Rice Pilaf. Complete Spinach Salad.
15 Minutes Before Dessert:	Make Turkish Coffee.

MINIATURE FILLO PASTRIES (Sigara Böregi)

Makes about 14 dozen appetizers

1   **package (1 pound) frozen fillo strudel leaves, thawed**

     Cheese Filling (recipe follows)

     Meat Filling (recipe follows)

¾   **cup unsalted sweet butter, melted**

     Heat oven to 350°

1.   Cut fillo leaves crosswise in half. Wrap half the fillo leaves tightly; refrigerate. Cut remaining sheets into 4 equal sections, about 8 x 4 inches each. Place fillo leaves between barely dampened kitchen towels to prevent drying.

2.   Make Cheese Filling.

3.   Make Meat Filling.

4.   Place 1 layer fillo section on clean surface; brush top with butter. Place ½ teaspoon of the Cheese Filling in center at narrow end of fillo piece; fold each long side of fillo ½ inch toward center. Roll up tightly, beginning at narrow end. Place seam side down in well-buttered jelly-roll pan, 15½ x 10½ x 1 inch. Repeat procedure with remaining fillo pieces.

5.   Cut reserved fillo leaves into sections, about 8 x 4 inches each. Repeat procedure in step 4 with 1 teaspoon Meat Filling.

6.   Brush tops with butter. Bake pastries until golden, about 25 minutes.*

TIP: *Pastries can be covered tightly with aluminum foil and frozen up to 10 days in advance. Heat in 350° oven until hot, about 15 minutes.

CHEESE FILLING

Makes about 1¼ cups

Combine all ingredients in medium-size bowl until smooth.

4   **ounces cream cheese, softened**
4   **ounces feta cheese**
½   **cup snipped fresh parsley**
2   **tablespoons grated Parmesan cheese**
1   **egg**
1   **tablespoon snipped fresh dill**

MEAT FILLING

Brown lamb and onion in butter in 10-inch skillet over medium heat; drain. Stir in remaining ingredients.

1   **pound ground lamb or beef**
2   **tablespoons grated onion**
1   **tablespoon butter or margarine**
¼   **cup snipped fresh parsley**
½   **teaspoon salt**
¼   **teaspoon freshly ground pepper**

STUFFED GRAPEVINE LEAVES (Yalanci Dolma)

Makes about 40

1   **jar (16 ounces) grapevine leaves, preserved in brine, drained**
2   **quarts boiling water**

4   **ounces pine nuts**
3   **tablespoons olive oil**
⅔   **cup uncooked regular rice**
2   **cups water**

½   **cup currants**
¼   **cup snipped fresh dill**
¼   **cup snipped fresh mint**
¼   **cup snipped fresh parsley**

1.   Boil grapevine leaves in 2 quarts boiling water 2 minutes; drain. Trim any tough stems or veins from leaves; pat dry on paper toweling.

2.   Sauté pine nuts in 1 tablespoon of the 3 tablespoons olive oil in large skillet over medium heat until golden, about 5 minutes; remove and reserve. Add the remaining 2 tablespoons olive oil to skillet. Sauté rice in hot oil over medium heat, stirring constantly, 2 to 3 minutes. Do not brown. Pour in 2 cups water; simmer covered over medium heat until water is absorbed, about 25 minutes.

3.   Combine cooked rice, reserved pine nuts, the currants, dill, mint, parsley, allspice, salt, pepper and lemon juice in medium-size bowl. Line skillet with torn and undersized grapevine leaves. To assemble stuffed

1½	teaspoons ground allspice
½	teaspoon salt
⅛	teaspoon freshly ground pepper
2	teaspoons lemon juice
1½	cups water
1	tablespoon olive oil

Lettuce leaves
Lemon slices
Tomato wedges, if desired

grapevine leaf, hold single leaf vein side up in palm of hand. Place about 1 tablespoon of the rice mixture, depending on size of leaf, on stem end of leaf. Fold end over filling; tuck in sides. Roll to form packet. Place seam side down in skillet. Repeat procedure with remaining filling and leaves. Pour 1½ cups water and 1 tablespoon olive oil over filled leaves. Simmer covered over low heat 50 minutes. Refrigerate covered.*

4.   Serve stuffed leaves cold on lettuce-lined plate with lemon slices and tomato wedges.

TIP: *Stuffed Grapevine Leaves can be prepared and refrigerated at this point 2 days in advance.

BEET SALAD (Pancar Salatasi)   *Makes 3 cups*

1	cup Yogurt (recipe follows)

1.   Make Yogurt.

2	cans (16 ounces each) whole beets, drained
2	tablespoons olive or vegetable oil
2	tablespoons lemon juice
¼	teaspoon garlic powder
½	teaspoon salt

Cucumber slices, if desired

2.   Coarsely grate beets; drain thoroughly. Place Yogurt, oil, lemon juice, garlic powder and salt in jar with tight-fitting lid; cover and shake.*

3.   Just before serving, toss yogurt mixture with beets. Garnish with cucumber slices.

TIP: *Beet Salad can be prepared to this point up to 4 hours in advance. Refrigerate beets and yogurt mixture, separately, covered.

1	quart milk
¼	cup instant nonfat dry milk solids
2	tablespoons commercial plain yogurt without preservatives

YOGURT*   *Makes about 1 quart*

Mix milk and dry milk solids in saucepan; scald. Cool to 110°. Pour milk into 3-quart glass bowl; stir in yogurt. Cover with plastic wrap. Wrap bowl in heavy towel or cloth. Let stand without stirring in warm place (oven with gas pilot light or electric range at warm setting) until thick, 4 to 6 hours. Remove towel and plastic wrap. Place several layers of unprinted paper toweling directly on top of yogurt to absorb excess moisture. Refrigerate covered until cold. Discard paper toweling. Store yogurt covered in refrigerator up to 1 week. Use 2 tablespoons as starter when preparing new yogurt.

TIP: *In recipes calling for Yogurt, commercial plain yogurt can be substituted.

CHICK-PEA DIP (Humus)   *Makes about 3 cups*

2	cans (15 ounces each) chick-peas*
⅓	cup fresh lemon juice
½	cup ground sesame seed oil**
3	cloves garlic, crushed
1	tablespoon snipped fresh mint
⅛	teaspoon salt

2	tablespoons olive oil

Mint leaves, if desired
Ripe olives, if desired
Toasted pita bread
    wedges or crackers

1.   Drain liquid from chick-peas; reserve ¼ cup liquid. Place chick-peas, lemon juice and reserved liquid in blender container; cover. Puree, scraping sides of container frequently with spatula, until smooth. Transfer chick-pea mixture to medium-size bowl; stir in sesame seed oil, garlic, snipped mint and salt. Refrigerate covered at least 6 hours.

2.   Pour chick-pea mixture into shallow serving bowl; make well in center. Pour olive oil into well. Let dip stand at room temperature 45 minutes before serving. Garnish with mint leaves and olives. Serve with pita bread.

TIPS: *Chick-peas are also called garbanzo beans or ceci peas.

**Sesame seed oil is also called tahini oil. It can be purchased in Middle Eastern sections of supermarkets or in health food stores.

Turkish hors d'oeuvres include Beet Salad, lamb meatballs, Pita Bread, fillo pastries, Chick-pea Dip, and Stuffed Grapevine Leaves.

APPETIZER MEATBALLS (Köfte)

Makes about 2 ½ dozen

4 slices thin white bread, crusts trimmed, torn into 1-inch pieces

Soak bread pieces in ⅓ cup water until most of the water is absorbed, about 10 minutes. Squeeze out excess water. Combine soaked bread, lamb, onion, salt and pepper. Shape rounded teaspoonfuls of the mixture into balls.

⅓	cup water
½	pound ground lamb
¼	cup minced onion
½	teaspoon salt
	Pepper
¼	cup all-purpose flour
	Vegetable oil

Roll each in flour. Heat oil (about 1 inch) in skillet to 400°. Fry meatballs until golden, about 5 minutes. Drain on paper toweling.

TIP: Appetizer Meatballs can be made up to 24 hours in advance. Cool thoroughly; refrigerate covered. Heat meatballs in 350° oven until hot, about 20 minutes.

PITA BREAD (Pide)

3 packages active dry yeast
4 cups warm water (105° to 115°)
1 tablespoon salt
¼ teaspoon sugar
⅓ cup olive oil
9½ to 10 cups all-purpose flour

Cornmeal

1. Dissolve yeast in 1 cup of the warm water in large bowl. Stir in remaining warm water, the salt, sugar, oil and 6 cups of the flour. Beat until smooth. Mix in enough of the remaining flour to make dough easy to handle.

2. Knead dough on lightly floured surface until smooth and elastic, about 10 minutes. Place in greased bowl; turn greased side up. Cover; let rise in warm place until double, about 1 hour.

3. Punch down dough; shape into 15 balls. Cover; let rise in warm place 30 minutes.

4. Sprinkle baking sheets with cornmeal. Roll each ball on lightly floured surface into circle, about 8 inches in diameter. Place 2 circles 2 inches apart on each baking sheet. Cover; let rise in warm place 30 minutes.

5. Heat oven to 500°. Bake pita bread until puffed and light brown, about 10 minutes.

TIPS: Bread can be refrigerated tightly wrapped in aluminum foil up to 3 days, and frozen no longer than 3 weeks. Heat in 350° oven until crisp, about 5 minutes.

Commercially prepared pita bread can be purchased in large supermarkets and some specialty stores.

CHICKEN AND YOGURT SOUP (Yogurtlu Tavuk Corbasi)

Makes 10 servings (about 1¼ cups each)

2 cups Yogurt (see recipe, page 135)

2 slices white bread, crusts removed, cut into ½-inch cubes
2 tablespoons butter or margarine

2 tablespoons butter or margarine, melted
1½ teaspoons paprika
½ teaspoon cayenne pepper

¾ cup all-purpose flour
1 egg

3 quarts chicken broth
1 medium onion
Parsley sprigs, if desired

1. Make Yogurt.

2. Brown bread cubes in 2 tablespoons butter in small skillet; reserve.

3. Mix 2 tablespoons melted butter, the paprika and cayenne; reserve.

4. Place Yogurt, flour and egg in blender container; cover. Blend until smooth.

5. Heat broth in Dutch oven. Pour yogurt mixture into broth gradually, stirring constantly. Heat over medium heat to boiling. Boil, stirring constantly, until creamy; reduce heat. Add onion; simmer uncovered over medium heat 5 minutes. Just before serving, remove onion; pour soup into tureen. Spoon reserved paprika mixture over soup; garnish with reserved bread cubes and the parsley sprigs.

SPIT-ROASTED LAMB AND BEEF ROLL (Kuzu Eti Gril)

Makes 10 servings

2 cups vegetable oil
1 cup lemon juice
1 lemon, minced
2 medium onions, grated
6 cloves garlic, crushed
1 tablespoon salt

1. Combine all ingredients except meat, watercress, kumquats and lemon slices; pour over meat in large glass baking dish. Refrigerate covered, turning occasionally, 3 days.

2. Remove meat from refrigerator; let stand at room temperature 2 hours before roasting.

1   tablespoon paprika
1   teaspoon cumin seeds
1   teaspoon cracked pepper
1   boneless leg of lamb (4½ to 5
      pounds), rolled and tied
      around 1 piece boneless
      sirloin steak (1 to 1½
      pounds)

Watercress, if desired
Kumquats, if desired
Lemon slices, if desired

3.   Open dampers on grill and cover. Make drip pan using double-thickness, heavy-duty aluminum foil (shiny side facing in); place pan on bottom rack of grill. Arrange 30 briquettes along each side of drip pan; light briquettes.

4.   Remove meat from marinade; reserve marinade. Place spit through center of meat. Insert meat thermometer so tip is in center of meat. Balance spit on grill when briquettes are white. Add 12 more briquettes to coals on each side. Roast meat, basting occasionally with reserved marinade, until temperature registers 160°, about 3 hours. Let stand 15 minutes before slicing. Garnish with watercress, kumquats and lemon slices.

TIP: Meat can be roasted on an electric oven rotisserie at 325°.

RICE PILAF (Pilav)   *Makes 10 servings (1 cup each)*

2   cups uncooked brown rice
1   tablespoon salt

1   cup chopped onion
6   tablespoons butter or margarine
3   tablespoons olive oil
¾   cup orzo (rice-shaped pasta)*
6   cups chicken broth
½   cup pine nuts, toasted
⅓   cup currants

Dill sprigs

1.   Cover rice with boiling water in large bowl; add salt. Let stand 10 minutes; drain and rinse.

2.   Sauté onion in butter and oil in Dutch oven over medium heat until golden, about 10 minutes. Add orzo; sauté until orzo is brown, about 10 minutes. Add drained rice; cook, stirring constantly, until rice sizzles, about 10 minutes. Pour in chicken broth; simmer covered over medium heat until broth is absorbed and rice is tender, 25 to 30 minutes. Stir in pine nuts and currants.

3.   Simmer pilaf uncovered over medium heat 2 minutes. Spoon into serving dish; garnish with dill.

TIPS: *Orzo can be purchased in specialty food stores or gourmet sections of supermarkets.*

Rice Pilaf can be made up to 1 day in advance; refrigerate covered. Simmer until hot, about 5 minutes.

SPINACH SALAD (Borani)   *Makes 10 servings*

1   cup Yogurt (see recipe, page 135)

2   quarts fresh spinach (about 2
      pounds), washed, trimmed
1   small red onion, thinly sliced
2   oranges, peeled, cut into
      1-inch pieces
3   tablespoons olive oil
1   tablespoon lemon juice
1   teaspoon sugar
½   teaspoon celery seeds
½   teaspoon salt
¼   teaspoon freshly ground pepper

1.   Make Yogurt.

2.   Combine spinach and onion in 2-quart glass bowl. Arrange orange pieces on spinach. Place Yogurt, oil, lemon juice, sugar, celery seeds, salt and pepper in jar with tight-fitting lid; cover and shake.

3.   Pour dressing into center of salad. Just before serving, toss salad.

Tempting Turkish pastries sweeten the dinner's end.

GOLDEN DOMES (Kayisi Hosafi)

Makes 10 servings

½ **pound dried pitted whole apricots***

1. Soak apricots in cold water to cover overnight.

1 **cup sugar**
¼ **cup water**
2 **teaspoons lemon juice**

2. Drain apricots. Place apricots, sugar, ¼ cup water and the lemon juice in small saucepan. Heat over medium heat, stirring constantly, to boiling; reduce heat. Simmer covered until syrup thickens, about 30 minutes. (Watch carefully during final cooking time that mixture doesn't burn.) Remove apricots from syrup; cover and refrigerate apricots and syrup separately until cool.

1 **cup whipping cream**
Blanched whole almonds
  (1 almond for each apricot)

3.   Whip cream in chilled small bowl. Fill pastry tube with whipped cream. Using large tip, pipe whipped cream into each apricot. Insert 1 almond into whipped cream filling in each apricot. Arrange apricots open side down in shallow serving dish. Pour syrup over apricots. (Heat syrup to pouring consistency, if it has hardened.) Store covered in refrigerator. Serve at room temperature.

TIP: *Dried whole apricots can be purchased in health food stores or specialty food shops. Dried apricot halves can be substituted for the whole apricots; press 2 halves together for each portion.*

BIRDS' NESTS (Farareer)

Makes 2 dozen

Walnut Filling (recipe follows)
24 **frozen fillo strudel leaves, thawed**
2   **cups unsalted sweet butter, melted**

Lemon Peel Syrup (recipe follows)

Heat oven to 400°

1.   Make Walnut Filling. Place fillo leaves between barely dampened kitchen towels to prevent drying. Place 1 fillo leaf on clean surface; brush top with butter. Fold lengthwise in half; brush with butter. Sprinkle 1 tablespoon of the Walnut Filling on long end of fillo leaf.

2.   Roll fillo leaf, starting at long folded edge, to 1 inch from edge. Form into ring, leaving 1 inch in center of ring. Fold overhanging fillo under ring. Place on buttered jelly-roll pan, 15½ x 10½ x 1 inch. Repeat procedure with remaining fillo leaves.

3.   Place 1 tablespoon of the Walnut Filling in center of each ring. Brush with butter. Bake pastries until golden, about 40 minutes.

4.   Make Lemon Peel Syrup. Pour syrup over each hot pastry. Cool completely. Store covered in refrigerator. Serve at room temperature.

WALNUT FILLING

3⅓ **cups finely chopped walnuts**
¼   **cup packed brown sugar**
½   **teaspoon ground cinnamon**

Mix all ingredients in medium-size bowl.

LEMON PEEL SYRUP

½   **lemon**
1½ **cups sugar**
1¼ **cups water**

Cut thin yellow peel from lemon. Cut peel into thin strips, 1 x ⅛ inch each. Juice lemon. Heat peel, juice, sugar and water in small saucepan over medium heat, stirring occasionally, to boiling; reduce heat. Simmer uncovered, stirring occasionally, 10 minutes.

TURKISH COFFEE (Türk Kahvesi)

*Makes 3 servings**

1   **cup cold water**
2   **tablespoons sugar**
⅛   **teaspoon ground cardamom**
2   **tablespoons pulverized dark roast coffee**

1.   Mix cold water and sugar in Turkish coffeepot.** Heat over high heat, stirring just until sugar is dissolved, to boiling. Add cardamom and coffee; stir constantly until mixture is smooth and thick, about 1 minute. Heat until thick foam rises, about 30 seconds. Remove pot from heat; spoon foam into each of 3 demitasse cups.

2.   Reduce heat; heat coffee to boiling twice more. Remove pot each time foam rises and divide foam evenly among 3 cups. Pour coffee into each cup. Let stand 2 minutes.

TIPS: *Turkish Coffee should be made in small amounts, no more than 3 to 4 servings at a time.*

***Turkish coffeepots are cone-shaped brass containers with long handles. A small saucepan or butter warmer can be substituted.*

A Scottish Picnic

Bagpipes, dancing lasses and the caber-toss are seen at Scottish Highland Games.

SCOTTISH PICNIC MENU

- **SCOTS EGGS**
- **SALMON CRESS SANDWICHES**
- **COCK-A-LEEKIE SALAD**

- **LADYFINGERS WITH LEMON CURD FILLING**
- **SHORTBREAD**
  FRESH FRUIT
  HOT OR ICED TEA

• Recipes included

The Scots glory in nature. Their serene and unspoiled countryside beckons them outdoors, and boosts their appetites for simple hearty fare. Enhance your own open-air revels with a Scottish picnic fit to be spread near loch or brae.

Traditional "take-along" favorites include Scots Eggs — delicious served warm or cold with a tangy mustard. These hard-cooked eggs coated in sausage and bread crumbs are deep-fat fried to a crusty golden brown. Salmon and watercress on wheat bread is a simple variation of a well-known teatime offering. And Cock-A-Leekie Salad combines chicken, rice and leeks into the cold version of a famous Scottish soup.

Sweet tooths never suffer from lack of variety in Scotland, even on a picnic. For dessert, try delicate ladyfingers with a luscious lemony filling. Or break off a bit of Shortbread — crisp butter-rich cake shaped in a decorative mold. Fresh fruit and tea, hot or cold, complete the out-of-the-ordinary outdoor menu. Serves 6.

Wine Suggestion: To make your repast in a natural setting even more beautiful, take with you a bottle of young and friendly Zinfandel, Sutter Home, or Châteauneuf-du-Pape.

142

PARTY PLAN FOR SCOTTISH PICNIC MENU

1 Day Before:
Prepare Cock-A-Leekie Salad through step 1 in recipe; refrigerate broth and chicken in separate covered containers.
Prepare Scots Eggs through step 3 in recipe.
Prepare Ladyfingers with Lemon Curd Filling through step 4 in recipe; wrap ladyfingers in aluminum foil and store at room temperature.

That Day:
Make Shortbread.

3 Hours Before Serving:
Complete Cock-A-Leekie Salad.
Make Salmon Cress Sandwiches.

30 Minutes Before Serving:
Complete Ladyfingers with Lemon Curd Filling.
Bake Scots Eggs uncovered at 350° 20 minutes, if serving hot.

Scots picnic foods: Salmon Cress Sandwiches, Cock-A-Leekie Salad, lemon-filled ladyfingers, Scots Eggs, and Shortbread.

SCOTS EGGS

1   **pound pork sausage**
¼   **cup dry bread crumbs**
2   **egg yolks**
2   **tablespoons milk**
1   **teaspoon Worcestershire sauce**
1   **cup all-purpose flour**
2   **egg whites, beaten**
1   **cup dry bread crumbs**

6   **hard-cooked eggs**

    Vegetable oil

    Salt
    Pepper
    Mustard
    Watercress, if desired
    Radishes, if desired

1. Mix sausage, ¼ cup bread crumbs, the egg yolks, milk and Worcestershire sauce in small bowl. Place flour, egg whites and 1 cup bread crumbs in separate bowls.

2. Coat each hard-cooked egg with flour. Pat ⅙ of the sausage mixture onto each egg. Dip sausage-coated eggs in flour, then egg whites, then bread crumbs.

3. Heat oil (4 to 5 inches) in deep-fat fryer or kettle to 350°. Fry eggs, 1 at a time, turning occasionally, until deep brown, about 5 minutes. Drain on paper toweling.*

4. Serve Scots Eggs hot or cold with salt, pepper and mustard. Garnish with watercress and radishes.

*TIP: *Eggs can be prepared to this point in advance; cover and refrigerate up to 24 hours.*

SALMON CRESS SANDWICHES

1   **can (7¾ ounces) salmon, drained**
½   **cup butter or margarine, softened**
⅓   **cup snipped fresh watercress**
    (about 1 bunch)
2   **tablespoons lemon juice**
6   **slices wheat bread, crusts**
    removed, buttered
    Watercress, if desired

Combine salmon, butter, ⅓ cup watercress and the lemon juice in small bowl. Spread salmon mixture on half the bread slices. Top with remaining slices. Cut sandwiches diagonally in half. Serve immediately or cover with damp towel and refrigerate until serving time. Garnish with watercress.

COCK-A-LEEKIE SALAD

1   **broiler-fryer chicken**
    (about 3 pounds)

    Salad Dressing (recipe follows)

1   **large leek, thinly sliced**
1   **cup cooked rice**
½   **cup chopped celery**
    Watercress
    Prunes

½   **cup olive or vegetable oil**
3   **tablespoons white wine vinegar**
1   **egg yolk**
¾   **teaspoon dried tarragon leaves**

1. Place chicken in boiling salted water to cover in 5-quart Dutch oven. Heat to boiling; reduce heat and cover. Simmer until tender, about 1 hour. Remove chicken, reserving broth; cool. Remove meat from bones and skin; dice meat.

2. Make Salad Dressing.

3. Heat reserved chicken broth to boiling. Cook leek in broth over high heat 5 minutes; drain. Combine chicken, leek, rice and celery. Toss with dressing 2 to 3 hours before serving; cover and refrigerate. Garnish with watercress and prunes.

SALAD DRESSING
Measure 2 tablespoons of the oil, the vinegar, egg yolk, seasonings and sugar into blender container; cover. Blend at high speed until smooth, about 10 seconds. Pour in remaining oil gradually, blending after each addition. Fold into whipped cream. Refrigerate.

¾ teaspoon dried chervil leaves
½ teaspoon dry mustard
½ teaspoon salt
½ teaspoon sugar
¼ cup whipping cream,
    whipped

LADYFINGERS WITH LEMON CURD FILLING   *Makes 12*

Lemon Curd Filling
  (recipe follows)

3 eggs, separated
½ teaspoon vanilla
Dash salt
½ cup powdered sugar

½ cup all-purpose flour

Powdered sugar

1 lemon
⅓ cup sugar
2 tablespoons butter or margarine,
    melted
1 egg, beaten
Dash salt

1.   Make Lemon Curd Filling.

2.   Heat oven to 350°. Beat egg yolks and vanilla in small bowl until thick and lemon colored. Beat egg whites and salt in medium-size bowl until foamy. Beat ¼ cup of the powdered sugar, 1 tablespoon at a time, into egg whites, until mixture forms stiff peaks.

3.   Fold beaten egg yolks into egg white mixture. Fold in remaining ¼ cup powdered sugar and the flour.

4.   Pipe batter through pastry tube with large tip onto brown paper-lined baking sheet in fingerlike shapes, 3½ x 1 inch each. Sprinkle with powdered sugar. Bake until edges are barely brown, 8 to 10 minutes. Transfer immediately to wire rack; cool.

5.   Spread Lemon Curd Filling on flat side of half the ladyfingers. Top with remaining ladyfingers, flat side down, to form sandwiches.

LEMON CURD FILLING
Grate peel and squeeze juice from lemon; strain juice. Measure all ingredients into small saucepan. Cook over medium heat, stirring constantly, until mixture thickens. Cover and refrigerate.

SHORTBREAD   *Makes three 6-inch cakes*

1 cup unsalted butter
½ cup superfine sugar
1½ cups rice flour
1½ cups all-purpose flour

Heat oven to 325°

1.   Mix butter and sugar in small bowl just until blended. Scrape onto cutting board. Work flours into butter-sugar mixture with hands until crumbly.

2.   Sprinkle 6-inch shortbread mold with sugar.* Press ⅓ of the dough firmly into mold. Invert onto brown paper-lined baking sheet, tapping mold on edges to loosen dough.

3.   Repeat 2 more times with remaining dough. Bake until edges are golden, 35 to 40 minutes. Cool 15 minutes on baking sheet. Transfer to wire rack; cool completely. Serve whole, allowing guests to break off pieces.

*TIP: *An 8-inch springform pan can be substituted for the shortbread mold.*

A Scottish Spread

Dinner in Scotland demonstrates that simple foods needn't be boring. With an eye to color and composition, the Scots transform plain fare into dishes that stick to the ribs, yet please the senses.

Cheddary gold disks called Ha' Pennies, and Brussels sprouts with a curried mayonnaise are elegant-looking but easy-to-prepare appetizers. The soup course features a warming, though not filling, beef broth, accompanied by Anchovy Toasts.

The numerous sheep that roam the countryside provide a favorite meat for Scotsmen. Our leg of lamb is highlighted with rosemary and Worcestershire sauce, and served with the traditional tatties, or potatoes. An array of side dishes — shimmering Parsley Jelly, stuffed tomatoes and Cauliflower with Egg Sauce — emphasizes the Scottish love of garden-grown vegetables. And fresh from the farm, a healthy loaf of oat bread carries a special country richness.

Nun's Pudding follows in the fine tradition of sweets for which Scotland is so renowned. The light and rich egg custard is laden with an apricot sauce and whipped cream, then decorated with cinnamon sticks in the shape of a cross. Serves 12.

Wine Suggestion: Complement this hearty fare with a fine, mellow burgundy — perhaps a Morgon Beaujolais from France — or the pride of Christian Brothers, a Pinot St. George.

Dinner starts with Ha' Pennies and Brussels sprouts appetizers, then proceeds to sherry-sparked beef broth.

PARTY PLAN FOR SCOTTISH DINNER MENU

1 Week Before:	Prepare Ha' Pennies through step 1 in recipe; freeze. Make Parsley Jelly.
1 Day Before:	Prepare Stuffed Baked Tomatoes through step 4 in recipe. Make Farm Bread. Wrap in aluminum foil and store at room temperature. Second loaf can be frozen up to 2 months, if desired. Prepare Nun's Pudding through step 2 in recipe.
That Afternoon:	Prepare Sherried Beef Broth with Anchovy Toasts through step 1 in recipe. Prepare Brussels Sprouts with Bombay Dip through step 2 in recipe.
3 Hours 30 Minutes Before Serving:	Make Leg of Lamb with Tatties. Measure and label ingredients to complete recipes; refrigerate perishables.
20 Minutes Before Guests Arrive:	Complete Ha' Pennies. Complete Brussels Sprouts with Bombay Dip.
30 Minutes Before Serving:	Complete Stuffed Baked Tomatoes. Make Cauliflower with Egg Sauce. Complete Sherried Beef Broth with Anchovy Toasts.
15 Minutes Before Dessert:	Complete Nun's Pudding.

Roast leg of lamb is accompanied by
potatoes, cauliflower and stuffed tomatoes.

HA' PENNIES

Makes about 9 dozen appetizers

8	ounces shredded sharp Cheddar cheese (2 cups)
1	cup all-purpose flour
½	cup butter or margarine, softened
3	tablespoons dry onion soup mix, crumbled

1. Place all ingredients in large bowl. Knead mixture into smooth ball. Divide dough in half. Shape each half into roll about 1 inch in diameter. Wrap in waxed paper.* Refrigerate at least 2 hours.

2. Heat oven to 375°. Cut rolls into ¼-inch slices. Bake on ungreased baking sheets until golden, 10 to 12 minutes. Serve immediately.

TIP: *Ha' Pennies can be prepared to this point and frozen up to 2 months. Thaw slightly in refrigerator before slicing and baking.*

BRUSSELS SPROUTS WITH BOMBAY DIP

Makes 12 servings

2	pounds fresh Brussels sprouts*
1	cup mayonnaise or salad dressing
2	tablespoons lemon juice
2	teaspoons grated onion
2	teaspoons sugar
1	teaspoon curry powder
	Orange slices

1. Heat 1 inch salted water (½ teaspoon salt to 1 cup water) to boiling. Add Brussels sprouts. Cover and heat to boiling; cook until crisp-tender, 6 to 8 minutes. Drain; refrigerate.

2. Mix remaining ingredients except orange slices in small bowl; cover. Refrigerate at least 2 hours.

3. To serve, arrange Brussels sprouts on orange slices around dip.

TIP: *3 packages (10 ounces each) frozen baby Brussels sprouts can be substituted for the fresh Brussels sprouts.*

SHERRIED BEEF BROTH WITH ANCHOVY TOASTS

Makes 12 servings (about ¾ cup each)

	Anchovy Toasts (recipe follows)
4	cans (10½ ounces each) beef consommé
4	cups water
¾	cup dry sherry
1	cup frozen peas, thawed
¼	cup butter or margarine, softened
1½	teaspoons anchovy paste
24	pieces melba toast

1. Make Anchovy Toasts.

2. Heat consommé and water in 3-quart saucepan, stirring occasionally, to boiling. Pour consommé into each of 12 soup bowls. Measure 1 tablespoon sherry and 1 heaping tablespoon peas into each bowl. Serve immediately with Anchovy Toasts.

ANCHOVY TOASTS

Mix butter and anchovy paste; spread very thinly on melba toast. Cover until serving time.

LEG OF LAMB WITH TATTIES

Makes 12 servings

1	lamb leg, whole (6 to 7 pounds)
¼	cup Worcestershire sauce
¼	cup all-purpose flour
2	teaspoons salt
1	teaspoon dried rosemary leaves, crumbled
½	teaspoon pepper
4	medium onions, thinly sliced
¼	cup butter or margarine, melted
½	teaspoon salt

1. Brush lamb with Worcestershire sauce. Mix flour, 2 teaspoons salt, the rosemary and pepper. Coat lamb with flour mixture. Place roast fat side up on rack in shallow roasting pan. Insert meat thermometer so tip is in center of thickest part of meat and does not touch bone or rest in fat.

2. Toss onions with butter and ½ teaspoon salt. Place in roasting pan around lamb. Heat oven to 325°. Roast lamb uncovered until thermometer registers 175°, about 3 hours.

3. Approximately 1 hour before end of cooking time, arrange potatoes in pan around roast. Spoon pan drippings over potatoes to coat. Let meat stand 15 minutes after removing from oven before carving; leave onions

| 8 | medium baking potatoes, pared, cut into quarters Watercress, if desired |

and potatoes in oven to keep warm. To serve, arrange onions and potatoes around roast on large platter. Garnish with watercress.

PARSLEY JELLY

Makes three 8-ounce glasses

6	cups packed parsley sprigs (about 12 ounces)
4	cups water
1	package (1¾ ounces) fruit pectin
2	tablespoons lemon juice
3¼	cups sugar
2	drops green food color
	Paraffin, melted

1. Check jelly glasses for nicks, cracks or sharp edges on sealing surfaces. Wash glasses in hot soapy water; rinse well. Place in pan with folded cloth or rack on bottom. Cover glasses with hot water. Heat to boiling; boil gently 15 minutes. Keep glasses in hot water until ready to use.

2. Chop parsley coarsely. Heat parsley and 4 cups water in Dutch oven to boiling; reduce heat. Simmer uncovered 15 minutes.

3. Drain parsley through cheesecloth, reserving liquid. Squeeze excess liquid from parsley into strained liquid. Discard parsley. Remove jelly glasses from water and invert on clean folded towel out of draft to drain.

4. Measure 2 cups of the reserved parsley liquid into small saucepan. Stir in fruit pectin and lemon juice. Heat to boiling. Stir in sugar and food color. Heat to boiling; boil and stir 1 minute. Remove from heat; immediately skim off foam.

5. Ladle hot jelly into 1 hot sterilized glass at a time, filling to within ½ inch of top. Hold ladle close to top of glass to prevent air bubbles from forming.

6. Cover hot jelly immediately with a ⅛-inch layer of hot paraffin. To ensure a good seal, paraffin must touch side of glass and be even. Pierce any bubbles that appear on paraffin as they can allow spoilage. When paraffin is hard, check seal. Cover glasses with metal or glass lids. Store in dark dry place. Once opened, store glasses covered in refrigerator.

STUFFED BAKED TOMATOES

Makes 12 servings

12	medium tomatoes Salt
2	packages (10 ounces each) frozen turnip greens
2	cups beef bouillon
1	tablespoon butter or margarine, melted
1	tablespoon fine dry bread crumbs
¼	teaspoon dried chervil leaves
	Butter or margarine
	Parsley, if desired

1. Cut thin slice from stem end of each tomato. Remove and discard seeds. Remove pulp; reserve. Salt insides of tomatoes lightly. Invert and drain 1 hour.

2. Cook turnip greens according to package directions using bouillon as the liquid. Pour into sieve; press liquid from greens using back of wooden spoon.

3. Chop turnip greens and reserved tomato pulp. Toss 1 tablespoon butter with the bread crumbs. Combine turnip greens, tomato pulp, bread crumbs and chervil.

4. Stuff each tomato with about ¼ cup of the vegetable mixture. Dot with butter. Place in greased baking dish.*

5. Heat oven to 325°. Bake tomatoes 20 minutes. Garnish with parsley.

*TIP: *Stuffed tomatoes can be prepared to this point in advance; cover and refrigerate up to 24 hours.*

CAULIFLOWER WITH EGG SAUCE

Makes 12 servings

2	medium heads cauliflower
2	hard-cooked eggs
3	tablespoons butter or margarine
3	tablespoons flour
¾	teaspoon salt
	Dash white pepper
	Dash ground nutmeg
1½	cups milk

1. Separate cauliflower into large flowerets. Place in 1 inch boiling salted water (½ teaspoon salt to 1 cup water). Heat to boiling; reduce heat and cover. Simmer until tender, about 10 minutes; drain.

2. Separate hard-cooked egg yolks from whites. Chop whites; reserve yolks. Melt butter in small saucepan over low heat. Stir in flour and seasonings. Cook over low heat, stirring constantly, until mixture is smooth and bubbly. Stir in milk gradually. Heat to boiling; boil and stir 1 minute. Stir in egg whites.

3. Pour white sauce over cauliflower in serving dish. Press egg yolks through sieve with back of spoon. Sprinkle over white sauce.

FARM BREAD

Makes 2 loaves

4	cups milk, scalded, cooled slightly
2	cups uncooked rolled oats
2	tablespoons lard
1	package active dry yeast
½	cup warm water (105° to 115°)
⅔	cup molasses
1	tablespoon salt
9	to 10 cups all-purpose flour
1	egg white
	Uncooked rolled oats

1. Place milk, 2 cups oats and the lard in large bowl. Stir until lard is melted; cover. Let stand at room temperature 1 hour.

2. Dissolve yeast in warm water. Stir dissolved yeast, the molasses and salt into oat mixture. Stir in enough flour to make dough easy to handle.

3. Turn dough onto lightly floured surface. Knead until smooth and elastic, about 5 minutes. Place in greased bowl; turn greased side up and cover. Let rise in warm place until double, about 2 hours. (Dough is ready if impression remains.)

4. Punch down dough. Knead on floured surface 15 minutes. Return to bowl; cover. Let rise until double, about 45 minutes.

5. Punch down dough; divide in half. Shape into 2 round loaves. Place on greased baking sheets. Let rise covered in warm place until double, about 45 minutes.

6. Heat oven to 325°. Brush loaves with egg white. Sprinkle oats over tops. Bake until loaves are golden and sound hollow when tapped, about 45 minutes. Cool on wire racks.

An apricot sauce and whipped cream top egg-rich Nun's Pudding.

NUN'S PUDDING

Makes 12 servings

½	cup apricot preserves
2	teaspoons ground cinnamon
4	cups milk
2	envelopes unflavored gelatin
¼	cup sugar
¼	teaspoon salt
8	egg yolks*
½	cup whipping cream
1	tablespoon sugar
2	cinnamon sticks

1. Mix preserves and ground cinnamon. Spread in bottom of 2-quart glass bowl. Refrigerate until set, about 1 hour.

2. Mix milk, gelatin, ¼ cup sugar, the salt and egg yolks in top of double boiler. Cook over simmering water, stirring constantly, until mixture thickens, 15 to 20 minutes. Pour mixture over preserves in bowl. Refrigerate until set, about 4 hours.

3. Beat whipping cream and 1 tablespoon sugar in chilled small bowl until stiff peaks form. Unmold pudding onto large serving plate; top with whipped cream and cinnamon sticks arranged in the form of a cross.

TIP: *Leftover egg whites can be used in angel food cake.*

A Tropical Island Feast

Offer shrimp and crab appetizers with sprightly Polynesian Punch.

ISLANDS MENU

• **POLYNESIAN PUNCH**

• **CRAB PUFFS**
• **CORAL SHRIMP**

• **CHARCOAL-BROILED
   ISLAND FISH**
• **GRILLED HAM WITH PLUM
   SAUCE**
• **COCONUT SWEET POTATOES**
• **SPINACH-SPROUT SALAD**
• **GINGERED CUCUMBER SLICES**

• **TROPICAL DESSERT**

• Recipes included

Who hasn't conjured up visions of an island paradise, complete with sparkling seas, luxuriant flora and endlessly enticing food and drink? So when summer breezes waft across the land, host a gala bash inspired by your daydreams.

Our tropical feast has a challenging menu that you might best accomplish with a little extra kitchen help. The party is also perfect for a cooperative venture, where guests bring different dishes. Drench the landscape in color — with bright linens, paper flowers, your own vibrant attire. Then sit back and revel in a South Pacific repast that friends will never forget.

Polynesian Punch sets the warm winds of conviviality stirring with a blend of light rum, cognac and peach brandy. Following is a delectable first course of Crab Puffs and Coral Shrimp, both served with a sweet chili-flavored sauce and a spunky peanut sauce.

The main courses will convince partygoers they're in a culinary paradise. Whole whitefish basted with a basil and sake mix, and Grilled Ham with Plum Sauce are charcoal cooked, then arranged on a bed of tropical ti leaves. Coconut Sweet Potatoes is a heavenly concoction with a hint of cumin and coriander. For a unique salad offering, toss fresh spinach and bean sprouts in a tangy dressing. Or diners may prefer cool and crisp Gingered Cucumber Slices.

The Tropical Dessert captures the essence of island bounty with luscious fruits in half-pineapple boats. Serves 12.

Wine Suggestion: A spicy, flowery Gewürztraminer — the one made in Alsace by Hügel or the one from California by Mirassou Vineyards — is the best choice for this feast.

Charcoal-cooked ham and fish are matched with cucumbers, sweet potatoes and Spinach-Sprout Salad.

PARTY PLAN FOR ISLANDS MENU

1 Week Before: Make Crab Puffs except for sauces.

1 Day Before: Make Chili Sauce and Peanut Sauce for Crab Puffs and Coral Shrimp; cover separately and refrigerate.
Prepare Coconut Sweet Potatoes through step 3 in recipe; cover and refrigerate.
Prepare Spinach-Sprout Salad through step 1 in recipe.
Make Gingered Cucumber Slices, except do not place in serving bowl.

That Afternoon: Prepare salad greens and bean sprouts for Spinach-Sprout Salad; refrigerate.
Prepare garnishes for menu; refrigerate.
Complete steps 2 and 3 of Coral Shrimp recipe; cover and refrigerate.
Prepare Polynesian Punch through step 1 in recipe.

3 Hours Before Serving: Prepare Charcoal-Broiled Island Fish through step 1 in recipe; cover and refrigerate.
Prepare Tropical Dessert through step 1 in recipe.

10 Minutes Before Guests Arrive: Remove Chili Sauce, Peanut Sauce and Coconut Sweet Potatoes from refrigerator.
Heat oven to 375°.
Heat oil (2 to 3 inches) in deep-fat fryer or kettle to 400°.

As Guests Arrive: Complete Polynesian Punch and serve.
Heat Crab Puffs in oven.
Complete Coral Shrimp.
Ignite coals in grill.

45 Minutes Before Serving: Increase oven temperature to 400°.
Complete Charcoal-Broiled Island Fish.
Make Grilled Ham with Plum Sauce.

30 Minutes Before Serving: Complete Coconut Sweet Potatoes.
Complete gingered cucumber slices.

15 Minutes Before Serving: Toss salad with dressing.

15 Minutes Before Dessert: Complete Tropical Dessert.

POLYNESIAN PUNCH

Makes 12 servings (1 cup each)

1   cup packed light
   brown sugar
1   cup water
2   cups fresh lemon juice
   (11 to 12 lemons)

1   bottle (⁴/₅ quart) light
   rum, chilled

1. Mix brown sugar and 1 cup water in small saucepan. Heat, stirring constantly, until sugar is dissolved. Remove from heat; stir in lemon juice. Refrigerate until cold.

2. Pour lemon mixture into chilled punch bowl. Stir in rum, cognac, peach brandy and 1 quart water. Garnish with lemon slices and mint sprigs.

1 pint cognac, chilled
¼ cup chilled peach brandy
1 quart water
Lemon slices
Mint sprigs

CRAB PUFFS

Makes about 3 dozen appetizers

Chili Sauce (recipe follows)
Peanut Sauce (recipe follows)

1 package (8 ounces) cream
  cheese, softened
1 can (7½ ounces) crabmeat,
  drained, cartilage removed
2 tablespoons minced green
  onion
2 tablespoons minced celery
2 tablespoons soft bread crumbs
¼ teaspoon salt
⅛ teaspoon red pepper sauce

9 commercial egg roll wrappers,
  cut into quarters

  Vegetable oil
  *Ti leaves, if desired

1 cup chili sauce
1 can (8 ounces) crushed
  unsweetened pineapple,
  drained
1 tablespoon sweet pickle relish
1 tablespoon chopped onion
1 tablespoon molasses
2 teaspoons prepared mustard

⅓ cup sugar
¼ cup fresh lemon juice
  (2 medium lemons)
2 tablespoons soy sauce
2 tablespoons prepared
  horseradish
¾ teaspoon ground ginger
¼ teaspoon crushed red pepper
⅓ cup peanut butter

1. Make Chili Sauce and Peanut Sauce.

2. Beat cream cheese until light and fluffy. Stir in crabmeat, onion, celery, bread crumbs, salt and red pepper sauce.

3. Spoon about 2 measuring teaspoonfuls of the crab filling onto center of each egg roll wrapper quarter. Moisten edges slightly; bring sides together and pinch to seal.

4. Heat oil (2 to 3 inches) in deep-fat fryer or kettle to 350°. Fry puffs in hot oil until golden, 2 to 3 minutes. Arrange puffs on ti leaves on platter. Serve with Chili Sauce and Peanut Sauce.

TIPS: Crab Puffs can be prepared in advance. Cool; wrap in aluminum foil. Freeze no longer than 2 weeks. To serve, heat oven to 375°. Heat Crab Puffs uncovered on baking sheets. Drain on paper toweling.

*Ti leaves can be purchased in florist shops.

CHILI SAUCE   *Makes 1⅔ cups*
Measure all ingredients into blender container; cover. Blend on medium speed 1 minute.

PEANUT SAUCE   *Makes 1 cup*
Mix sugar, lemon juice, soy sauce, horseradish, ginger and pepper. Stir in peanut butter; mix until smooth.

CORAL SHRIMP

Makes about 6 dozen appetizers

Chili Sauce (see recipe above)
Peanut Sauce (see recipe
  above)

2 packages (7¾ ounces each)
  bean threads

1½ pounds medium shrimp,
  shells removed

1. Make Chili Sauce and Peanut Sauce.

2. Place bean threads, ½ package at a time, in blender container; cover. Blend on medium-high speed until coarsely ground.

3. Sprinkle shrimp with salt and monosodium glutamate. Coat shrimp with cornstarch; dip into eggs and coat with ground bean threads.

1	teaspoon salt
1	teaspoon monosodium glutamate
1	cup cornstarch
3	eggs, beaten
	Vegetable oil
	Ti leaves, if desired

4. Heat oil (2 to 3 inches) in deep-fat fryer or kettle to 400°. Fry shrimp in hot oil until golden, 4 to 5 minutes. Arrange shrimp on ti leaves on platter. Serve with Chili Sauce and Peanut Sauce.

CHARCOAL-BROILED ISLAND FISH
Makes 12 servings

1	dressed whole whitefish (4 to 5 pounds)*
	Salt
	Pepper
	Lime slices
	Onion slices
3	large bay leaves
½	cup butter or margarine, melted
½	cup sake (Japanese rice wine)
2	teaspoons dried basil leaves
	Ti leaves
	Lime slices
	Fresh anise or parsley

1. Rub cavity of fish with salt and pepper. Alternate slices of lime and onion in cavity of fish. Place bay leaves on lime and onion slices. Close opening with skewers; lace.

2. Mix butter, sake and basil leaves. Place fish in wire basket on grill 4 inches from medium coals. Cook, turning 3 times and basting with butter mixture, until fish flakes easily with fork, about 45 minutes. Arrange fish on ti leaves on platter. Garnish with lime slices and anise.

*TIP: *Lake trout or red snapper can be substituted for the whitefish.*

GRILLED HAM WITH PLUM SAUCE
Makes 12 servings

2	jars (10 ounces each) plum jelly
¾	cup water
2	tablespoons vinegar
¼	cup catsup
½	teaspoon ground ginger
2	tablespoons cornstarch
¼	cup water
1	canned ham (7 pounds), cut lengthwise in half
	Ti leaves
	Parsley

1. Heat jelly, ¾ cup water, the vinegar, catsup and ginger over medium heat, stirring constantly, until jelly is melted.

2. Mix cornstarch and ¼ cup water; stir into jelly mixture. Heat, stirring constantly, to boiling; boil and stir 2 minutes.

3. Place ham on grill 4 inches from medium coals. Cook, basting frequently with plum sauce, until meat thermometer registers 140°, about 15 minutes on each side. Arrange ham on ti leaves on platter. Garnish with parsley. Serve remaining plum sauce with ham.

COCONUT SWEET POTATOES
Makes 12 servings

3	cans (3½ ounces each) flaked coconut
2	cups light cream or half-and-half
3	cans (18 ounces each) vacuum-packed sweet potatoes
½	teaspoon ground cumin
1¼	teaspoons salt
¼	teaspoon ground coriander

1. Reserve ¾ cup of the coconut. Heat remaining coconut and the cream to boiling; remove from heat. Let stand 30 minutes. Drain; reserve liquid and coconut.

2. Beat potatoes until fluffy; beat in reserved coconut liquid gradually. Stir in drained coconut, the cumin, salt and coriander.

3. Turn potato mixture into buttered 1½-quart casserole or baking dish, 8 x 8 x 2 inches. Toss reserved ¾ cup coconut and the butter; sprinkle over potatoes.

2 tablespoons butter or
    margarine, melted

Watercress, if desired

4. Heat oven to 400°. Bake mixture until potatoes are hot, about 20 minutes. Garnish with watercress.

SPINACH-SPROUT SALAD

Makes 12 servings

½ cup olive or vegetable oil
¼ cup red wine vinegar
½ teaspoon salt
½ teaspoon grated lemon peel
½ teaspoon soy sauce
½ teaspoon honey
    Dash pepper

6 cups bite-size pieces assorted
    salad greens
6 cups torn fresh spinach
1 can (16 ounces) bean sprouts,
    drained

1. Shake all ingredients except salad greens, spinach and bean sprouts in jar with tight-fitting lid. Refrigerate 24 hours.

2. Combine salad greens, spinach and bean sprouts in large salad bowl. Pour dressing over salad; toss.

GINGERED CUCUMBER SLICES

Makes 12 servings

3 large unpared cucumbers,
    thinly sliced (about 8 cups)

1 cup green onion strips,
    1 x ¼ inch each
1¼ cups distilled white vinegar
⅓ cup water
¼ cup sugar
2 tablespoons minced gingerroot
1 teaspoon salt
¼ teaspoon pepper
    Lemon leaves, if desired

1. Soak cucumber slices in ice water until crisp, about 1 hour; drain.

2. Combine remaining ingredients except lemon leaves; pour over cucumbers and cover. Refrigerate until flavors are blended, at least 3 hours. Place cucumber mixture in bowl lined with lemon leaves.

TROPICAL DESSERT

Makes 12 servings

3 pineapples
2 pints strawberries, halved
3 cups cubed cantaloupe or
    honeydew melon

¾ cup mayonnaise or salad
    dressing
1½ tablespoons fresh lemon
    juice
1 tablespoon powdered sugar
1½ cups whipping cream,
    whipped
½ cup chopped dates
⅓ cup chopped nuts
    Ti leaves
    Fresh mint, if desired

1. Cut pineapples lengthwise in half. Remove fruit from pineapples with grapefruit knife, leaving shells intact. Cut fruit into cubes. Combine pineapple, strawberries and melon. Spoon fruit into pineapple shells and cover. Refrigerate until serving time.

2. Mix mayonnaise, lemon juice and sugar; fold into whipped cream. Fold in dates and nuts. Arrange pineapple boats on ti leaves on large tray. Garnish with fresh mint. Serve with date-nut dressing.

A Cantonese Sampling

Vegetables, fruits and meats on display in Oriental shops.

CANTONESE DINNER MENU

- SOY-HONEY SPARERIBS
- FRAGRANT WATERCRESS SOUP

- CHICKEN ALMOND WITH
  STEAMED RICE
- RED-COOKED BEEF WITH
  SESAME NOODLES
- CHILLED SHRIMP, SNOW
  PEAS AND BEAN CURD
  SOY SAUCE, PLUM
  SAUCE AND MUSTARD
  SAUCE

  FRUIT BOWL
- ALMOND CAKES
  TEA

- Recipes included

Cantonese cuisine needs no introduction to most American palates. This popular fare harmonizes sweet and sour, bland and bitter, salty and hot into an indescribable taste experience. Our Cantonese menu assembles a table of traditional favorites certain to tantalize diners.

Soy-Honey Spareribs with a splash of ginger is a savory opening course. Follow this appetizer with an aromatic fresh watercress soup dotted with green onions.

The entrée choices use the versatile *wok* — or a large skillet — and basic Cantonese cooking techniques. In Chicken Almond with Steamed Rice, bits of chicken and Oriental vegetables are stir fried in peanut oil to retain maximum flavor and freshness. The red-cooked beef acquires its name from the color of the soy sauce mixture it's simmered in. Serve the beef with coriander-accented Sesame Noodles. Snow peas, shrimp and bean curd are Cantonese staples that form a refreshing pastel-colored salad.

Almond Cakes provide a customary conclusion to the meal. But guests will also delight in a cooling and colorful fruit bowl. Try combining the fresh fruits in season, plus canned loquats, litchis and kumquats — Oriental delectables — and arranging them all in a scooped-out watermelon, if possible. Serves 6.

Wine Suggestion: Renowned wine master Sichel has created the pleasant and interesting Wan-Fu from white Bordeaux wines to complement Chinese dishes.

Cantonese dishes include beef with Sesame Noodles, Soy-Honey Spareribs, Chilled Shrimp, Snow Peas and Bean Curd, and chicken with almonds.

PARTY PLAN FOR CANTONESE DINNER MENU

2 Days Before:	Make Almond Cakes.
That Afternoon:	Prepare fruits. Assemble in melon shell or bowl; cover and refrigerate. Prepare Soy-Honey Spareribs through step 2 in recipe. Measure and label ingredients for remaining recipes; refrigerate perishables. Prepare garnishes for menu; refrigerate perishables.
2 Hours Before Serving:	Complete Soy-Honey Spareribs.
1 Hour 30 Minutes Before Serving:	Prepare Red-Cooked Beef with Sesame Noodles through step 3 in recipe. Make Chilled Shrimp, Snow Peas and Bean Curd.
45 Minutes Before Serving:	Prepare Chicken Almond with Steamed Rice through step 1 in recipe.
30 Minutes Before Serving:	Complete Chicken Almond with Steamed Rice. Make Fragrant Watercress Soup. Complete Red-Cooked Beef with Sesame Noodles.

SOY-HONEY SPARERIBS
Makes 6 appetizer servings

4   **pounds lean pork spareribs, cut in half across bones**

⅓   **cup soy sauce**
⅓   **cup honey**
3   **tablespoons cider vinegar**
2   **tablespoons sherry**
1   **tablespoon sugar**
1   **teaspoon minced peeled fresh or canned gingerroot**
2   **medium cloves garlic, minced or 1 teaspoon garlic powder**
1½   **cups beef broth or bouillon**

    Green onion tassels*
    Plum sauce or mustard sauce

1. Cut spareribs between the bones into individual ribs; trim excess fat.

2. Combine remaining ingredients except green onion tassels and plum or mustard sauce in glass or ceramic bowl large enough for marinating ribs; mix until sugar is dissolved. Marinate ribs, stirring every 30 minutes, 2 to 3 hours.

3. Heat oven to 350°. Drain ribs, reserving marinade. Place ribs on rack in shallow roasting pan; cover with aluminum foil. Cook 45 minutes. Uncover and baste; cook 25 minutes longer. Turn and baste with reserved marinade. Cook, basting occasionally, until ribs are tender, about 25 minutes. Arrange ribs on platter; garnish with green onion tassels. Serve with plum sauce or mustard sauce.

*TIP: *To make onion tassels, see tip under Fried Chicken Pieces in Spicy Sauce recipe on page 124.*

FRAGRANT WATERCRESS SOUP
Makes 6 servings (about 1 cup each)

6   **cups chicken stock**
1   **teaspoon monosodium glutamate, if desired**
3   **slices (⅛ inch thick each) peeled fresh or canned gingerroot**

1. Combine chicken stock, monosodium glutamate and gingerroot in saucepan. Heat to boiling; cook over high heat 5 minutes.

2. Wash watercress thoroughly; discard tough stems and cut watercress into 2-inch lengths. Clean green onions and slice thinly. Remove gingerroot from broth; add watercress.

The Chinese slicing cleaver is a helpful tool in food preparation.

2	large bunches watercress (1½ to 2 cups)*
2	green onions
	Salt

3. Cook soup over medium heat 15 minutes. Season to taste with salt. Serve in bowls or cups garnished with green onion slices.

TIP: *Fresh spinach can be substituted for the watercress. Wash spinach thoroughly; discard tough stems and shred spinach coarsely to measure 2 to 3 cups. Cook in broth 5 minutes.

CHICKEN ALMOND WITH STEAMED RICE
Makes 6 servings

	Steamed Rice **(recipe follows)**
3	tablespoons peanut oil
½	teaspoon salt
6	large chicken breasts, halved, skinned, boned, cut into 1-inch cubes
1	can (8½ ounces) water chestnuts, drained, diced
1	can (8 ounces) bamboo shoots, drained, diced or about 1 cup diced peeled fresh bamboo shoots
¾	cup diced celery
¾	cup diced fresh mushrooms or canned button mushrooms
½	teaspoon monosodium glutamate, if desired
¾	cup chicken broth or bouillon
2	teaspoons soy sauce
2	tablespoons cornstarch
2	tablespoons water
½	cup blanched whole almonds, French fried*

1. Make Steamed Rice.

2. Heat *wok* (at least 14 inches) or large heavy skillet. Add peanut oil and salt; heat until sizzling or very hot. Add chicken and stir over high heat until almost done, at least 5 minutes.

3. Add vegetables and monosodium glutamate. Stir just until all ingredients are thoroughly combined and heated.

4. Stir in chicken broth and soy sauce; reduce heat and cover. Simmer 6 minutes. Mix cornstarch and water; stir into chicken mixture slowly. Mix gently but rapidly until sauce thickens and all ingredients are very hot. Place in serving bowl; garnish with French fried almonds. Serve with Steamed Rice.

TIP: *To French fry almonds, heat 2 inches peanut oil in 1-quart saucepan or skillet to 365°. Add almonds, ¼ cup at a time, frying until golden, about 2 minutes. Remove with slotted spoon and drain on paper toweling. Repeat procedure until all almonds are fried. Almonds can be fried, cooled and stored in covered jar several days in advance.

On next pages: Soy-Honey Spareribs, almond chicken, Chilled Shrimp, Snow Peas and Bean Curd, beef with Sesame Noodles, and watercress soup.

STEAMED RICE

2 cups uncooked long grain rice
   Water

Makes about 6 cups

1. Wash rice, rubbing grains between hands until water is fairly clear and not milky; repeat procedure 3 times. Place rice in heavy 3-quart saucepan; add water to 1 inch above rice (about 4 cups) and cover.

2. Heat rice to boiling; remove cover and stir with fork. Cook uncovered over high heat until water has evaporated to the level of the rice. Cover; reduce heat to very low.

3. Cook until rice is quite dry and grains are tender, 15 to 20 minutes. Fluff with fork and cover until just before serving.

RED-COOKED BEEF WITH SESAME NOODLES

Makes 6 servings

2 pounds beef chuck steak, boneless
1½ cups water
1 slice peeled fresh or canned gingerroot
1 clove garlic, cut in half
1 green onion, cut lengthwise in half
¼ cup soy sauce
2 tablespoons dry white wine or sherry
1 tablespoon sugar
⅛ teaspoon white pepper

3 tablespoons peanut oil

   Sesame Noodles
   (recipe follows)

   Coriander leaves
   or parsley
   Toasted sesame seeds

1 package (10 ounces) fine Chinese egg noodles or any fine egg noodles
2 quarts boiling water
2 teaspoons salt

1 tablespoon peanut oil, warmed

¼ teaspoon salt
2 green onions with tops, minced
¼ cup fresh coriander leaves, minced or parsley*
1 slice peeled fresh or canned gingerroot, minced
2 teaspoons soy sauce
¾ teaspoon sesame oil, if desired

1. Cut beef into 1½-inch cubes. Combine water, gingerroot, garlic, onion, soy sauce, wine, sugar and pepper in small bowl.

2. Heat *wok* or large heavy skillet. Add 2 tablespoons of the peanut oil and heat to very hot. Add half the beef cubes; toss for 2 minutes until brown on all sides. Remove browned beef to 3-quart saucepan. Add remaining oil to *wok* and heat to very hot; add remaining beef and toss until brown. (If oil smokes, reduce heat slightly.)

3. Place remaining beef cubes in saucepan; add water mixture. Heat over high heat to boiling; reduce heat and cover. Simmer, stirring every 20 minutes, until meat is tender and liquid is reduced to ⅓ cup, about 1 hour.

4. While beef cubes are simmering, make Sesame Noodles.

5. Place beef in serving bowl. Garnish with small sprigs of coriander leaves and sprinkle with toasted sesame seeds. Serve with Sesame Noodles.

SESAME NOODLES

1. Stir noodles into 2 quarts boiling water in saucepan; stir in 2 teaspoons salt. Cook until tender, 3 or 4 minutes.

2. Drain noodles in large strainer or colander; rinse thoroughly with cold water. Return to saucepan; toss warm peanut oil with noodles and heat over low heat.

3. Stir in ¼ teaspoon salt, the green onions, coriander leaves, gingerroot, soy sauce and sesame oil when noodles are heated through. Toss; heat until hot.

CHILLED SHRIMP, SNOW PEAS AND BEAN CURD

Makes 6 servings

1	bean curd cake (about ½ pound)
1	quart boiling water
½	pound cleaned fresh or frozen raw shrimp
2	quarts boiling water
2	teaspoons salt
¾	cup fresh or frozen snow peas
1	quart boiling water
1	green onion, minced
2	tablespoons soy sauce
¼	teaspoon monosodium glutamate, if desired
1	tablespoon sesame oil

1. Cut bean curd cake into 3 slices. Carefully place slices in sieve. Plunge into 1 quart boiling water 30 seconds; drain. Cut each slice diagonally into 1-inch pieces. Arrange on serving platter; cool.

2. Stir shrimp into 2 quarts boiling water; stir in 2 teaspoons salt. Cook until shrimp turn pink, 2 to 3 minutes. Drain, rinsing with cold water; reserve shrimp. If shrimp are large, cut diagonally into 1-inch pieces.

3. Break ends off fresh snow peas. Cook snow peas in 1 quart boiling water 2 minutes. Drain, rinsing with cold water. Cut snow peas diagonally in half.

4. Top bean curd with snow peas, reserved shrimp and the green onion. Mix soy sauce, monosodium glutamate and sesame oil; pour over shrimp mixture and toss lightly. Cover; chill 1 hour.

ALMOND CAKES

Makes about 5 dozen cookies

1	cup lard, butter or margarine, softened
1	cup sugar
1	egg
1	teaspoon almond extract
2½	cups all-purpose flour
½	teaspoon salt
30	blanched almonds, cut lengthwise in half
1	egg yolk
1	teaspoon water
	Heat oven to 375°

1. Beat lard, sugar, egg and almond extract in medium-size bowl. Stir in flour and salt.

2. Shape dough into 1-inch balls; place 2 inches apart on ungreased baking sheets. Flatten slightly with heel of hand. Press almond half into center of each cookie. Beat egg yolk and water; brush lightly on each cookie.

3. Bake cookies until golden, 10 to 12 minutes. Cool on wire racks.

TIP: Almond Cakes can be made 2 or 3 days in advance. Cool completely and store in airtight container.

A Nova Scotian Christmas

Stilton, a regal English cheese, is savored with celery sticks and glasses of wine.

NOVA SCOTIAN CHRISTMAS DINNER MENU

- OYSTER LOAVES
  MEAD

- PARSLEY SOUP
- ROAST GOOSE WITH APPLE
  STUFFING AND POTATOES
- BUTTERED BRUSSELS SPROUTS
- TURNIP SOUFFLE
  WHOLE STILTON CHEESE
  CELERY STICKS

- CHRISTMAS PUDDING WITH
  BRANDY BUTTER
- MINCEMEAT TARTLETS
- POSSET
  TEA OR COFFEE

- ICED CHRISTMAS CAKE
- TURKISH DELIGHT
  MUSCATEL RAISINS
  WHOLE ALMONDS
  CRYSTALLIZED GINGER

• Recipes included

A bountiful board is the most celebrated aspect of an English Christmas. And nowhere is the tradition of roast goose and flaming pudding more faithfully followed than in Nova Scotia. The English influence is strong in this Canadian province, where more than three-fourths of the population are of British descent. When Yuletide arrives, they set out a feast that bridges the ocean between the peninsula and the parent country.

The holiday dinner begins with the Oyster Loaves appetizer. Sherried Parsley Soup, prepared from a goose broth base, readies the taste buds for the tantalizing entrée. The succulent goose is surrounded by the customary side dishes: apple stuffing, potatoes, Brussels sprouts, and turnips transformed into a golden soufflé.

All the desserts that follow have histories dating from the Middle Ages. Brandy-steeped Christmas pudding traces its origin to frumenty, a gruel of wheat, strained milk and eggs. Traditionally, everyone should help stir the pudding, while the cook places silver trinkets in it. Mincemeat Tartlets figure in the fun, too, since the number consumed portends the number of pleasant months in the coming year. As a lighter alternative, feasters might turn to lemony Posset. Later in the day, additional sweets await revelers. A magnificent Iced Christmas Cake, decorated with holly, and squares of Turkish Delight are presented with bowls of raisins, nuts and candied ginger. Serves 8.

Wine Suggestion: This traditional dinner should be served in the grand manner — with two different wines. First, with the Oyster Loaves, a white, such as Simi Winery's Johannisberg Riesling or Trimbach's Sylvaner. Then, for the goose, you will want a robust red, perhaps the superb Zinfandel from Clos Du Val or the Hungarian Egri Bikavér.

Guests cross arms to open holiday favors before
sampling sherried Parsley Soup (above).

PARTY PLAN FOR NOVA SCOTIAN CHRISTMAS DINNER MENU

4 Weeks Before: Prepare Mincemeat Tartlets through step 1 in recipe.

3 Weeks Before: Prepare Iced Christmas Cake through step 3 in recipe.
Prepare Christmas Pudding with Brandy Butter through step 1 in recipe.

1 Week Before: Make Brandy Butter.

3 Days Before: Complete steps 4 and 5 of Iced Christmas Cake recipe.

2 Days Before: Prepare Bread Loaves through step 2 in recipe.
Thaw goose if frozen.

1 Day Before: Make broth from goose neck and giblets for Parsley Soup.
Complete Bread Loaves; cool and wrap in aluminum foil.
Make Apple Stuffing; cover and refrigerate.
Make Posset.
Prepare Turkish Delight through step 1 in recipe.
Complete Mincemeat Tartlets.
Complete Iced Christmas Cake.

4 Hours Before Serving: Complete steps 2 and 3 of Oyster Loaves recipe. Cover loaves; cover and refrigerate oysters.
Prepare Parsley Soup through step 1 in recipe; cover and refrigerate.
Complete steps 2 and 3 of Roast Goose with Apple Stuffing and Potatoes recipe.
Measure and label ingredients for remaining recipes; refrigerate perishables.
Prepare garnishes; cover and refrigerate.

2 Hours Before Serving: Make Turnip Soufflé mixture and pour into soufflé dish; refrigerate.
Complete Turkish Delight; arrange on serving trays with muscatel raisins, whole almonds and crystallized ginger.
Remove Stilton cheese from refrigerator.

45 Minutes Before Serving: Complete Roast Goose with Apple Stuffing and Potatoes.
Complete Parsley Soup.
Bake Turnip Soufflé.
Complete Christmas Pudding with Brandy Butter.

20 Minutes Before Serving: Complete Oyster Loaves.
Make Buttered Brussels Sprouts.

15 Minutes Before Dessert: Heat Mincemeat Tartlets.

After Dessert: Arrange Iced Christmas Cake, Turkish Delight, muscatel raisins, whole almonds and crystallized ginger on buffet.

OYSTER LOAVES

Makes 8 servings

8   **Bread Loaves
(recipe follows)**

1. Make Bread Loaves.

½   **cup butter or margarine,
melted**

2. Heat oven to 425°. Slice each loaf horizontally in half; scoop soft bread out of bottom half leaving ¼-inch shell. Brush insides and outsides of loaves with ½ cup melted butter. Bake on baking sheet until crisp and golden, about 10 minutes.

32   **oysters in shells***

3. To shuck oysters, grip narrow end with flat side of shell down. Insert

2 tablespoons butter or
      margarine
½ cup dairy sour cream
¼ cup dry white wine
   Dash cayenne pepper
   Salt
   Freshly ground white
      pepper

oyster knife near narrow end. Press knife firmly against top shell; hold open with thumb. Cut center and rim muscles. With knife blade, free meat and membrane from top shell. Open shell; cut meat from bottom shell. Drain.

4. Heat oysters and 2 tablespoons butter in 1-quart saucepan over medium heat until oysters are opaque, about 1½ minutes. Remove oysters from saucepan. Cut into 1-inch pieces; reserve. Add sour cream, wine and cayenne pepper to pan juices. Cook over medium heat, stirring constantly, until mixture thickens and is reduced to 1 cup. Stir in oysters; season with salt and white pepper. Fill bottom of each bread loaf with about 2 table-spoons of the oyster mixture; cover with tops of loaves. Serve immediately.

TIP: *1 pint fresh or 2 cans (10 ounces each) frozen thawed oysters, rinsed and well drained, can be substituted for the oysters in shells. Omit step 3 in recipe.

1 package active dry yeast
1 cup warm water (105° to 115°)
¼ cup sugar
¼ cup shortening
1 teaspoon salt
1 egg
½ cup instant nonfat dry
      milk solids
3 to 3½ cups all-purpose flour

BREAD LOAVES   Makes 16

1. Dissolve yeast in warm water in large mixer bowl. Add sugar, shortening, salt, egg, dry milk solids and 1½ cups of the flour. Beat on low speed until ingredients are moistened. Beat on medium speed until smooth, about 1 minute.

2. Stir in enough of the remaining flour to make dough easy to handle. Place in greased bowl; turn greased side up and cover loosely with plastic wrap. Refrigerate at least 8 hours or overnight.

3. Divide dough in half. Roll half the dough on lightly floured surface into 8-inch square. Cut into 8 rectangles, 4 x 2 inches each. Place on greased baking sheet. Repeat procedure with remaining dough. Let rise in warm place until double, 1½ to 2 hours.

4. Heat oven to 375°. Bake loaves until golden, 15 to 20 minutes. Cool on wire rack.

TIP: Remaining loaves can be stored tightly wrapped in freezer up to 2 months.

PARSLEY SOUP   Makes 8 servings (about ½ cup each)

4 cups goose broth (from neck
      and giblets of goose)
      or chicken broth
2 cups firmly packed parsley,
      stems removed (about
      ¼ pound)
½ cup chopped onion
1 teaspoon sugar
½ teaspoon salt
   Dash freshly ground
      pepper

1 cup milk
2 cups diced pared potatoes
      (about 2 medium)
2 tablespoons butter or
      margarine
¼ cup all-purpose flour
1 tablespoon dry sherry
1 tablespoon snipped fresh
      parsley

1. Place broth, 2 cups parsley, the onion, sugar, salt and pepper in 2-quart saucepan. Heat to boiling; reduce heat. Simmer covered 30 minutes. Strain; reserve broth.

2. Heat milk and potatoes covered in small saucepan over medium heat until potatoes are tender, about 15 minutes. Heat butter in medium-size saucepan over low heat. Stir in flour; cook and stir over low heat until smooth and bubbly. Stir in reserved broth slowly. Heat to boiling; cook, stirring constantly, until slightly thickened, about 2 minutes. Reduce heat; add potato mixture and sherry. Heat until hot. Pour into soup tureen. Garnish with snipped parsley.

169

ROAST GOOSE WITH APPLE STUFFING AND POTATOES

Makes 8 servings

**Apple Stuffing
(recipe follows)**

1 goose (8 to 10 pounds)
**1 tablespoon butter or
margarine**

1. Make Apple Stuffing.

2. Heat oven to 350°. Fill goose cavity loosely with stuffing. Close ends of cavity. Insert meat thermometer so tip is in thickest part of inside thigh muscle, away from bone. Place goose breast side up on rack in open shallow roasting pan. Mix 1 tablespoon butter, ½ teaspoon salt, ½ tea-

A Christmas tradition — magnificent roast goose is accompanied by Apple Stuffing, potatoes, Brussels sprouts and Turnip Soufflé.

½	teaspoon salt
½	teaspoon pepper
¼	teaspoon ground ginger, if desired
¼	cup port
8	medium potatoes, pared
¼	cup butter or margarine

spoon pepper and the ginger; spread over goose.

3.   Roast goose uncovered, basting occasionally with wine and draining excess fat from roasting pan, until thermometer registers 185°, 3½ to 4 hours.

4.   While goose is roasting, cook potatoes in boiling water 5 minutes. Drain on paper toweling. Place potatoes in baking dish with ¼ cup butter and the shortening.

171

2 tablespoons shortening

2 tablespoons flour
1 cup water
1 teaspoon salt
½ teaspoon pepper

Snipped fresh mint

5. Remove goose from oven. Cover goose loosely with aluminum foil; let stand 30 minutes before carving. Increase oven temperature to 425°. Bake potatoes until tender, about 30 minutes.

6. Drain all but 2 tablespoons of the fat from roasting pan. Stir in flour. Cook over low heat, stirring constantly, until mixture is bubbly. Remove from heat. Stir in 1 cup water, 1 teaspoon salt and ½ teaspoon pepper. Heat to boiling, stirring constantly; boil and stir 1 minute.

7. Transfer stuffing to serving bowl. Serve goose on platter surrounded with potatoes; garnish with snipped fresh mint. Pass stuffing and gravy.

APPLE STUFFING *Makes about 6 cups*

3 medium onions, pared, chopped
¼ cup boiling water
1 tablespoon crumbled dried sage leaves
4 cups fresh bread crumbs
1 large cooking apple, pared, cored, diced
1 egg
1½ tablespoons butter or margarine, melted
2 tablespoons grated lemon rind
2 tablespoons lemon juice
2 tablespoons apple cider
  Salt
  Pepper

Cover onions with water in medium-size saucepan. Heat to boiling; reduce heat. Simmer covered 5 minutes. Drain on paper toweling. Pour ¼ cup boiling water over sage in large bowl; let stand 5 minutes. Add onions, bread crumbs and apple. Beat egg; stir in butter, lemon rind, juice and apple cider.* Toss bread crumb and egg mixtures lightly; season with salt and pepper.

*TIPS: *If egg mixture is dry, add another tablespoon of apple cider to bind. Stuffing should be moist.*

Stuffing can be made 1 day in advance and refrigerated covered.

BUTTERED BRUSSELS SPROUTS *Makes 8 servings*

2 pounds Brussels sprouts, washed, outer leaves removed*
2 tablespoons butter or margarine
1 teaspoon sugar
  Salt
  Freshly ground white pepper

Cook Brussels sprouts covered in 1 inch boiling salted water in large saucepan until tender, 12 to 15 minutes; drain. Add butter and sugar; season with salt and pepper.

*TIP: *3 packages (10 ounces each) frozen Brussels sprouts can be substituted for the fresh. Cook according to package directions. Season as above.*

TURNIP SOUFFLE *Makes 8 servings*

1 pound white turnips, pared, diced (about 4 cups)
1 cup water

2 tablespoons butter or margarine
1 tablespoon flour
⅓ cup whipping cream
1 teaspoon sugar
¼ teaspoon salt
  Dash freshly ground white pepper
3 eggs, separated

1. Heat turnips and water in 2-quart saucepan to boiling; reduce heat. Simmer covered until tender, about 20 minutes. Drain; mash (makes about 1½ cups). Keep warm.

2. Melt butter in medium-size saucepan; stir in flour. Cook and stir over low heat until smooth and bubbly. Stir in cream. Heat to boiling; boil and stir until thickened, about 1 minute. Stir in mashed turnips, sugar, salt and pepper, stirring constantly, until mixture boils and thickens. Remove from heat; stir ¼ cup of the mixture into slightly beaten egg yolks. Gradually return to turnip mixture. Cool to lukewarm.

3. Heat oven to 425°. Beat egg whites until stiff peaks form. Fold turnip mixture into egg whites. Pour into ungreased 1-quart soufflé dish.* Bake until golden and dry, about 20 minutes. Serve immediately, dividing soufflé into sections with 2 forks.

CHRISTMAS PUDDING WITH BRANDY BUTTER

Makes two 1-quart molds (8 servings each)

1   cup golden raisins
1   cup dark raisins
¾   cup currants
½   cup chopped mixed candied
    fruit
½   cup slivered almonds
1   medium cooking apple, pared,
    cored, chopped
¼   pound minced suet, membrane
    trimmed (about 1 cup)
1   tablespoon grated orange
    peel
1   teaspoon grated lemon peel
2   cups fresh bread crumbs
1   cup all-purpose flour
½   cup packed dark brown
    sugar
½   teaspoon salt
½   teaspoon ground allspice
    Dash ground nutmeg
3   eggs
¼   cup brandy
¼   cup stout or dark ale
2   tablespoons fresh orange
    juice
2   tablespoons fresh lemon
    juice

    Brandy Butter
    (recipe follows)

    Brandy, heated

6   tablespoons butter
6   tablespoons sifted powdered
    sugar
2   to 3 tablespoons brandy

1.   Combine raisins, currants, candied fruit, almonds, chopped apple, suet, and orange and lemon peel in large bowl. Mix bread crumbs, flour, brown sugar, salt and spices. Stir into fruit mixture. Beat eggs until foamy; add ¼ cup brandy, the stout, and orange and lemon juices. Stir into fruit mixture. Spoon 3 cups of the batter into each of 2 well-greased, 1-quart molds. Cover tightly with aluminum foil.* Place molds on rack in deep kettle; add 1 inch water. Heat water to boiling; reduce heat and cover kettle. Steam until wooden pick inserted in center of pudding comes out clean, about 2 hours. (Add boiling water to kettle, if necessary.) Remove molds from kettle. Remove aluminum foil; cool molds on wire rack. Wrap securely in foil; refrigerate at least 3 weeks.

2.   Make Brandy Butter.

3.   To serve, steam molds on rack in covered kettle with 1 inch boiling water until heated, about 1 hour. Remove molds from kettle; cool slightly and unmold. Flame with heated brandy. Serve with Brandy Butter.

TIP: *Pudding can be prepared to this point 2 hours before steaming; refrigerate.

BRANDY BUTTER
Makes 1 cup

Cream butter until light and fluffy; add sugar gradually, beating until light and fluffy. Add brandy, 1 tablespoon at a time, beating well after each addition. Beat until mixture is light in color and holds shape. Spoon into serving dish. Refrigerate at least 1 hour, no longer than 1 week.

MINCEMEAT TARTLETS

Makes 12

1   cup chopped cored pared
    cooking apples
1   cup dark raisins
½   cup currants
½   cup minced suet, membrane
    trimmed
⅓   cup chopped mixed
    candied fruit
⅓   cup packed brown sugar
¼   cup chopped almonds
¼   teaspoon ground allspice
¼   teaspoon ground cinnamon
⅛   teaspoon ground cloves
⅓   cup brandy
¼   cup rum

1.   Combine apples, raisins, currants, suet, candied fruit, brown sugar, almonds, spices, brandy and rum in large bowl. Place in sterilized 1-quart jars and seal; refrigerate 4 weeks. Check occasionally, adding more rum if mixture becomes dry.

2.   Make Short-Crust Pastry.

3.   Heat oven to 375°. Measure 3 tablespoons of the mincemeat mixture into each tart shell; press lightly with back of spoon. Roll remaining pastry dough ⅛ inch thick on lightly floured surface. Cut into 12 circles with 2¾-inch cookie cutter. Place circles over filling; seal edges and flute. Pierce several times with fork. Bake until crusts are golden, about 20 minutes. Remove tartlets from pans; cool on wire rack.* Sprinkle lightly with powdered sugar.

Short-Crust Pastry
(recipe follows)

Powdered sugar,
    if desired

3   cups all-purpose flour
¼   teaspoon salt
¾   cup chilled butter or
      margarine
¼   cup plus 2 tablespoons
      shortening

4   to 5 tablespoons cold water

TIPS: *Remaining mincemeat can be stored covered in refrigerator up to 1 year. It is excellent served heated over ice cream.*

**Mincemeat Tartlets* can be made up to 24 hours in advance. Store covered in refrigerator. Heat covered at 350° until warm, about 15 minutes.*

SHORT-CRUST PASTRY   *Makes twelve 2½-inch tart shells*

1. Mix flour and salt in medium-size bowl. Add chilled butter and shortening; work into flour by rubbing rapidly between fingers until mixture resembles oatmeal.

2. Sprinkle mixture with cold water, 1 tablespoon at a time, mixing until all flour is moistened and dough almost cleans side of bowl. Gather dough into ball. Sprinkle lightly with flour; wrap securely in waxed paper. Place in freezer just until firm, about 1 hour.

3. Divide dough into 2 parts, 1 twice the size of the other. Roll larger part of dough ⅛ inch thick on lightly floured surface. Cut into 12 circles with 4½-inch cookie cutter. Press circles into well-greased and floured 2½-inch muffin cups, allowing ¼ inch dough to remain above each rim.

POSSET   *Makes 8 servings*

4   eggs, separated
⅔   cup fresh lemon juice
¼   cup plus 2 tablespoons
      sugar
3   tablespoons grated lemon
      peel
¼   teaspoon salt
2   tablespoons dry sherry
1   envelope unflavored gelatin
⅓   cup white port
3   tablespoons dry sherry
½   cup whipping cream,
      whipped

Mix egg yolks, lemon juice, sugar, lemon peel and salt in top of 2-quart double boiler. Cook over hot water, stirring constantly, until thickened. Remove from heat; cool to lukewarm, stirring occasionally. Stir 2 tablespoons sherry and the gelatin in small saucepan over low heat until gelatin is dissolved, about 3 minutes. Stir into lemon mixture; stir in port and 3 tablespoons sherry. Fold whipped cream into lemon mixture. Beat egg whites until stiff peaks form; fold into lemon mixture. Pour into 2-quart glass bowl. Refrigerate until set, about 2 hours.

ICED CHRISTMAS CAKE   *Makes 8 servings*

1   cup golden raisins
1   cup dark raisins
1   cup currants
3   tablespoons chopped candied
      orange peel
3   tablespoons chopped candied
      lemon peel
2   tablespoons chopped candied
      cherries
¼   cup apple cider
¼   cup brandy or apple cider
1½ cups all-purpose flour
½   teaspoon ground cinnamon
½   teaspoon ground cloves
½   teaspoon ground nutmeg

1   cup butter or margarine
1   cup packed brown sugar
4   eggs

1. Combine raisins, currants, orange and lemon peel, cherries, cider and ¼ cup brandy in small bowl. Mix flour and spices; stir into fruit mixture until thickened.

2. Cream butter and sugar until light and fluffy. Add eggs, 1 at a time, beating well after each addition. Beat in golden syrup until smooth. Fold in fruit mixture. Spoon batter into greased 9-inch springform pan lined with well-greased waxed paper. Bake until wooden pick inserted in center comes out clean, about 2¼ hours. Do not open oven during baking. Cool in pan 10 minutes; remove from pan. Cool completely on wire rack.

3. Store cake uncovered at room temperature 3 weeks. Invert and pierce daily with wooden pick; sprinkle lightly with brandy.

4. Stir apricot jam until smooth. Brush top and sides of cake.

5. Make Almond Paste. Divide paste in half. Roll half the paste on surface sprinkled with powdered sugar into 9-inch circle. Roll remaining paste into 4 strips, 7½ x 2 inches each. Place paste circle on cake. Wrap strips

Yuletide sweets are Turkish Delight, Mincemeat Tartlets, Posset, Iced Christmas Cake, and Christmas Pudding with Brandy Butter.

3   tablespoons golden syrup*

Brandy or apple cider

¼   cup apricot jam

Almond Paste
  (recipe follows)

Christmas Icing
  (recipe follows)

Holly or ribbon,
  if desired

Heat oven to 300°

1¼ cups finely ground almonds
1   cup sifted powdered sugar
¾   cup granulated sugar
2   egg whites
⅛   teaspoon almond flavoring

3   egg whites
¼   teaspoon cream of tartar
5   to 5½ cups sifted
      powdered sugar
1   teaspoon strained fresh
      lemon juice
1   teaspoon glycerine*

around rim of cake; press firmly, sealing seams. Let dry at room temperature 3 days.

6.   Make Christmas Icing.

7.   Spoon icing on cake (icing should hold stiff peaks). Decorate with holly or ribbon.

TIP: *Golden syrup can be purchased at gourmet food shops. Light molasses can be substituted.

ALMOND PASTE
Mix almonds and sugars in medium-size bowl until smooth; stir in egg whites and almond flavoring to make soft paste. Knead on surface sprinkled with powdered sugar until smooth.

CHRISTMAS ICING
Beat egg whites and cream of tartar until mixture forms stiff peaks. Stir powdered sugar into mixture ½ cup at a time. Add lemon juice and glycerine. Continue adding powdered sugar until icing forms very stiff peaks.

TIP: *Glycerine can be purchased at drugstores.

TURKISH DELIGHT   *Makes about 5 dozen candies*

1   cup orange juice
1   cup water
1   tablespoon rose water
4   envelopes unflavored gelatin
2   cups granulated sugar
1   teaspoon grated lemon
      peel
1   teaspoon grated orange
      peel

Sifted powdered sugar

1.   Stir orange juice, water, rose water and gelatin in 2-quart saucepan over low heat until gelatin is dissolved, about 4 minutes. Stir in granulated sugar and fruit peel until dissolved. Heat to boiling; reduce heat. Simmer uncovered, stirring occasionally, 20 minutes. Pour into ungreased baking dish, 8 x 8 x 2 inches. Refrigerate until set, about 4 hours.

2.   Cut candy into 1-inch squares; roll in powdered sugar.

A Swiss Party Supper

RACLETTE MENU

- **RACLETTE**
  BOILED POTATOES
  COOKED TINY WHITE ONIONS
  CORNICHONS
  FRENCH BREAD

  FRESH FRUIT
  COFFEE OR TEA

• Recipe included

Raclette cheese before and after heating.

From the canton of Valais comes raclette, a Swiss cheese ritual that's ripe for import to party tables everywhere.

Raclette began with big wheels of local Valaisan cheese — soft creamy Bagnes or Conches. That first inventive host rested half the cheese, its cut face towards the flames, on a stone in his fireplace. As the cheese melted, he would scrape the delectable runny surface onto a waiting plate. His guests helped themselves to glasses of wine, and portions of potatoes, pickles and onions to round out their dinner.

This custom of raclette, which means "scraper" in French, soon spread from Valais to other parts of Switzerland. Special ovens were developed to simplify the melting. And cheesemakers engraved the word "raclette" on those cheeses best suited to the process.

Raclette is ideal for a novel party offering or light supper. Since the cheese is the main course of the meal, allow a minimum of one-fourth pound for each guest. And you have a choice of modern methods (see below) to present the cheese at its creamiest. Besides the traditional accompaniments, serve crusty bread, and fruit for dessert.

Wine Suggestion: When I last enjoyed raclette in Switzerland, everyone was sipping a young Beaujolais with it. Try the one from Paul Bocuse, or a Gamay Beaujolais by Parducci of California.

PARTY PLAN FOR RACLETTE MENU

45 Minutes Before Serving: Cut cheese into wedges or slices.
Cook boiled potatoes and onions.

At Serving Time: Cook cheese according to desired method.

SUGGESTIONS FOR SERVING THE RACLETTE

Swiss raclette cheese can be purchased at most large cheese and gourmet shops. But we tested other cheeses too, in case the raclette-stamped cheese is not readily available. We found that Port-Salut (French) and Fontina (Italian) are equally creamy and delicious when melted.

Raclette stoves can be rented for a modest sum, or purchased, at many cheese and gourmet shops. If you cannot, or do not wish to, obtain a raclette stove, you can still enjoy the Swiss tradition. When using other methods, be sure that serving plates are warmed either in the oven (oven-**Wedges of cheese are melted, then served with traditional accompaniments.**

proof plates only!), in a dishwasher set for the dish-warming cycle or in a sink full of hot water. Here are 4 alternatives to the raclette stove.

1. The fireplace: You can toast a large wedge of cheese on a long fork held close to the fire and scrape the melted surface onto a warm plate. Or you can build a makeshift platform of bricks or concrete blocks and top it with a cast-iron skillet or a griddle to hold the cheese.

2. A toaster oven: We found this appliance to be the best alternative to a raclette stove. Not only can it be conveniently placed on the dining table, but it also melts the cheese most effectively. Cut the cheese in a large wedge or slice, about 1½ to 2 inches thick. You can vary the size of the wedge depending on the size of your oven. But make sure that there is a 2-inch space between the cheese and the oven's heating coils. Set cheese on a shallow pan. Turn oven heat to high and place cheese in oven. As top melts, remove cheese from oven for guest to scrape; then return cheese to oven to melt next portion. The toaster oven will hold enough cheese to serve 4 to 6 people.

Creamy raclette cheese makes a special supper with potatoes, onions and tiny pickles called *cornichons*.

3. Regular oven preheated to 350°: Place ½-inch-thick slices of cheese on oven-proof plates and put plates in the oven until cheese melts, about 7 to 9 minutes. Remove plates from the oven with hot pads and serve immediately. Four dinner or 6 luncheon plates will fit in the oven. For additional servings, place 2 portions of cheese on 1 plate for 2 guests to share, and serve potatoes and other side dishes separately. The inconvenience of this method is that the hot plates must be transferred from oven to table.

4. Regular oven preheated to broil and/or 550°: Place ½-inch-thick slices of cheese on a jelly-roll pan or metal plates or steak platters. (Do not use regular oven-proof plates at this temperature; see directions above for oven set at 350°.) Place cheese in oven until it melts, about 3 to 4 minutes. The inconvenience of this method is that if you use a pan to hold the cheese, you must transfer portions to warmed plates and carry them to the table. But you can serve many people quickly this way; 8 to 10 servings will fit on a jelly-roll pan.

A Hungarian Buffet

A statue of Hungary's first king, Stephen, watches over the Castle Hill in Budapest.

HUGARIAN BUFFET MENU

- **FISH PAPRIKA**
- **MIXED MEAT GOULASH**
  HOT RED AND GREEN PEPPERS
- **CUCUMBER SALAD WITH DILL**
  DRESSING

- **WILTED LETTUCE**
  BREAD

- **CHERRY STRUDEL**
  COFFEE

- Recipes included

Beyond goulash and strudel, many people never venture into the exuberant world of Hungarian cookery. But this robust and romantic cuisine offers numerous other delights worthy of sampling. For a unique ethnic buffet, enjoy the famous Hungarian favorites with some less widely known specialties.

Paprika — that staple spice of Hungary — perks up whitefish fillets in a main dish of the dinner. Goulash is derived from *gulyás*, one of the four classic types of Hungarian stews. In its native land, the beef, pork and veal combination would be cooked in a *bogrács*. This caldron is a contribution of early Magyar herdsmen, who wielded it over their open fires.

Vegetables abound in Hungarian cuisine. So diners have a choice of a cool cucumber salad sparked with dill, or Wilted Lettuce — romaine tossed with a bacon dressing. A plate of hot red and green peppers should also appear on an authentic table.

The bold-flavored fish, meat and vegetables give way to an incredibly delicate Cherry Strudel for the banquet's conclusion. The dessert is a heavenly example of *rétes*, a popular Hungarian confection. And it features timesaving frozen fillo leaves to wrap around the fruit. Serves 10.

Wine Suggestion: A glass of Hungarian Villányi Burgundi will create the perfect atmosphere for this buffet. The California counterpart might be a Pinot Noir made by the master, Robert Mondavi.

This hearty Hungarian menu features spicy Fish Paprika, dill-sparked cucumber salad, Wilted Lettuce and Mixed Meat Goulash.

PARTY PLAN FOR HUNGARIAN BUFFET MENU

1 Day Before:	Make Cucumber Salad with Dill Dressing. Prepare Mixed Meat Goulash through step 2 in recipe.
That Afternoon:	Make Cherry Strudel. Let cool; cover loosely with aluminum foil. Prepare Wilted Lettuce through step 1 in recipe; refrigerate romaine and bacon separately. Measure and label ingredients to complete recipes; refrigerate perishables.
45 Minutes Before Serving:	Make Fish Paprika. Complete Wilted Lettuce. Complete Mixed Meat Goulash.
20 Minutes Before Dessert:	Heat Cherry Strudel uncovered at 350° 15 minutes.

FISH PAPRIKA (Hal Paprikás)

Makes 10 servings

3	tablespoons lard or shortening
3	cups chopped onions
2	tablespoons paprika
⅛	to ¼ teaspoon cayenne pepper
4	pounds whitefish fillets, cut into serving pieces
1	cup water
2	teaspoons salt
½	teaspoon black pepper
1	cup dairy sour cream
	Watercress, if desired
	Dairy sour cream, if desired

1. Heat lard until hot. Sauté onions, paprika and cayenne pepper in lard until onions are brown. Divide onion mixture between 2 large skillets. Arrange 2 pounds of the fish on onions in 1 skillet; add ½ cup of the water. Sprinkle with 1 teaspoon salt and ¼ teaspoon black pepper. Repeat procedure using remaining fish, water, salt and black pepper in second skillet. Heat to boiling; reduce heat and cover. Cook until fish flakes easily with fork, 5 to 7 minutes.

2. Transfer fish to serving platter. Stir remaining fish stock and onions into 1 skillet. Stir 1 cup sour cream gradually into fish stock. Cook and stir just until boiling. Spoon sauce over fish. Garnish with watercress and sour cream.

MIXED MEAT GOULASH (Bogrács Gulyás)

Makes 10 servings

3	tablespoons lard or shortening
3	cups thinly sliced onions
3	tablespoons paprika
1½	pounds beef for stew, cut into 1-inch cubes
1½	pounds veal for stew, cut into 1-inch cubes
1½	pounds pork for stew, cut into 1-inch cubes
1	cup thinly sliced green pepper
1	cup beef broth
1	can (6 ounces) tomato paste
2½	teaspoons salt
½	teaspoon black pepper
½	teaspoon caraway seeds
¼	teaspoon cayenne pepper
2	medium potatoes, pared, cubed (about 2 cups)
1½	cups dairy sour cream

1. Heat lard in Dutch oven until hot. Sauté onions and paprika in lard 10 minutes. Stir in meat and green pepper; sauté until meat is brown.

2. Stir remaining ingredients except potatoes and sour cream into meat mixture. Heat to boiling; reduce heat and cover. Simmer 45 minutes. Add potatoes. Heat to boiling; reduce heat and cover. Simmer until meat is tender, 30 to 45 minutes.*

3. Stir in sour cream. Heat until hot. Ladle into serving dishes.

TIP: *Mixed Meat Goulash can be prepared to this point 2 days in advance. Refrigerate covered. To serve, heat until hot and proceed with step 3.*

CUCUMBER SALAD WITH DILL DRESSING (Uborkasaláta)

Makes 10 servings

4	cucumbers, pared, thinly sliced (about 2 pounds)
1½	teaspoons salt
½	cup distilled white vinegar
½	cup water
1	tablespoon dried dillweed
1	teaspoon sugar
	Dash pepper

1. Sprinkle cucumber slices with salt in medium-size bowl; toss. Let stand 30 minutes; drain.

2. Mix remaining ingredients; pour over cucumbers and cover. Refrigerate at least 3 hours, no longer than 2 days.

WILTED LETTUCE (Fejes Saláta)   *Makes 10 servings*

1	head romaine (about 1¼ pounds)
6	slices bacon
½	cup water
⅓	cup distilled white vinegar
1	tablespoon vegetable oil
2	teaspoons sugar
1	teaspoon salt
1	teaspoon Dijon-style mustard

1. Tear romaine into bite-size pieces into large salad bowl. Fry bacon until crisp. Drain and crumble; reserve. Discard all but 1 tablespoon bacon fat.

2. Stir remaining ingredients into bacon fat. Heat dressing to boiling; pour over romaine. Toss lightly and cover. Let stand 30 minutes. Toss; sprinkle with reserved bacon.

CHERRY STRUDEL (Cseresznyés Rétes)   *Makes 2*

1	cup bread crumbs
¼	cup butter or margarine, melted
¾	cup granulated sugar
2	teaspoons grated lemon peel
1½	teaspoons ground cinnamon
½	box (16-ounce size) frozen fillo strudel leaves, thawed
1¼	cups butter or margarine, melted
4	cans (16 ounces each) pitted sour cherries, rinsed, drained thoroughly
	Powdered sugar, if desired
	Heat oven to 375°

1. Cook and stir bread crumbs in ¼ cup butter until light brown; reserve. Mix granulated sugar, lemon peel and cinnamon; reserve.

2. Place 1 fillo leaf on kitchen towel; brush with melted butter. Place another leaf on top; brush with butter. Repeat using 5 fillo leaves and about ½ cup of the melted butter.

3. Sprinkle top leaf with half the reserved bread crumbs (reserve 2 tablespoons for topping). Mound half the cherries along narrow end of leaves in a 3-inch strip, leaving a 2-inch border. Sprinkle with half the reserved cinnamon mixture.

4. Lift towel, using it to roll leaves over cherries, jelly-roll fashion, starting from narrow end. Brush strudel with melted butter after each turn. Brush top of strudel with butter; sprinkle with reserved 2 tablespoons bread crumbs. Place strudel on greased jelly-roll pan, 15½ x 10½ x 1 inch. Repeat procedure from step 2 for second strudel. Bake until brown and crisp, about 20 minutes. Sprinkle with powdered sugar. Serve warm.

Tantalizing Cherry Strudel is a time-honored delicacy.

A Pasta Festa

A rustic village in the Roman countryside.

Say "pasta," and most peoples' mouths begin to water as they imagine their favorite Italian dishes. So what better basis for a good-eating get-together than noodles that are made right at the party?

Before everyone gets down to creating the pasta, they can sip sparkling Campari Punch and dunk assorted vegetables and bread slices in a sour cream-anchovy dip. Pasta making should then proceed — with guests mixing the dough, kneading it, shaping it by hand or machine into thin sheets and finally cutting it into ribbons and cooking it. They might even vary the basic recipe with spinach and beet for green and red noodles (*pasta verde* and *pasta rossa*).

The cooks can enjoy their handiwork with an array of tantalizing sauces, some familiar, some not so well-known. Meat and seafood choices are Bolognese Ragu Sauce, Hearty Sausage Sauce, White Clam Sauce, and Shrimp and Artichoke Sauce. Unusual Zucchini-Basil Sauce and Tomato-Vegetable Sauce are hot vegetarian varieties. And cold vegetable sauces include the classic Pesto — made with fresh spinach — and Cold Tomato-Sweet Pepper Sauce. Orange Pico Salad and crusty bread round out the main course.

For dessert, Spiced Coffee Ice will refresh the feasters. Complement it with Italian cookies, almond-flavored liqueur and plenty of espresso. Serves 12.

Wine Suggestion: To complement the casual mood of this party, offer a young and light red wine. You might select an Almadén Barbera or, from Verona, Ricasoli Valpolicella.

Begin dinner with Bagna Cauda Dip and Campari Punch.

Picturesque Italian scenes show pasta cooked over a wood fire and a quaint old building in Modena.

PARTY PLAN FOR PASTA PARTY MENU

1 Week Before:	Make the following sauces, if used: Bolognese Ragu Sauce; Tomato-Vegetable Sauce; Pesto Sauce. Prepare Hearty Sausage Sauce, if used, through step 2 in recipe.
1 Day Before:	Make Cold Tomato-Sweet Pepper Sauce, if used. Prepare Spiced Coffee Ice through step 2 in recipe.
That Afternoon:	Prepare White Clam Sauce, if used, through step 1 in recipe. Prepare assorted vegetables for Bagna Cauda Dip; cover and refrigerate. Cut zucchini for Zucchini-Basil Sauce, if used. Wrap in damp paper toweling; refrigerate. Make Orange Pico Salad, except do not toss with dressing. Chill Campari Punch ingredients. Prepare spinach and beet, if used, for Homemade Pasta; cover and refrigerate separately. Thaw artichokes for Shrimp and Artichoke Sauce, if used. Fill dessert dishes with Spiced Coffee Ice; freeze.
30 Minutes Before Guests Arrive:	Slice French bread and arrange assorted vegetables on platter for Bagna Cauda Dip; cover. Make Bagna Cauda Dip. Complete Campari Punch.
2 Hours Before Serving:	Set out Pesto Sauce. Prepare and shape Homemade Pasta dough.
45 Minutes Before Serving:	Heat water to boiling in covered pot for cooking pasta. Make the following sauces, if used: Zucchini-Basil Sauce; Shrimp and Artichoke Sauce. Complete Hearty Sausage Sauce and White Clam Sauce, if used. Heat the following sauces, if used: Bolognese Ragu Sauce; Tomato-Vegetable Sauce.
At Serving Time:	Cook pasta. Toss salad with dressing.
15 Minutes Before Dessert:	Complete Spiced Coffee Ice.

Zucchini-Basil Sauce, Hearty Sausage Sauce, Pesto Sauce, and Artichoke Sauce are served with fresh homemade noodles and Orange Pico Salad.

CAMPARI PUNCH *Makes 12 servings (4½ ounces each)*

1½ cups Campari liqueur
1½ cups dry vermouth
1½ cups unsweetened grapefruit
     juice*
1   lime, thinly sliced, seeded
2¼ cups (18 ounces) chilled club
     soda
1   tray ice cubes

Mix Campari, vermouth, grapefruit juice and lime slices in glass punch bowl; chill. Just before serving, stir in club soda and ice.

*TIP: *Campari Punch has a refreshingly dry, slightly bitter taste. Sweetened grapefruit juice or club soda may be substituted for the unsweetened grapefruit juice. If soda is used, add just before serving.*

BAGNA CAUDA DIP

Makes 12 servings (about 3 cups)

1   cup butter or margarine
⅔   cup olive oil
2   cans (2 ounces each) flat
    anchovy fillets, drained,
    finely chopped
1   tablespoon minced garlic
¼   teaspoon freshly ground black
    pepper
1½ to 2 cups dairy sour cream
    Assorted fresh vegetables
    Thinly sliced French bread

Heat butter and oil in saucepan over medium heat until butter foams. Sauté anchovies and garlic in butter mixture 3 to 5 minutes. Stir in pepper; remove from heat. Stir in sour cream gradually until smooth. Heat until hot; pour into chafing dish or fondue pot. Keep warm over low flame, stirring occasionally. Serve with assorted vegetables and French bread.

The lush fields of Tuscany.

HOMEMADE PASTA

Makes 2 servings (about 8 ounces dry pasta)

1   **cup all-purpose flour**
1   **egg**
1   **egg white**
1   **tablespoon olive or vegetable oil**
     Dash salt

2   **quarts water**
1   **teaspoon salt**
     Melted butter or margarine

1.   Measure 1 cup flour into mound on breadboard; shape deep well in center. Place egg, egg white, oil and dash salt in well.*

2.   Beat egg mixture in well with fork until smooth; stir flour from well gradually into egg mixture to make a stiff sticky dough. Scrape fork. Knead remaining flour into dough until smooth and elastic, about 10 minutes. Cover with towel; let stand 10 minutes. (Scrape gummy particles from board; discard.)

TO SHAPE PASTA BY HAND: Roll dough on lightly floured surface into oval $^{1}/_{16}$ inch thick, turning dough over occasionally and dusting with flour to prevent sticking. (Dough should be thin enough to read through.) Dust top surface of oval lightly with flour. Roll oval into cylinder from narrow end. Cut cylinder crosswise into ribbons $^{1}/_{8}$ to $^{1}/_{4}$ inch wide each; immediately unroll onto dry towel. Let stand uncovered to dry pasta, turning occasionally with floured hands to prevent sticking, about 30 minutes.

TO SHAPE PASTA BY MACHINE: Divide dough in half. ** Pass half the dough through smooth rollers of pasta machine on widest setting. Dust lightly with flour; fold dough crosswise into thirds and press to flatten. Repeat rolling, dusting and folding until dough becomes smooth, soft and pliable (like chamois), 10 to 15 times.

Move roller width gauge to next widest setting. Pass dough through rollers; dust lightly with flour. DO NOT FOLD. Continue moving width gauge in decreasing widths and passing dough through rollers once at each setting. Dust dough with flour, if necessary. (Dough sheet will become longer and thinner with each pass.) Roll dough to narrowest machine setting or to desired thinness, about $^{1}/_{16}$ inch thick. (Dough should be thin enough to read through.)

Lay dough sheet smoothly on dry towel. Cut sheet crosswise in half for easier handling. Repeat entire procedure with remaining dough. Let stand uncovered to dry dough, 10 minutes. If dough is too moist, dust lightly with flour.

Pass each dough sheet through cutting rollers of machine to form pasta ribbons. Spread ribbons on dry towels; let stand, turning occasionally to prevent sticking, 30 minutes.

TO COOK FRESH PASTA: Heat water and 1 teaspoon salt*** to boiling;**** stir in pasta. Boil until pasta rises to surface and is tender but firm to the bite (*al dente*), 2 to 3 minutes. Drain; toss lightly with melted butter. Serve immediately; keep hot, covered on electric warming tray set at 200°.

TO DRY AND STORE PASTA: If not cooked immediately, cover pasta ribbons with paper toweling. Let stand at room temperature overnight to dry *completely*. Refrigerate in airtight container no longer than 2 weeks.

*TIPS: *To make green pasta (pasta verde) or red pasta (pasta rossa), omit egg white from basic recipe. Add 2 tablespoons minced dry-squeezed cooked spinach or 2 tablespoons minced cooked beet to egg mixture in well. Proceed with step 2.*

***If recipe is doubled, divide dough into quarters.*

****Add 2 tablespoons cider vinegar to water, if cooking red pasta.*

*****If cooking 12 servings of pasta, use 6 quarts water and 1 tablespoon salt.*

BOLOGNESE RAGU SAUCE

Makes 4½ cups

¼ cup chopped celery
¼ cup chopped carrot
¼ cup chopped onion
¼ cup olive or vegetable oil
1½ pounds lean ground beef
1 teaspoon salt

1½ cups dry white wine
1 cup milk
¼ teaspoon ground nutmeg
1 can (28 ounces) Italian-style plum tomatoes, undrained, cut into small pieces
   Salt
   Hot cooked Homemade Pasta (see recipe, page 188)
   Freshly grated Parmesan cheese

1. Sauté celery, carrot and onion in oil in 2-quart saucepan over medium heat until tender, about 5 minutes. Stir in beef and 1 teaspoon salt. Sauté, breaking up beef, until beef is brown, 3 to 5 minutes.

2. Stir wine into beef mixture. Heat to boiling; reduce heat. Simmer uncovered until almost all wine is absorbed, about 20 minutes. Stir in milk and nutmeg. Heat to boiling; reduce heat. Simmer uncovered, stirring occasionally, about 10 minutes. Stir in tomatoes; simmer uncovered over medium heat until sauce is thickened, about 1 hour and 20 minutes. Season to taste with salt. Serve sauce over hot cooked pasta. Pass grated Parmesan.

TIP: Sauce can be made up to 1 week in advance. Store covered in refrigerator or freezer. Heat to boiling; reduce heat and cover. Simmer about 10 minutes before serving.

HEARTY SAUSAGE SAUCE

Makes 6 cups

2 ounces lean salt pork, diced (about ⅓ cup)
1 tablespoon olive or vegetable oil
½ cup chopped onion
3 cloves garlic, minced
1¼ pounds mild Italian sausage, casing removed, cut into ½-inch pieces

1 can (28 ounces) Italian-style plum tomatoes, undrained, cut into small pieces
1 can (12 ounces) tomato juice
½ cup snipped fresh parsley
2 tablespoons tomato paste

2 small green peppers, seeded, cut into thin strips
1 tablespoon olive or vegetable oil
   Hot cooked Homemade Pasta (see recipe, page 188)
   Freshly grated Parmesan cheese

1. Sauté salt pork in 1 tablespoon oil in 3-quart saucepan over medium heat until golden, about 5 minutes. Stir in onion and garlic; sauté until tender, about 3 minutes. Stir in sausage pieces; sauté until brown, about 5 minutes.

2. Stir tomatoes, tomato juice and parsley into sausage mixture. Heat to boiling; reduce heat and cover. Simmer, stirring occasionally, 40 minutes; uncover. Stir in tomato paste. Cook over medium heat, stirring occasionally, until sauce is thickened, about 30 minutes. Skim off excess fat. *

3. Sauté pepper strips in 1 tablespoon oil in small skillet until barely tender, about 3 minutes; stir into sauce. Serve sauce over hot cooked pasta. Pass grated Parmesan.

*TIP: *Recipe can be prepared to this point up to 1 week in advance. Store covered in refrigerator or freezer. Skim off excess fat. Heat to boiling; reduce heat and cover. Simmer 10 minutes; proceed with step 3.*

WHITE CLAM SAUCE

Makes 1½ cups

2	**dozen littleneck clams**
1	**tablespoon chopped shallot or green onion**
1	**teaspoon chopped garlic**
½	**cup olive or vegetable oil**
¼	**cup dry white wine or bottled clam juice**
¼	**teaspoon crushed red pepper**
1	**to 1½ teaspoons cornstarch**
2	**tablespoons cold water**
2	**tablespoons snipped fresh parsley**
2	**tablespoons freshly grated Parmesan cheese**
1	**tablespoon butter or margarine, softened**
	Hot cooked Homemade Pasta (see recipe, page 188)
	Freshly grated Parmesan cheese

1. Scrub clams under cold water. Place in 2-quart saucepan; cover. Cook over medium heat until shells open, 3 to 5 minutes; cool. Shuck clams into small bowl; pour pan juices over clams.*

2. Sauté shallot and garlic in oil in 10-inch skillet over low heat until tender, about 5 minutes. Stir in wine and red pepper. Heat to boiling; boil until liquid is reduced by half. Remove from heat.

3. Chop clams and reserve. Pour juice from clams through cheesecloth-lined sieve to measure ⅔ cup; stir juice into wine mixture. Heat to boiling; boil until liquid is reduced by half. Dissolve cornstarch in 2 tablespoons cold water; stir into sauce. Cook and stir until thickened, about 1 minute.

4. Stir clams, parsley, 2 tablespoons Parmesan and the butter into sauce. Cook and stir until Parmesan is melted, about 1 minute. Serve sauce immediately over hot cooked pasta. Pass additional Parmesan.

*TIP: *Recipe can be prepared to this point up to 6 hours in advance. Store covered in refrigerator. Proceed with step 2.*

SHRIMP AND ARTICHOKE SAUCE

Makes 3½ cups

2	**ounces bacon, chopped (about ⅓ cup)**
¼	**cup chopped onion**
2	**tablespoons butter or margarine**
1	**cup whipping cream**
1	**package (8 or 9 ounces) frozen artichoke hearts, thawed, halved**
½	**cup canned tomatoes, undrained, chopped**
1	**teaspoon dried basil leaves or dried marjoram leaves, crumbled**
½	**teaspoon salt**
¼	**teaspoon ground nutmeg**
⅛	**teaspoon freshly ground black pepper**
4	**ounces cooked small shrimp or 1 can (4½ ounces) tiny shrimp, drained**
	Hot cooked Homemade Pasta (see recipe, page 188)
	Freshly grated Parmesan cheese

1. Sauté bacon and onion in butter in 2-quart saucepan over medium heat until bacon is barely crisp, 3 to 5 minutes. Stir remaining ingredients except shrimp, pasta and Parmesan into bacon mixture. Heat to boiling; reduce heat. Simmer uncovered until artichokes are tender and sauce is thickened, 8 to 10 minutes.*

2. Stir shrimp into artichoke mixture. Heat until hot. Serve sauce over hot cooked pasta. Pass grated Parmesan.

*TIP: *Recipe can be prepared to this point up to 6 hours in advance. Store covered in refrigerator. Heat to boiling; reduce heat and cover. Simmer 10 minutes. Proceed with step 2.*

ZUCCHINI-BASIL SAUCE

Makes 3 cups

2	**tablespoons vegetable oil**
1	**pound zucchini (about 3 medium), unpared, cut into sticks 2 x ⅛ inch each**

1. Heat 1 tablespoon of the oil in 10-inch skillet over medium heat. Sauté half the zucchini sticks in oil until golden, about 3 minutes. Remove with slotted spoon; drain on paper toweling. Repeat procedure with 1 tablespoon oil and remaining zucchini.

3   tablespoons butter or margarine
3   tablespoons vegetable oil
2   teaspoons flour
⅔   cup milk

¾   cup freshly grated Parmesan
     cheese
3   tablespoons butter or margarine,
     softened
1   egg yolk, slightly beaten
1   teaspoon dried basil leaves,
     crumbled
¼   teaspoon salt
     Hot cooked Homemade Pasta
     (see recipe, page 188)
     Freshly grated Parmesan cheese

2. Heat 3 tablespoons butter and 3 tablespoons oil in same skillet over medium heat. Dissolve flour in milk; stir into skillet. Cook and stir until thickened, about 1 minute.

3. Stir zucchini, ¾ cup Parmesan, 3 tablespoons butter, the egg yolk, basil and salt into sauce. Stir until Parmesan is melted and sauce is smooth, about 1 minute. Serve sauce immediately over hot cooked pasta. Pass additional Parmesan.

TOMATO-VEGETABLE SAUCE   *Makes 5 cups*

2   cans (28 ounces each) Italian-
     style plum tomatoes, undrained,
     cut into small pieces
1   cup minced onion
1   cup minced celery
⅔   cup minced carrots
½   cup snipped fresh parsley
1   bay leaf
2   teaspoons dried marjoram leaves,
     crumbled
1½ teaspoons sugar
1   teaspoon salt
1   teaspoon dried thyme leaves,
     crumbled
½   teaspoon dried basil leaves,
     crumbled
⅛   teaspoon freshly ground black
     pepper
     Hot cooked Homemade Pasta
     (see recipe, page 188)
     Freshly grated Parmesan cheese

Measure all ingredients except pasta and Parmesan into 3-quart saucepan. Heat to boiling; reduce heat and partially cover. Simmer, stirring occasionally, 1 hour; uncover. Simmer, stirring occasionally, until thickened, 1 to 1½ hours. Remove bay leaf. Serve sauce over hot cooked pasta. Pass grated Parmesan.

TIP: Sauce can be made up to 1 week in advance. Store covered in refrigerator or freezer. Heat to boiling; reduce heat and cover. Simmer 10 minutes before serving.

COLD TOMATO-SWEET PEPPER SAUCE   *Makes 3½ cups*

1½ pounds tomatoes (about 4
     medium), coarsely chopped
1   medium green pepper, seeded,
     chopped
1   teaspoon salt
1   teaspoon dried basil leaves,
     crumbled
1   teaspoon chopped garlic
⅛   teaspoon freshly ground black
     pepper
½   cup olive or vegetable oil
¼   cup freshly grated Parmesan
     cheese
     Hot cooked Homemade Pasta
     (see recipe, page 188)
     Freshly grated Parmesan cheese

Measure half each of the tomatoes and green pepper, the salt, basil, garlic and black pepper into blender container. Add ¼ cup of the oil; cover. Blend until smooth, about 30 seconds. Transfer to medium-size bowl. Blend remaining tomatoes, green pepper and oil until smooth; add to mixture in bowl. Stir in ¼ cup Parmesan; cover. Refrigerate at least 3 hours.* Serve sauce cold over hot cooked pasta. Pass additional Parmesan.

*TIP: *Sauce can be made up to 2 days in advance. Store covered in refrigerator.*

PESTO SAUCE

2   cups packed torn fresh
    spinach
½   cup snipped fresh parsley
3   tablespoons toasted pine nuts
    or toasted chopped walnuts
2   cloves garlic, sliced
2   teaspoons dried basil leaves,
    crumbled
½   teaspoon salt
¾   cup olive or vegetable oil
¾   cup freshly grated Parmesan
    cheese
3   tablespoons butter or margarine,
    softened
    Hot cooked Homemade Pasta
    (see recipe, page 188)

Measure spinach, parsley, nuts, garlic, basil and salt into blender container. Pour oil over mixture; cover. Blend 20 seconds; remove cover. Push mixture into blades using rubber spatula; cover. Blend until smooth, about 25 seconds. Do not overblend. Transfer to bowl; stir in Parmesan and softened butter. Serve sauce at room temperature over hot cooked pasta.

TIPS: Sauce can be made up to 1 week in advance. Store covered in refrigerator. Bring to room temperature before serving. If sauce is too thick, stir in 1 or 2 teaspoons hot water.

If recipe is doubled, blend mixture in 2 batches.

ORANGE PICO SALAD

4   oranges, peeled, sliced, seeded,
    drained (reserve juice)
1   cucumber (about 10 ounces),
    unpared, thinly sliced
6   cups torn fresh spinach
    (about 1½ pounds)
2   heads (about 4 ounces each)
    Bibb lettuce, torn
1   small red onion, sliced, separated
    into rings
½   cup coarsely chopped toasted
    walnuts

½   cup vegetable oil
2   tablespoons cider vinegar
1½ teaspoons sugar
¼   teaspoon salt
⅛   teaspoon freshly ground
    black pepper

1. Arrange several orange and cucumber slices alternately around side of chilled, large, glass salad bowl. Arrange spinach, Bibb lettuce, remaining orange and cucumber slices, the onion rings and walnuts in layers in bowl.

2. Measure reserved orange juice and remaining ingredients into jar with tight-fitting lid; cover and shake.* Just before serving, pour dressing over salad; toss.

*TIP: *Recipe can be prepared to this point up to 4 hours in advance. Store salad and dressing covered, separately, in refrigerator. Just before serving, toss salad with dressing.*

SPICED COFFEE ICE

2   cups water
1   cup granulated sugar
4   whole allspice
1   quart boiling water
½   cup instant espresso coffee
    powder

1   cup whipping cream
2   tablespoons powdered sugar
    Almond-flavored liqueur
    (optional)

1. Measure 2 cups water, the granulated sugar and allspice into 3-quart saucepan. Heat to boiling; boil, stirring occasionally, until a light syrup is formed, about 8 minutes. Discard allspice. Mix the boiling water and coffee powder; stir into syrup and cool. Pour mixture into 2 to 3 ice cube trays with dividers; freeze overnight.

2. Measure coffee cubes, 3 at a time, into blender container; cover. Blend until coarse crystals are formed, about 30 seconds. Transfer to bowl. (Keep bowl in freezer while blending remaining cubes.) Measure ¼ of the crystals at a time into blender container; blend until smooth and dark brown, about 30 seconds. Do not overblend. Transfer to bowl; cover and freeze until consistency of firm sherbet, about 2 hours.*

3. Scoop about ⅔ cup of the coffee ice into each of 12 chilled dessert dishes or stemmed glasses; freeze until firm, about 30 minutes, or overnight.

Spiced Coffee Ice with a hint of almond makes an elegant light dessert.

4. Just before serving, beat whipping cream and powdered sugar in chilled small bowl until mixture forms stiff peaks. Drizzle 1 to 2 tablespoons of the almond-flavored liqueur over each serving of coffee ice.** Top each with dollop of whipped cream. Serve immediately.

TIPS: *Recipe can be prepared to this point up to 2 days in advance. Let stand at room temperature until consistency of firm sherbet, about 10 minutes. Proceed with step 3.

**Almond-flavored liqueur can be served in cordial glasses on the side, if desired.

A Quebec Feast

Ice sculptures in Quebec.

QUEBEC DINNER MENU

- **GALANTINE OF PORK**

- **GLAZED DUCKLINGS**
- **RICE CANADIAN**
- **SPINACH WITH ONIONS**
- **ENDIVE SALAD WITH LEMON
    DRESSING**
  BREAD AND BUTTER

- **SUGAR PIE**
  COFFEE

• Recipes included

Views of Quebec city's historical old section (above and below).

Canada's *"belle province,"* Quebec, enjoys many outstanding culinary traditions. The oldest is French — brought there by settlers in the early 1600s. Our dinner selections team the flavors of France with some favorite Canadian foods.

With a definite French flair, Galantine of Pork makes an elegant molded first course. Duck is popular in Quebec. And the duckling here is highlighted by orange — a hint of the entrée's French origins. But a measure of pure maple syrup in the glaze is a special Canadian touch.

Rice Canadian features mushrooms, celery and onion in a sturdy brown and wild rice blend. Another accompaniment for the duckling garnishes fresh cooked spinach with green onions. On the salad, a spirited Lemon Dressing adds zest to endive, watercress and spinach.

For the dinner's finale, set out a distinctive Quebec sweet — Sugar Pie. This cream and brown sugar spectacular will be an unforgettable treat for your diners. Serves 6.

Wine Suggestion: Gewürztraminer from Trimbach or Mirassou will go well with the pork. With the duckling, try to find a good bottle of Chambertin. Or enjoy a fine Pinot Noir from Hanzell.

194

Present Galantine of Pork as the dinner's first course.

PARTY PLAN FOR QUEBEC DINNER MENU

1 Day Before:	Prepare Galantine of Pork through step 2 in recipe. Prepare Endive Salad with Lemon Dressing through step 1 in recipe; refrigerate.
That Afternoon:	Complete step 2 of Endive Salad with Lemon Dressing recipe. Make Sugar Pie; let cool. Store loosely covered with aluminum foil at room temperature. Measure and label ingredients for remaining recipes; refrigerate perishables.
3 Hours Before Serving:	Make Glazed Ducklings.
1 Hour 15 Minutes Before Serving:	Make Rice Canadian.
20 Minutes Before Serving:	Make Spinach with Onions. Complete Galantine of Pork. Complete Endive Salad with Lemon Dressing.
15 Minutes Before Dessert:	Heat Sugar Pie at 350° 15 minutes.

GALANTINE OF PORK*

Makes 6 servings

1	pork shoulder roast (2 to 2½ pounds)
1	pork hock (1 to 1½ pounds)
¾	cup chopped onion
2	teaspoons coarse salt
1	clove garlic, chopped
½	teaspoon dried savory leaves
⅛	teaspoon ground cloves
½	cup water
¼	cup warm tea (105° to 115°)
	Lemon slices, if desired
	Celery leaves, if desired

Heat oven to 325°

1. Place pork roast, pork hock, onion, salt, garlic, savory and cloves in Dutch oven. Bake uncovered 2 hours. Add water; bake covered 1 hour. Refrigerate covered until cold.

2. Remove meat from bones. Break meat into 1-inch pieces. Pass pork hock skin through fine blade of meat grinder. Combine meat, ground skin and onion; spoon into 1-quart mold. Remove solidified fat from pan juices. Stir warm tea into pan juices. Work tea mixture into meat mixture with fork gradually. Refrigerate covered until set, at least 4 hours.

3. Unmold galantine onto serving platter; garnish with lemon slices and celery leaves.

GLAZED DUCKLINGS*

Makes 6 servings

3	ducklings (4½ to 5 pounds each)
	Salt
	Pepper
¼	teaspoon rosemary or sage leaves
¼	cup orange juice
¼	cup pure maple or maple- flavored syrup
1	cup orange juice
1	cup black currant jelly
1	cup beef broth
1	tablespoon grated fresh gingerroot or ½ teaspoon ground ginger
1	teaspoon curry powder
¼	teaspoon ground nutmeg
	Orange slices, if desired
	Watercress, if desired

Heat oven to 400°

1. Rinse ducklings with cold water; pat dry on paper toweling. Sprinkle cavity and skin of ducklings with salt and pepper; rub cavity with rosemary. Place ducklings on rack in roasting pan; bake 15 to 20 minutes. Drain fat. Reduce oven temperature to 350°; bake until thigh moves easily, about 2 hours. Mix ¼ cup orange juice and the maple syrup. During last 30 minutes of cooking time, baste ducklings with orange juice mixture every 5 minutes.

2. Remove ducklings to serving platter; keep warm. Drain all but 2 tablespoons of the pan juices. Stir in remaining ingredients except orange slices and watercress. Simmer over low heat, stirring constantly, until sauce is smooth, about 15 minutes. Pour ¼ cup of the sauce over ducklings; garnish with orange slices and watercress. Pass remaining sauce.

RICE CANADIAN

Makes 6 servings

1	cup uncooked brown rice
1	cup uncooked wild rice*
1	cup chopped onion
1	cup sliced celery
½	cup butter or margarine
1	pound fresh mushrooms, sliced
1	quart chicken broth
¼	cup snipped fresh parsley
½	teaspoon salt
¼	teaspoon dried thyme leaves
	Pepper

Heat brown and wild rice, onion, celery and butter uncovered in 2-quart saucepan over medium heat, stirring frequently, 5 minutes. Stir in remaining ingredients; simmer covered, stirring occasionally, 1 hour.

*TIP: *1 cup additional brown rice can be substituted for the wild rice.*

This table of delicacies features Glazed Ducklings, Spinach with Onions, Rice Canadian, and lemon-sparked endive salad.

In the maple syrup country of Quebec.

SPINACH WITH ONIONS

Makes 6 servings

10	green onions with 2-inch tops
3	tablespoons chopped onion
½	teaspoon salt
¼	teaspoon white pepper
½	cup butter or margarine
3	pounds fresh spinach, stems removed, torn into 2-inch pieces

Cut green onions lengthwise in half. Cook in 1 inch lightly salted boiling water 1 minute; drain and reserve. Sauté chopped onion with salt and pepper in butter in small skillet over low heat until transparent, about 5 minutes. Meanwhile, cook spinach with water that clings to leaves from washing covered in Dutch oven over medium heat 3 minutes; drain. Spoon spinach onto serving platter. Pour chopped onion mixture over spinach; toss. Garnish with reserved green onions.

ENDIVE SALAD WITH LEMON DRESSING

Makes 6 servings (about 1 cup each)

Lemon Dressing (recipe follows)

6	large heads Belgian endive
2	cups loosely packed watercress, stems trimmed to 2 inches
4	cups loosely packed torn fresh spinach

1. Make Lemon Dressing.

2. Separate endive leaves; trim and reserve hearts. Arrange 1½ cups of the watercress on bottom of large bowl. Beginning with largest leaves and overlapping slightly, arrange half the endive leaves over watercress, with tips of leaves toward rim of bowl. Arrange 3 cups of the spinach over endive; arrange remaining endive leaves over spinach. Arrange remaining watercress over endive. Chop reserved endive hearts; combine with remaining spinach in small bowl. Sprinkle spinach mixture over salad. Refrigerate covered until cold.

3. Just before serving, pour Lemon Dressing over salad.

LEMON DRESSING

Makes ½ cup

Place all ingredients in jar with tight-fitting lid; cover and shake.

¼	cup olive or vegetable oil
2	tablespoons lemon juice
1	tablespoon tarragon-flavored white wine vinegar
1	teaspoon salt
¼	teaspoon dry mustard
¼	teaspoon sugar
¼	teaspoon freshly ground white pepper

Sugar Pie is the sensational conclusion of the Quebec repast.

SUGAR PIE

Makes 6 to 8 servings

Pie Pastry (recipe follows)

2½ cups packed brown sugar
¾ cup all-purpose flour
1 cup whipping cream
1 egg, slightly beaten

1 tablespoon butter or margarine,
    melted
    Whipping cream

1½ cups all-purpose flour
1 teaspoon salt
⅓ cup lard
4 to 5 tablespoons cold water

Heat oven to 350°

1. Make Pie Pastry.

2. Increase oven temperature to 400°. Mix sugar and flour in 2-quart saucepan. Mix 1 cup cream and the egg in small bowl; stir into sugar mixture. Heat sugar mixture over medium heat, stirring constantly, just until sugar is dissolved, 3 to 5 minutes. Pour into prepared pastry.

3. Gather reserved pastry trimmings into ball. Shape into flattened round. Roll dough ¼ inch thick on lightly floured surface. Cut pastry into ten ½-inch strips; arrange in lattice pattern over filling. Brush strips with melted butter. Bake 15 minutes. Serve pie warm with whipping cream.

PIE PASTRY

1. Mix flour and salt in medium-size bowl; cut in lard until mixture resembles coarse crumbs. Sprinkle with cold water, 2 tablespoons at a time, mixing with fork until all flour is moistened and dough almost cleans side of bowl. Gather dough into ball.

2. Shape dough into flattened round. Roll dough on lightly floured surface into 11-inch circle. Fold pastry into quarters; unfold and ease into 9-inch pie plate. Trim overhanging edge 1 inch larger than plate; reserve pastry trimmings. Flute edges of pastry; pierce bottom and side with fork. Bake until pastry is golden, about 10 minutes.

*Reprinted, by permission, from *The Canadiana Cookbook*, © 1970 Pagurian Press Limited.

A Country French Buffet

LE BUFFET CAMPAGNARD MENU

- **FRESH VEGETABLES WITH VINAIGRETTE**

  RACK OF SAUSAGES
  PROSCIUTTO HAM
- **POTTED MINCED PORK**
- **TERRINE OF CHICKEN LIVERS**
- **BUTCHER-STYLE LIVER PATE**
- **GALANTINE OF VEAL AND PORK**

  ASSORTED CHEESES

- **MARINATED ONIONS**
- **MIXED VEGETABLES**
  SOUR PICKLES
- **MAYONNAISE WITH HERBS**
  DIJON-STYLE MUSTARD
  COARSE SALT

  WHOLE GRAIN BREADS
  TUB OF BUTTER

200   **FRUIT JUICES, CIDER OR WINE**

• Recipes included

Parisians are looking to the provinces for the latest inspiration in casual entertaining. *Le buffet campagnard,* or country buffet, has recently become a popular party idea in the fashionable city. It's a charming and economical way to serve even large groups stylishly.

The buffet is easy to set up. A long table covered with a gay rough cloth is the groaning board for bountiful country fare. Dishes and flatware are at a minimum, since guests help themselves, using healthy slices of whole grain breads as plates.

The "centerpiece" is a huge bouquet of *crudités.* These colorful vegetables are ripe and waiting to be picked and dipped in a light vinaigrette or herbed mayonnaise. Flanking the vegetables are a rack of European sausages and a wood paddle strewn with prosciutto ham — both spectacular means of presenting cold meats.

Our menu provides the special French country flavor with hearty dishes typical of a rural feast: pork liver pâté, rillettes (bits of pork slow cooked in their own fat), Galantine of Veal and Pork, and Terrine of Chicken Livers. Condiments, such as Marinated Onions and piquant Mixed Vegetables, along with coarse salt, mustard and pickles, are laid out in earthenware bowls to accent the spread. The dairy's contributions are cheeses and a quaint tub of butter. Instead of expensive liquors, diners quench their thirsts with fruit juices and cider in pitchers and jugs, and wine drawn from a keg. Serves 16 to 20.

Wine Suggestion: An imaginative country buffet such as this requires a choice of red or white wine. The red might be a Gamay Beaujolais from Monterey Vineyard, or a Beaujolais Villages by Louis Jadot. And for the white, try Gold Seal's celebrated Pinot Chardonnay, or the Sylvaner from Trimbach.

Crisp fresh vegetables are surrounded by such French country fare as pork liver pâté, Terrine of Chicken Livers, herbed mayonnaise, Marinated Onions, Mixed Vegetables, Galantine of Veal and Pork, and rillettes.

PARTY PLAN FOR LE BUFFET CAMPAGNARD MENU

1 Week Before:	Prepare Butcher-Style Liver Pâté through step 4 in recipe. Prepare Potted Minced Pork through step 4 in recipe.
3 Days Before:	Make Mixed Vegetables. Make Marinated Onions. Prepare Terrine of Chicken Livers through step 4 in recipe.
1 Day Before:	Make Mayonnaise with Herbs. Prepare Galantine of Veal and Pork through step 5 in recipe. Prepare Fresh Vegetables with Vinaigrette through step 1 in recipe.
That Afternoon:	Complete steps 6, 7 and 8 of Galantine of Veal and Pork recipe. Assemble condiments for menu; refrigerate perishable ingredients. Slice ham, if serving; refrigerate covered.
1 Hour Before Serving:	Complete Terrine of Chicken Livers. Complete Potted Minced Pork. Complete Galantine of Veal and Pork. Complete Butcher-Style Liver Pâté. Complete Fresh Vegetables with Vinaigrette. Arrange ham, sausages, cheeses, breads and condiments on table.

FRESH VEGETABLES WITH VINAIGRETTE (Crudités au Vinaigrette)　　　*Makes about 2 cups dressing*

1½ cups vegetable or olive oil
¼ cup plus 2 tablespoons white
　　wine vinegar
2 tablespoons lemon juice
1 teaspoon dry mustard
½ teaspoon salt
⅛ teaspoon freshly ground pepper
3 tablespoons snipped fresh
　　parsley
1 tablespoon snipped fresh chives
　　or green onion tops

Assorted fresh vegetables
　　(radishes, green and red
　　peppers, carrots, artichokes, red
　　cabbage, fennel, endive, cauli-
　　flower, cherry tomatoes, cucum-
　　bers, celery, onions)

1.　Measure oil, vinegar, lemon juice, mustard, salt and pepper in large jar with tight-fitting lid; cover. Shake vigorously until blended. Stir in parsley and chives. Refrigerate covered at least 3 hours or overnight.

2.　Arrange assorted vegetables on large tiered serving platter or as shown in photo on pages 200-201. Serve with vinaigrette dressing.

TIP: Vegetables are also excellent dipped into Mayonnaise with Herbs (see recipe on page 205).

POTTED MINCED PORK (Rillettes de Tours)　　　*Makes about 1 quart*

2 pounds boneless pork
　　Salt

1½ pounds pork suet
1 bay leaf
1 teaspoon dried thyme leaves
1 teaspoon dried chervil leaves
1 clove garlic, crushed
3 whole cloves
1 teaspoon salt
⅛ teaspoon pepper

1.　Arrange pork in 1 layer in shallow dish. Sprinkle both sides generously with salt; cover. Refrigerate overnight.

2.　Drain pork; pat dry on paper toweling. Cut pork and suet into thin strips, about 2 x 1 x ½ inch each. Tie remaining ingredients except 1 teaspoon salt and the pepper in cheesecloth bag. Place pork, suet and spice bag in Dutch oven; sprinkle with 1 teaspoon salt and the pepper.

3.　Cook mixture uncovered over medium-low heat, stirring occasionally, until most of the suet is rendered and meat is tender, but still soft, 2 to 2½ hours. Remove from heat. Drain mixture through sieve; reserve fat. Discard spice bag and unrendered suet.

4.　Pull meat strips apart with 2 forks until finely shredded. Place in 1-quart terrine or individual earthenware crocks, leaving about 1-inch headspace. Pour strained fat over meat, sealing completely; cover with plastic wrap. Refrigerate at least 1 day before serving.

5.　One hour before serving, let rillettes stand at room temperature to soften. Serve with knife for spreading on bread.

TIP: Leftover rillettes can be stored covered with additional fat or plastic wrap in refrigerator up to 3 weeks.

Crudités, **prosciutto ham and a medley of terrines and pâtés highlight the feast.**

TERRINE OF CHICKEN LIVERS (Terrine de Foies de Volaille)
Makes 10 servings (about ¼ cup each)

5   **ounces unsmoked unsalted bacon (fatback), rind removed***

10 **ounces chicken livers, veins removed**

1   **bay leaf**

2   **tablespoons minced shallots**

¾   **teaspoon dried thyme leaves**

½   **teaspoon salt**
     Dash pepper

½   **cup port, cognac or Madeira**

½   **cup butter or margarine, softened**

3   **egg whites**

5   **to 7 thin slices unsmoked unsalted bacon, rind removed, if desired**

1.   Dice 5 ounces bacon; cook in 10-inch skillet over medium heat until fat is rendered, about 10 minutes. Stir in chicken livers, bay leaf, shallots, thyme, salt and pepper; sauté until livers are barely pink in center, about 5 minutes. Drain; discard fat and bay leaf.

2.   Place liver mixture and port in medium-size bowl; cover. Let stand at room temperature about 1 hour. Force liver-wine mixture through sieve or food mill, or pass through fine blade of meat grinder, until smooth.

3.   Beat butter until light and fluffy. Beat egg whites in small mixer bowl until almost stiff (whites should be firm but still soft). Beat butter into liver mixture gradually until light and fluffy; fold in egg whites gradually.

4.   Line 1-quart terrine, loaf pan or decorative ceramic bowl with bacon slices. Spoon pâté into terrine, smoothing top with rubber spatula. Cover with plastic wrap, pressing to surface of mixture. Refrigerate at least 1 day before serving.

5.   One hour before serving, let pâté stand at room temperature to soften; remove plastic wrap. Serve with spoon dipped into hot water.

*TIPS: *Regular smoked bacon can be substituted for the unsmoked bacon. Heat bacon in water to cover to boiling; reduce heat. Simmer 10 minutes to remove salt and smoked flavor. Drain and rinse under cold water; pat dry on paper toweling. Proceed with step 1.*

Leftover pâté can be stored covered securely with plastic wrap in refrigerator up to 1 week.

BUTCHER-STYLE LIVER PATE (Pâté de Foie des Charcutiers)
Makes 16 servings

1   **pound unsmoked unsalted bacon (fatback), rind removed***

12 **ounces pork liver**

8   **ounces pork suet**

½   **cup minced onion**

1   **tablespoon butter or margarine**

1   **teaspoon salt**

1   **teaspoon dried thyme leaves**

¾   **teaspoon ground nutmeg**

½   **teaspoon pepper**

1   **bay leaf, crumbled**

1.   Cut 1 pound bacon, the pork liver and suet into small pieces. Pass mixture twice through fine blade of meat grinder until smooth.

2.   Sauté onion in butter in small skillet over medium heat until golden, about 5 minutes. Stir onion mixture, the salt, thyme, nutmeg, pepper and crumbled bay leaf into pork mixture. Stir in eggs and flour until smooth.

3.   Line 2-quart terrine, deep casserole or loaf pan with about 5 bacon slices. Spoon pork mixture into terrine, smoothing top with rubber spatula. Cover mixture with remaining bacon slices. Decorate with bay leaf and cloves; cover with terrine lid or aluminum foil.

2   eggs
1   tablespoon flour

8   to 10 thin slices unsmoked
       unsalted bacon, rind
       removed
1   bay leaf, if desired
     Whole cloves or peppercorns,
       if desired

     Parsley sprigs, if desired

4.   Place terrine on rack in Dutch oven. Pour hot water into Dutch oven, filling ⅔ up side of terrine; cover. Heat to boiling; reduce heat. Simmer, adding more hot water as necessary, until knife inserted into center of pâté comes out clean and meat juices flow clear, about 1 hour and 15 minutes. Remove terrine from water; cool slightly. Refrigerate covered at least 1 day before serving.

5.   To serve, remove pâté from terrine; scrape off surrounding fat, if desired. Place pâté on serving platter and slice thinly. Decorate with parsley sprigs.**

TIPS: *Regular smoked bacon can be substituted for the unsmoked bacon. Heat bacon in water to cover to boiling; reduce heat. Simmer 10 minutes to remove salt and smoked flavor. Drain and rinse under cold water. Proceed with step 1.

**Pâté can be surrounded with cubed aspic jelly (see recipe for Galantine of Veal and Pork below).

Leftover pâté can be stored covered securely with plastic wrap in refrigerator up to 10 days.

GALANTINE OF VEAL AND PORK (Galantine de Veau et de Porc)   *Makes 16 servings*

1   pound boneless pork
1   pound unsmoked unsalted
       bacon (fatback), rind
       removed*
12   ounces boneless veal or
       boneless skinned chicken

⅓   cup cognac or brandy
1½   teaspoons salt
½   teaspoon pepper
¼   teaspoon ground ginger
¼   teaspoon ground nutmeg
¼   teaspoon ground cinnamon
¼   teaspoon ground cloves
2   eggs

8   cups chicken broth

1   cup dry white wine

2   egg whites

2   to 3 envelopes unflavored
       gelatin
1   to 1½ cups cold water

1.   Cut pork, bacon and veal into small pieces. Pass mixture twice through fine blade of meat grinder until smooth.

2.   Stir cognac, salt, pepper, ginger, nutmeg, cinnamon and cloves into meat mixture; stir in eggs until smooth. Place mixture on center of large square cheesecloth; fold ends up and press and squeeze mixture into firm ball. Tie cheesecloth closed to hold shape.

3.   Place wrapped ball in Dutch oven; add chicken broth and cover. Heat to boiling; reduce heat. Simmer gently until meat is tender and juices flow clear when meat is pierced, 2½ to 3 hours.

4.   Remove ball from broth; place on rack over bowl to drain, about 30 minutes. Wrap ball in clean kitchen towel; place in bowl and cover with a light weight. Refrigerate overnight.

5.   Add wine to broth in Dutch oven. Heat to boiling; boil until broth is reduced to 6 cups, 20 to 30 minutes. Cool slightly; cover and refrigerate overnight.

6.   Skim fat from broth and discard. Beat 1 cup of the broth with the egg whites in large bowl with wire whisk until foamy. Heat remaining broth to boiling; pour into egg white mixture gradually, stirring constantly. Return mixture to 2-quart saucepan; heat until mixture begins to boil. Reduce heat to low; simmer gently, stirring occasionally, until egg whites and sediment float to surface, 10 to 15 minutes.

7.   Ladle broth gently through cheesecloth into clean bowl. Measure clarified broth and return to clean saucepan; heat to simmering. Sprinkle 1 envelope (1 tablespoon) unflavored gelatin for each 2 cups broth into ½ cup cold water. Let stand 5 minutes; stir into simmering broth until dissolved.

8. Place saucepan in bowl of water and ice; stir aspic occasionally until it begins to thicken. Pour into clean jelly-roll pan, 15½ x 10½ x 1 inch. Refrigerate until firm, about 1½ hours.

9. To serve, remove towel and cheesecloth from galantine; place on serving platter and cut a few thin slices. Cut aspic jelly into small cubes; arrange around galantine on platter.**

TIPS: *Regular smoked bacon can be substituted for the unsmoked bacon. Heat bacon in water to cover to boiling; reduce heat. Simmer 10 minutes to remove salt and smoked flavor. Drain and rinse under cold water. Proceed with step 1.

**Leftover aspic jelly can be used to decorate other terrines and pâtés.

MARINATED ONIONS (Petits Oignons Marinés)　　　　　　　Makes about 1½ pints

1　pound tiny white boiling onions
1½　cups white wine vinegar

Heat onions in water to cover to boiling; reduce heat and cover. Simmer until onions are barely tender, about 10 minutes; drain. Pack in clean glass jars; pour vinegar over. Screw lids in place; refrigerate at least 2 days before serving.

TIPS: Marinated Onions can be stored covered in refrigerator indefinitely without change in flavor or texture.

One large jar commercially prepared marinated or pickled pearl onions can be substituted for the above recipe.

MIXED VEGETABLES (Variante de Légumes)　　　　　　　Makes about 1 quart

2　cups white wine vinegar
1　bay leaf
1　teaspoon dried thyme leaves
4　cups sliced or chunked mixed raw vegetables (carrots, turnips, celery, cauliflower, pearl onions, fennel, pimiento)

Heat vinegar, bay leaf and thyme in small saucepan to boiling; pour over vegetables in clean glass jars or medium-size bowl. Screw lids in place or cover. Refrigerate at least 2 days before serving.

TIP: Mixed Vegetables can be stored covered in refrigerator up to 10 days without change in flavor or texture.

MAYONNAISE WITH HERBS (Mayonnaise aux Fines Herbes)　　　　　Makes about 2 cups

2　cups mayonnaise or salad dressing
2　tablespoons snipped fresh chives or green onion tops
1　tablespoon dried chervil leaves

Mix mayonnaise, chives and chervil in small bowl until smooth; cover and refrigerate at least 3 hours or overnight. Serve as sauce for sausages and dip for fresh vegetables.

A Tunisian Temptation

Grilled Shrimp with Sauce Kerkennaise makes a savory beginning for dinner.

TUNISIAN DINNER MENU

- **GRILLED SHRIMP WITH SAUCE KERKENNAISE**
  OR
- **PASTRY TRIANGLES STUFFED WITH EGG AND TUNA**

- **CHICKEN WITH STUFFED OLIVES**
- **TUNISIAN EGGPLANT SALAD WITH ROASTED PEPPER STRIPS**
  FRENCH BREAD

- **TUNISIAN CREAM SWEET**
  ORANGES WITH POMEGRANATE SEEDS
  FRESH DATES
- **MINT TEA**

• Recipes included

Tunisia is an exotic blend of many cultures built upon the ruins of ancient history. This small strip of North Africa holds vestiges of Carthage, the Phoenicians and Roman rule. But the Berbers, Arabs, Andalusians, Turks and French who settled there have also shaped the land — and created an excitingly unique cuisine from its rich resources.

Our Tunisian dinner party begins with a choice between country and cosmopolitan delicacies. Broiled shrimp served with zestful Sauce Kerkennaise is a first course from the Mediterranean shores. Or you might try a *brik* — tuna and a whole egg hidden in a crisp fillo crust — like those sold in the bustling streets of Tunis.

The entrée combines boned chicken breasts with a rousing potpourri of spices, plus onions, potatoes, Chicken Meatballs and olives, one of Tunisia's major crops. Highly prized coriander and red pepper spark a salad of baked eggplant, tomatoes and green peppers.

After these exuberant flavor experiences, the dessert course is delicate and cooling. Tunisian Cream Sweet is a thin custard with a hint of rose water and a sprinkling of sugar and ground almonds. Orange segments with pomegranate seeds, fresh dates and soothing Mint Tea complete the luxurious repast. Serves 8.

Wine Suggestion: For your appetizer, I recommend a fine Chenin Blanc from Almadén, or a dry white Pouilly-Fumé by Ladoucette. With the entrée, change to a pleasantly chilled rosé — Paul Masson's Vin Rosé Sec, for example, or the Tavel from Domaine de Longval.

206

PARTY PLAN FOR TUNISIAN DINNER MENU

1 Day Before:	Prepare Tunisian Eggplant Salad with Roasted Pepper Strips through step 4 in recipe; cover and refrigerate. Prepare Chicken with Stuffed Olives through step 4 in recipe. Prepare Tunisian Cream Sweet through step 1 in recipe.
That Afternoon:	If serving Grilled Shrimp with Sauce Kerkennaise, make sauce; cover and refrigerate.
45 Minutes Before Guests Arrive:	If serving Pastry Triangles Stuffed with Egg and Tuna, make triangles; bake 10 minutes before guests arrive. If serving Grilled Shrimp with Sauce Kerkennaise, prepare shrimp; broil 10 minutes before guests arrive.
45 Minutes Before Serving:	Complete Chicken with Stuffed Olives. Complete Tunisian Eggplant Salad with Roasted Pepper Strips.
15 Minutes Before Dessert:	Make Mint Tea. Complete Tunisian Cream Sweet.

GRILLED SHRIMP WITH SAUCE KERKENNAISE (Crevettes Grilles à la Kerkennaise)   *Makes 8 servings*

Sauce Kerkennaise (recipe
  follows)

3   pounds large shrimp, cleaned,
      deveined
    Olive or vegetable oil
    Salt
    Pepper

    Lime wedges
    Parsley sprigs, if desired

2   medium tomatoes, peeled,
      chopped (about 1½ cups)
⅓   cup olive or vegetable oil
¼   cup snipped fresh parsley
2   tablespoons minced green onion
1   clove garlic, crushed
1   teaspoon salt
½   teaspoon black pepper
½   teaspoon crushed red pepper
¼   teaspoon sugar

1. Make Sauce Kerkennaise.

2. Set oven control to broil and/or 550°. Dip shrimp in oil; season with salt and pepper. Thread shrimp on skewers. Broil 4 inches from heat until shrimp turn pink, 3 to 4 minutes on each side.

3. Remove shrimp from skewers. Arrange shrimp, lime wedges and small pot of Sauce Kerkennaise on individual serving dishes. Garnish with parsley sprigs.

SAUCE KERKENNAISE   *Makes about 2 cups*
Combine all ingredients; refrigerate.

PASTRY TRIANGLES STUFFED WITH EGG AND TUNA (Brik au Thon)   *Makes 8 servings*

8   fillo strudel leaves
1½ cups butter or margarine,
      melted

½   cup snipped fresh parsley
1   can (6½ ounces) tuna,
      drained, flaked
3   tablespoons minced green onion

1. Brush 1 fillo leaf with butter. Fold leaf into quarters, forming a rectangle, 8 x 6 inches. Fold in end to make a square. Brush with butter.

2. Arrange 1 tablespoon of the snipped parsley, 1½ tablespoons of the tuna and about 1 teaspoon of the onion in 1 corner of square, making a well in center of mixture. Slip 1 of the eggs into center of well. Brush edges of square with beaten egg.

Fillo pastries filled with egg and tuna are another first-course choice.

8	eggs*	
1	egg, slightly beaten	
	Lemon slices	
	Parsley sprigs, if desired	

3.   Heat oven to 525°. Fold fillo leaf over egg to form triangle, sealing edges. Brush with butter. Place triangle in buttered jelly-roll pan, 15½ x 10½ x 1 inch. Repeat procedure for remaining triangles.

4.   Bake triangles until light brown, 5 to 7 minutes. Serve hot with lemon slices. Garnish with parsley sprigs.

TIP: *Fresh grade AA large eggs should be used.*

CHICKEN WITH STUFFED OLIVES (Poulet aux Olives Farcies)   *Makes 8 servings*

	Chicken Meatballs (recipe follows)
4	whole chicken breasts, split, boned
	Salt
	Black pepper
½	teaspoon ground cumin
2	tablespoons olive or vegetable oil
2	tablespoons butter or margarine
⅓	cup olive or vegetable oil
⅓	cup butter or margarine
3	cups minced onions
¾	cup chopped pimiento-stuffed olives
½	cup snipped fresh parsley
3	cloves garlic, minced
2	tablespoons lemon juice
1	to 1½ teaspoons ground cumin
1	teaspoon salt
¾	teaspoon paprika
½	teaspoon crushed red pepper
½	teaspoon black pepper
¼	teaspoon sugar
32	pimiento-stuffed olives

1.   Make Chicken Meatballs.

2.   Sprinkle chicken breasts with salt, black pepper and ½ teaspoon cumin. Heat 2 tablespoons oil and 2 tablespoons butter in large skillet until hot. Brown chicken breasts in oil and butter; arrange in single layer in roasting pan.

3.   Brown Chicken Meatballs in oil and butter in skillet (add more oil, if necessary); place in roasting pan with chicken breasts. Heat ⅓ cup oil and ⅓ cup butter in skillet until hot. Sauté onions in oil mixture until tender.

4.   Stir remaining ingredients except 32 olives, potatoes and parsley into onions. Spoon onion mixture over chicken in roasting pan; add olives and cover.*

5.   Heat oven to 375°. Bake chicken 25 minutes; remove cover. Bake until hot, about 5 minutes longer. Arrange chicken breasts, meatballs and hot potatoes on platter. Spoon onion mixture over chicken. Garnish with parsley.

TIP: *Chicken with Stuffed Olives can be prepared to this point 24 hours in advance. Cover and refrigerate. Proceed with step 5, increasing baking time to 40 minutes.*

24 small new potatoes, cooked,
      pared
    Parsley, if desired

¾ pound ground cooked chicken
¼ cup fine bread crumbs
¼ cup snipped fresh parsley
1 egg, beaten
1 tablespoon water
1 tablespoon grated onion
¼ teaspoon salt
⅛ teaspoon pepper
⅛ teaspoon ground cumin

CHICKEN MEATBALLS   *Makes about 2 dozen*

Combine all ingredients. Shape into 1-inch balls.

The chicken entrée features olives, potatoes and a lively blend of spices.

TUNISIAN EGGPLANT SALAD WITH ROASTED PEPPER STRIPS (Salade d'Aubergines)   *Makes 8 servings*

Roasted Pepper Strips
  (recipe follows)

3   eggplants (about 1½ pounds
     each)
2½   teaspoons salt

6   cloves garlic, minced
1   large green pepper, cut
     into thirds
3   medium tomatoes, halved
     Olive or vegetable oil

⅓   cup olive or vegetable oil
1   tablespoon red wine vinegar
3   tablespoons crushed coriander
     seeds
2½   teaspoons salt
¾   teaspoon crushed red pepper

     Fresh coriander or parsley

3   green peppers
¼   cup olive or vegetable oil
1½   tablespoons red wine vinegar
½   teaspoon salt
¼   teaspoon black pepper
1   clove garlic, cut into quarters

1. Make Roasted Pepper Strips.

2. Cut each eggplant lengthwise into 6 wedges. Cut flesh diagonally almost to skin at 1-inch intervals. Sprinkle with 2½ teaspoons salt. Place eggplant flesh side down on paper toweling; let stand 30 minutes. Pat dry.

3. Increase oven temperature to 450°. Place garlic deep in slits in eggplant. Coat eggplant, green pepper and tomatoes generously with oil. Bake in lightly greased roasting pan until eggplant is tender, about 20 minutes.

4. Remove skin from eggplant. Mash eggplant gently with fork. Mince green pepper. Peel tomatoes; chop. Mix eggplant, green pepper, tomatoes, ⅓ cup oil, the vinegar, coriander seeds, 2½ teaspoons salt and the red pepper.

5. Mound eggplant mixture on individual serving plates; garnish with fresh coriander. Arrange Roasted Pepper Strips around salad.

ROASTED PEPPER STRIPS
1. Remove seeds from peppers; cut lengthwise into ¼-inch strips. Place peppers in baking dish, 13½ x 8¾ x 1¾ inches. Combine remaining ingredients; pour over peppers. Let stand, turning occasionally, at least 1 hour.

2. Heat oven to 375°. Bake peppers until crisp-tender, about 25 minutes.

TUNISIAN CREAM SWEET (Crème Tunisienne)   *Makes 8 servings (about ½ cup each)*

6   egg yolks
3   cups half-and-half
¾   cup sugar
⅛   teaspoon salt
2   tablespoons rose water

½   cup coarsely ground lightly
     toasted almonds
1   tablespoon sugar

1. Beat all ingredients except rose water, almonds and 1 tablespoon sugar in saucepan. Cook over medium heat, stirring constantly, until slightly thickened. Remove from heat; stir in rose water. Pour egg mixture into 8 stemmed dessert dishes; cover and refrigerate.

2. To serve, mix almonds and 1 tablespoon sugar. Sprinkle over each dessert.

TIP: The consistency of dessert is quite thin.

MINT TEA (Thé à la Menthe)   *Makes 8 servings*

2   tablespoons tea leaves
2   cups fresh mint leaves
¼   to ½ cup sugar
1   quart boiling water

Measure tea leaves into heated teapot; add mint leaves and sugar. Pour in boiling water; cover. Let stand 8 minutes. Stir. Serve immediately.

Cap the meal with Tunisian Cream Sweet, oranges with pomegranate seeds, dates and refreshing Mint Tea.

Argentine Fiesta Barbecue

Accompany the appetizers — cold stuffed round steak and sizzling Parmesan cheese — with glasses of red wine.

ARGENTINE BARBECUE
DINNER MENU

- **GRILLED PARMESAN CHEESE**
- **ROLLED STUFFED ROUND STEAK**

- **MIXED MEAT BARBECUE**
- **COMBINATION VEGETABLE SALAD**
  FRENCH BREAD

- **FRESH FRUIT SALAD**
- **CHOCOLATE-CARAMEL TORTE**

• Recipes included

Gauchos, the legendary herdsmen of Argentina, enjoyed meat roasted over a blazing fire as their staple food. Today, the spirit of the gauchos lives on at the *asado*, or barbecue party, the most popular form of entertaining for Argentines of all ages.

As guests gather round the grill — your version of the Argentine *parrilla* — delight them with the customary appetizers. Serve Italian-style cheese slices hot from the grill, or the famous cold beef roll called *matambre*, which means "kill hunger." This savory opener features marinated round steak stuffed with carrots, olives and hard-cooked eggs.

The heart of the feast is a Mixed Meat Barbecue of chicken, beef ribs and sausages liberally splashed with *chimichurri* (hot chili) sauce. To complement the zesty meats, set out a cool and colorful salad of tomatoes, onions and green peppers, and basketfuls of crusty bread.

Traditionally, the *asado* ends with two mouth-watering desserts. The Fresh Fruit Salad presents a luscious mélange of the season's best offerings. But no one can resist the tempting *torta de chocolate* — layers of rich chocolate cake and creamy caramel filling topped with a fluffy meringue. Serves 8.

Wine Suggestion: A heady, full-bodied wine should accompany your gaucho-style feast. California's marvelously fruity Barberas would be ideal. Two of the best come from the Heitz Cellars and Louis M. Martini.

Barbecued meats team with Hot Chili Sauce and a colorful vegetable salad.

PARTY PLAN FOR ARGENTINE BARBECUE MENU

1 Day Before:

Prepare Rolled Stuffed Round Steak through step 4 in recipe.
Prepare Mixed Meat Barbecue through step 1 in recipe.
Prepare Chocolate-Caramel Torte through step 2 in recipe; wrap cake layers in aluminum foil and store at room temperature.

3 Hours Before Serving:

Make Combination Vegetable Salad.
Complete step 3 of Chocolate-Caramel Torte recipe; cover loosely with aluminum foil.
Prepare Fresh Fruit Salad through step 1 in recipe.
Prepare garnishes for menu; refrigerate perishable ingredients.

213

10 Minutes Before Guests Arrive:	Complete Rolled Stuffed Round Steak. Make Grilled Parmesan Cheese.
At Serving Time:	Complete Mixed Meat Barbecue.
15 Minutes Before Dessert:	Complete Chocolate-Caramel Torte. Complete Fresh Fruit Salad.

GRILLED PARMESAN CHEESE

Makes 8 servings

16 ounces Parmesan cheese, cut
    into ½-inch-thick slices,
    2½ x 2 inches each
Vegetable oil
Dried oregano leaves, crumbled

Brush cheese slices lightly with oil. Place in jelly-roll pan, 15½ x 10½ x 1 inch. Place on grill 6 to 8 inches from medium coals. Cook until cheese slices are slightly brown on the bottom, 5 to 8 minutes; turn with spatula. Cook until cheese is soft, but still holds its shape, and other side is slightly brown. Remove from grill; sprinkle with oregano. Serve immediately with knife and fork.

ROLLED STUFFED ROUND STEAK

Makes 8 servings

1 beef round steak, boneless,
    ¾ inch thick (about 3 pounds),
    butterflied
1 teaspoon salt
½ teaspoon pepper

½ cup vegetable oil
½ cup red wine vinegar
2 tablespoons snipped fresh
    parsley
2 bay leaves, broken into
    pieces
2 cloves garlic, minced
1 teaspoon crushed red pepper
    flakes
¼ teaspoon dried oregano leaves

1 large onion, minced
3 small carrots, cut into thin
    julienne strips, about 2
    inches long each
4 slices uncooked bacon, diced
10 pimiento-stuffed olives, chopped
3 hard-cooked eggs, cut into sixths
2 tablespoons snipped fresh parsley
½ teaspoon dried oregano leaves
½ teaspoon salt
⅛ teaspoon pepper

2 cups hot water

1. Trim excess fat from meat. Open up meat to lie flat. Pound with meat mallet or side of cleaver until meat is about ¼ inch thick. Sprinkle with 1 teaspoon salt and ½ teaspoon pepper.

2. Place meat in large glass baking dish; sprinkle with oil, vinegar, 2 tablespoons parsley, the bay leaves, garlic, pepper flakes and ¼ teaspoon oregano. Refrigerate covered overnight.

3. Remove meat from marinade; remove bay leaves. Lay meat out on board. Distribute minced onion evenly over meat. Arrange carrots, bacon, olives and eggs over onion. Sprinkle with 2 tablespoons parsley, ½ teaspoon oregano, ½ teaspoon salt and ⅛ teaspoon pepper. Sprinkle any remaining marinade over filling.

4. Heat oven to 350°. Roll up meat from long side; secure with skewers. Tie with string at ½-inch intervals. Place meat roll in baking pan, 13 x 9 x 2 inches. Pour hot water into pan. Cover securely with aluminum foil. Bake until tender, about 1 hour. Remove meat from pan; place on wooden board. Cool to room temperature. Wrap in aluminum foil and refrigerate.

5. Cut meat into ½-inch slices and arrange on platter. Serve cold.

MIXED MEAT BARBECUE
Makes 8 servings

Hot Chili Sauce (recipe follows)

2   broiler-fryer chickens
     (2½ to 3 pounds each),
     cut into quarters
     Salt
     Pepper
3   to 3½ pounds beef chuck short ribs
4   smoky-cheese sausages
4   Thuringer sausages

     Vegetable oil
1   lemon, cut into quarters
1   lime, cut into quarters

½   cup vegetable oil
½   cup malt vinegar
¼   cup water
2   tablespoons snipped fresh
     parsley
4   small cloves garlic, minced
1   teaspoon cayenne pepper
1   teaspoon salt
¾   teaspoon dried oregano leaves
½   teaspoon black pepper

1. Make Hot Chili Sauce.

2. Season chicken with salt and pepper. Trim excess fat from ribs. Slash sausages diagonally. Sprinkle Hot Chili Sauce over ribs and sausages. Place all meats on grill 6 to 8 inches from medium coals.

3. Cook meats, turning frequently, brushing chicken with oil, and seasoning ribs and sausages with Hot Chili Sauce until done. Allow about 45 minutes cooking time for chicken, 30 minutes for ribs and 10 minutes for sausages. Remove meats from grill as they are done and serve. Cut sausages in half. Serve ribs and sausages with remaining Hot Chili Sauce. Serve chicken with lemon and lime quarters.

HOT CHILI SAUCE
Makes about 1½ cups

Combine all ingredients in a bottle with a cork, or a jar with a metal lid. Cover and shake. Let stand at room temperature 24 hours. Cut a hole about ¼ inch in diameter through the lid to shake sauce from bottle.

COMBINATION VEGETABLE SALAD
Makes 8 servings

3   medium tomatoes, coarsely
     chopped
3   medium onions, coarsely chopped
3   green peppers, coarsely chopped
2   tablespoons snipped fresh parsley
1   clove garlic, minced
1   teaspoon salt
½   teaspoon pepper
¾   cup red wine vinegar
2   tablespoons vegetable oil

Combine all ingredients in medium-size glass bowl; toss. Refrigerate covered 3 to 4 hours.

FRESH FRUIT SALAD
Makes 8 servings

4   medium apples, unpared, cored,
     diced
4   bananas, sliced
     Juice of 1 lemon
1   fresh pineapple, pared, cored,
     cubed
1   cup fresh berries
1   cup cream sherry

     Mint sprigs

1. Combine apples and bananas in large bowl; sprinkle with lemon juice. Add remaining ingredients except mint sprigs; toss. Refrigerate covered 1 to 2 hours.

2. Toss again before serving. Garnish with mint sprigs.

Chocolate-Caramel Torte and a cooling fruit salad are customary Argentine desserts.

CHOCOLATE-CARAMEL TORTE

½ cup butter or margarine,
    softened
1½ cups sugar
4 egg yolks
2 cups cake flour
2 teaspoons baking powder
¼ teaspoon salt
5 squares (1 ounce each)
    unsweetened chocolate
1 cup hot milk
1 teaspoon vanilla

4 egg whites

Caramel Filling (recipe follows)

Meringue Topping (recipe follows)

1 can (15 ounces) sweetened
    condensed milk
2 tablespoons whipping cream
1½ teaspoons vanilla

2 egg whites
⅛ teaspoon cream of tartar
    Dash salt
½ teaspoon vanilla
¼ cup sugar

1. Cream butter and sugar in medium-size bowl. Beat in egg yolks alternately with flour, baking powder and salt. Melt chocolate in hot milk in small saucepan over low heat; stir in vanilla. Mix into batter.

2. Heat oven to 350°. Beat egg whites until stiff peaks form. Fold into batter. Pour into 3 greased and floured layer pans, 9 x 1½ inches each. Bake until wooden pick inserted in center comes out clean, about 20 minutes. Loosen edges of cake layers from pans with spatula. Cool in pans 10 minutes; remove from pans. Cool completely.

3. Make Caramel Filling. Spread 2 of the layers with ½ cup of the filling each; stack. Top with remaining layer.

4. Just before serving, make Meringue Topping. Spread on top layer.

CARAMEL FILLING
Mix all ingredients in heavy medium-size saucepan. Cook over low heat, stirring frequently, until mixture becomes thick and caramel colored, about 30 minutes. Cool 5 minutes.

MERINGUE TOPPING
Beat egg whites, cream of tartar and salt in small bowl until mixture forms soft peaks; add vanilla. Beat in sugar, 1 tablespoon at a time, until stiff and glossy. Do not underbeat.

Index

Mail-Order Sources

SPECIALTY FOOD ITEMS

Marshall Field and Co.
Gourmet Foods Section
Mail Order Department
111 N. State Street
Chicago, Illinois 60602
(312) 781-1000
No minimum order if C.O.D.;
otherwise, $10.00 minimum
order

Stop & Shop
16 W. Washington Street
Chicago, Illinois 60602
(312) 726-8500
$2.00 delivery charge for orders
under $50.00 in Chicago and
suburbs; parcel service charges
elsewhere

INDIAN FOODS

Bezjian Grocery
4725 Santa Monica Blvd.
Hollywood, California 90029
(213) 663-1503
$1.00 handling charge for orders
under $10.00

India Grocers
5002 N. Sheridan Road
Chicago, Illinois 60640
(312) 334-3351
No minimum order

CHINESE FOODS

Wing Chong Lung Co.
922 S. San Pedro Street
Los Angeles, California 90015
(213) 627-5935
No minimum order

Star Market
3349 N. Clark Street
Chicago, Illinois 60657
(312) 472-0599
No minimum order

Oriental Import-Export Co.
2009 Polk Street
Houston, Texas 77002
(713) 223-5621
$10.00 minimum order

Legal Sea Foods Market
237 Hampshire Street
Cambridge, Massachusetts 02139
(617) 547-1410
No minimum order

MIDDLE EASTERN FOODS

Kasso Brothers
570 Ninth Avenue
New York, New York 10036
(212) 736-7473
$30.00 minimum order

American Oriental Grocery
20736 Lahser Road
Southfield, Michigan 48075
(313) 352-5733
No minimum order

Photography Credits

Cover Photo: John Stewart

Pages 10-13: John Stewart; 14-19: Tim Schultz; 21-23, 27: Fred Brodersen; 28-29, 31, 34: Frances McLaughlin-Gill; 36-37, 39-41, 43, 45: Don Levey; 46-47, 49-53, 55: John Stewart; 56 (left): Japan Air Lines; 56 (right) India Tourist Office; 57-59, 65-66, 68-73: Richard Tomlinson and Giovanni Lunardi; 77-78: John Stewart; 80-81, 85: Richard Tomlinson; 86-87, 89-91, 94: Jim Wood; 98-99, 101-103, 105: John Stewart and Otto Stupakoff; 110-112, 115: Max Henriquez; 117-119, 122: Richard Foster; 126-127: Richard Jeffery; 128-129: John Widmer; 130-131, 133: John Stewart and Turkish American Cultural Alliance; 132, 136-137: Tim Schultz; 140: John Stewart; 142: Jonas Dovydenas; 143, 146-147, 151-153: Robert Keeling; 158-159, 161-163: Pete Segura; 166-167, 170-171, 175: Richard Jeffery; 176-179: John Stewart; 180 (left): Szathmáry Archives, Chicago; 180-181, 183: Robert Keeling; 184-185: Tutt Esquerre; 186-187: Robert Keeling; 188: Tutt Esquerre; 193: Robert Keeling; 194-195, 197, 198-199: André Gillardin; 200-203: John Stewart; 206, 208-209, 211: Robert Keeling; 212-213, 216: Robert Keeling.